WAGES & WHITLAM

The Wages Policy of the Whitlam Government

WAGES & WHITLAM

The Wages Policy of the Whitlam Government

P A McGAVIN

Melbourne
OXFORD UNIVERSITY PRESS
Oxford Auckland New York

OXFORD UNIVERSITY PRESS

Oxford New York Toronto Delhi Bombay Calcutta
Madras Karachi Singapore Hong Kong Tokyo Nairobi
Dar es Salaam Cape Town Melbourne Auckland
and associates in
Beirut Berlin Ibadan Nicosia

First published 1987

National Library of Australia
Cataloguing-in-Publication data:

McGavin, P.A. (Paul A.) 1943-
Wages and Whitlam.

Bibliography.
Includes index.
ISBN 0 19 554732 2.

1. Wages — Government policy — Australia — History. 2. Australia — Economic policy — 1972-1975. 3. Australia — Economic conditions — 1972-1975. I. Title.

331. 2'994

Edited by Dugald McLellan
Cover design by Steve Randles
Typeset by Asco Trade Typesetting Ltd, Hong Kong
Printed in Singapore by Singapore National Printers (Pte Ltd)
Published by Oxford University Press,
7 Bowen Crescent, Melbourne
OXFORD is a trademark of Oxford University Press

Contents

To Ern

GLORIA DEO PATRI FILIO SPIRITUI

Preface

The profound effects on Australian economy and society of the brief and tumultuous period of the Whitlam Government are of vital interest in the search to understand the problems of contemporary Australia. An economic evaluation of the wages policy of the Whitlam Government attracted my attention as a subject for a doctoral thesis. Turning the thesis into a book involved a substantial amount of editorial work by the author, although the basic shape of the work remains the same as that which earned me the degree of Doctor of Philosophy and the joint award of the Harbison-Higinbotham Research Scholarship of the University of Melbourne.

I wish to express my gratitude to many who have assisted me during the preparation of this book. I have a particular debt to Dr E. A. Boehm, sometime Reader in Economics in the University of Melbourne, for the courtesy, fine scholarship and generosity of his supervision, and for his encouragement at all points. Particular gratitude is due also to Professors R. H. Snape and F. G. Davidson for their comments on the thesis as examiners.

I am thankful also to a large number of colleagues, especially those who have kindly read and commented on various parts of my work—including Drs R. J. Dixon, R. G. Gregory, D. Pope, L. S. Williams, P. L. Williams, G. Withers, Associate Professor B. L. J. Gordon, Professor R. A. Williams, and the referees and editors of *Australian Economic Papers, Australian Economic Review, The Economic Record*, and the *Journal of Industrial Relations*. None of the above bears responsibility for the deficiencies of this work.

My thanks are also due to the officers of the Australian Bureau of Statistics for supplying unpublished data; to the staff of the

Australian Department of Employment and Industrial Relations for aiding my access to Commonwealth submissions to National Wage Cases; to the Librarian of the Australian Conciliation and Arbitration Commission for access to Transcripts and Exhibits of the National Wage Cases; and to the Librarians of the Giblin Library, Faculty of Economics and Commerce, University of Melbourne. The University supported this work in providing a fine research environment and, during the first year of my candidacy, a University of Melbourne Postgraduate Research Scholarship. I am grateful also to the National Institute of Labour Studies and to the School of Social Sciences at the Flinders University of South Australia in the work of preparing my thesis for publication. Dugald E. McLellan did a meticulous job as consultant editor, and efficient help was given by Ev Beissbarth, production editor with Oxford University Press Australia. The exacting job of preparing the index was done by Elmar Zalums.

P. A. McGavin

Chapter 1
Introduction

Labor's first priority will be to restore genuine full employment—without qualification, without hedging.

Will you again entrust the nation's economy to men who deliberately, but needlessly, created Australia's worst unemployment for ten years?

(Australian Labor Party, *Policy Speech 1972*, pp. 10, 3)

[The fall in seasonally adjusted civilian employment] is the biggest fall in the history of the series ...

The number of persons registered for employment with the Commonwealth Employment Service at the end of December [is] ... the largest number unemployed since the 1930s.

(*Treasury Information Bulletin*, January 1975, pp. 1, 3)

December 1972 to November 1975

At the General Elections for the House of Representatives on 2 December 1972, a majority was gained by the Australian Labor Party. On the morning of Tuesday, 5 December 1972, Sir Paul Hasluck, then Governor-General, received the resignation of the Leader of the Liberal Party of Australia, the Rt Hon. William McMahon. He then commissioned the Hon. Edward Gough Whitlam, Leader of the Parliamentary Labor Party, to form a Government for the Commonwealth of Australia. The following afternoon, His Excellency swore in an interim Ministry consisting of Mr Whitlam and his Deputy (the Hon. Lance Herbert Barnard), thereby forming the first Labor Party Government of the Commonwealth for twenty-three years. Two weeks later, a Ministry of twenty-seven members was sworn in, with the Hon. Clyde Robert Cameron, taking office as Minister for Labour. Mr Cameron held his portfolio until 6 June 1975 when, at Mr Whitlam's request, Sir John Kerr, then Governor-General, revoked his commission and swore in Senator the Hon. Douglas McClelland as Minister for Labour and Immigration. On the afternoon of Tuesday, 11 November 1975, His Excellency withdrew Mr Whitlam's commission, and dissolved Parliament. At the General Elections for both Houses of Parliament on 13 December 1975, the Liberal Party gained a majority, and the Hon. John Malcolm Fraser (who at the Governor-General's request had acted as 'caretaker' Prime Minister) was called upon by Sir John to form a Government for the Commonwealth of Australia.

This book focuses on that brief, but eventful, period between December 1972 and November 1975: the 'Whitlam period'. The turbulent history of that period is given only to the extent necessary for an economic evaluation of the wages policy of the Whitlam Government.

'Wages policy' (defined in the following section) was a central aspect of the Labor Government's policy, and an area in which Mr Whitlam at times took a leading role. The day following the formation of the interim Cabinet, Mr Whitlam 'authorised an application to the Industrial Registrar asking to have the recent hearing on equal pay [for female employees] before the Full Bench of the Arbitration Commission reopened' (Whitlam, Press Statement, 6 December 1972). The day following the formation of the second Whitlam Ministry, the Prime Minister announced 'that the Australian Government will support a claim by Australian Public Service Unions for four weeks annual leave' (Whitlam, Press Statement, 20 December 1972). These actions signified the pattern and the priority of wages policy as set by the incoming government.

Scope and Perspective of this Book

'Wage' is the reward for market labour services. A government's wages policy treats all aspects of government policy which relate to reward for labour services and includes such topics as policy concerning wage rates and employment, relative wages, wage maintenance, non-monetary rewards in employment, transfer payments, etc. Each of these areas comprises a complex of policies. 'Relative wages' policy, for example, comprises government policies concerning wage remuneration for skilled compared with unskilled workers; female compared with male workers; and junior compared with adult workers. 'Wage maintenance' policy comprises government policy towards cost-of-living adjustments, and compensatory taxation cuts. 'Non-monetary rewards in employment' concern government policy towards a wide range of 'fringe benefits' and employment conditions which affect the non-monetary rewards attaching to employment. 'Transfer payments' policies involve government policies about unemployment benefits and other welfare transfer payments which represent an opportunity cost of employment or of non-participation in the work force. 'Wages and employment' policy involves the overall understanding and policy response concerning the role of wages and wage variation for labour employment.

There are a variety of perspectives from which the issue of government 'wages policy' may be examined: for example, from the viewpoints of law, ethics, politics, industrial relations, and economics. In this book these issues are examined from the viewpoint of economic analysis. However, not all questions of economic significance will be addressed: for example, the large and interesting question of the impact of wages policy upon the distribution of income remains largely unexamined.

The principal economic question examined is the relationship of 'wages and employment'. The term 'employment' has a wider use than wage employment. Both 'self-employment' and 'engagement in gainful non-market activities' (for example, 'home duties') may fall within normal English usage of the term 'employment'. The interest followed in this book is *wage* employment, and the term 'employment' is used to denote this. It is, however, not the author's intention to give 'wage employment' a higher 'status' than other forms of market, or of non-market, labour engagement. Occasionally, therefore, the term 'wage employment' is used—especially where the discussion concerns the examination of allocation decisions as between market and non-market labour activity. Similarly, the term 'labour force' is used to comprise those in wage employment and those actively seeking wage employment. Yet this usage does not connote that persons not in the 'labour force' are not gainfully engaged in rendering labour services. Thus the term 'labour force' applies to *market* provision of labour services. The term 'work force' is used to denote those members of the labour force in wage employment: that is, the 'work force' does not include 'unemployed' persons. However, no connotation is intended that persons not in the 'work force' necessarily do not 'work': the usage denotes only that the activities of such persons do not comprise the relationship of wage employment. 'Wages and employment' therefore deals with a restricted set of labour activity: with *market* labour activity.[1]

In examining the economic question of 'wages and employment', the perspective adopted is chiefly that of market analysis conceived in terms of interaction of 'demand' and 'supply', deriving a market outcome (or indicating the direction in which movement in market outcome may be anticipated). That is, the economic perspective of this book is chiefly that of 'neoclassical' economics. As has already been noted, there are large areas of interest under the general heading of the evaluation of government 'wages policy' which are not here examined (for instance: legal, ethical, political, and industrial relations considerations receive little or no direct attention). Employment is dealt with in market terms only, and the very relevant question of the relationship between social valuation of labour activity in market and in non-market terms does not receive direct attention. This, then, is the perspective from which the wages policy of the Whitlam Government is examined.

The focus is on the wages policy 'of the Whitlam Government'. But the Labor Government did not 'happen' in a vacuum. An outline of Australian institutions and principles of wage determination, and an explanation of some of the language used in this study are given in Appendix 1.1. The following section gives a 'lead up' to the Whitlam period. The last section briefly surveys the contents of the book and outlines the main conclusions.

Lead up to December 1972

The Background to Labor's Assuming Office

The years 1970 and 1971 were a period of strong growth in employment in Australia: aggregate weekly hours worked according to the August survey of the Australian Bureau of Statistics (ABS) were up on the previous year by 4.4 per cent in 1970, and by 3.2 per cent in 1971. At August 1972, however, aggregate weekly hours worked had risen on 1971 by only a further 0.4 per cent. The slowing of growth in employment during 1971 was accompanied by a rise in unemployment from 1.4 to 1.7 per cent of the labour force. At August 1972, measured unemployment had increased to 2.5 per cent, a rise of nearly 50 per cent on a year earlier. With the exception of 1961, this was the highest unemployment rate recorded in post-World War II Australia.[2] Commonwealth Employment Service (CES) data on persons seeking full-time employment and on registrations of job vacancies show an unemployed:vacancies ratio of 1.30 at June 1970. This ratio rose to 2.06 at June 1971, and had doubled to 4.12 at June 1972.

During 1969–70 the Consumer Price Index (CPI) increased by 3.2 per cent, and by a further 4.8 per cent in 1970–71. The rate of inflation during 1971–72 of 6.8 per cent was clearly the highest rate since the Korean War boom of 1950–51/1951–52. Although average weekly earnings (AWE) continued to grow strongly, male hourly earnings after allowing for the effects of inflation (that is, 'real' male hourly earnings) increased during the year to August 1972 by only 2.9 per cent, compared with increases of 4.3 per cent in 1970, and 8 per cent in 1971.

The downturn in the growth of earnings, and the record rate of unemployment, together with a sharp worsening in the ratio of persons registered as seeking employment to job vacancies, are indicative of the serious deterioration in labour market conditions. Although these data may not be taken in isolation from other economic and political considerations, they may nevertheless serve as barometers of the favour or disfavour with which governments are viewed by the electorate. The indications for an expression of electoral disfavour towards the McMahon Government were clear. The tune *It's Time* was catching: 'It's time for a change'.[3]

On 2 December the choice for 'change' was made by the Australian electorate. The popular saying, 'Governments do not win elections, only lose them', seems to the author more persuasive than Mr Whitlam's interpretation of events as a 'mandate' for Labor Party policies. To the present author it would seem that the Liberal Party lost the 2 December 1972 election principally because—relative to accustomed Australian experience—there appeared to be a deterioration in economic performance. The Labor Party lost the 13 December 1975 election principally because—relative to accustomed experience—there was clearly a deterioration in economic performance.[4, 5]

In reading the record of the Labor administration, it should therefore be kept in mind that the failures of the Whitlam period cannot simply be attributed to the policies of the Labor Government. The Whitlam Government took charge of the management of an economy in which there had already emerged trends unfavourable to the restoration of economic balance and growth. The challenge for the Whitlam Government was for them to recognize emerging unfavourable trends in economic indicators, and to adopt policies which would reverse (or at least modify) the direction of changes so as to make for the restoration of balance in the Australian economy. To the author, this would seem the primary test of whether, given opportunity, the Australian electorate would express favour or disfavour towards an outgoing government. The expression of disfavour on 13 December 1975 is therefore viewed as a failure of Labor's policies to meet the *political* objective of reversing or of moderating the direction of change in the Australian economy.

This book is concerned with the *economic* evaluation of an important subset of the policies of the Whitlam Government: with the economic evaluation of policies falling under the heading of 'wages policy'. As has been indicated, it is chiefly from the perspective of 'wages and employment' that this evaluation is undertaken. The indicators of economic circumstances at the advent of the Whitlam Government serve as reminders: that evaluation of the Labor administration needs to be made within the context of the economic situation which was inherited—and within the context of economic trends already emerging when Labor took office.

Shifts in Australian Wage-setting at the Advent of Labor

During the period leading up to the Whitlam years there was a tendency towards decline in the proportion of union members to all wage and salary earners. The proportion of male unionists to male employees fell fairly steadily from 60 per cent at December 1966 to 58 per cent at December 1972. At the same time, however, there was some tendency for decline in the number of separate trade unions—implying an increase in concentration of unions. The most notable shift, however, in the profile of trade union membership during this period was the increase in the number of unions in the largest membership category (80 000 and over). Their number increased from three to eight between 1969 and 1972.

In his August 1973 ANZAAS Presidential address, Dr J. E. Isaac (later a Deputy President of the Australian Conciliation and Arbitration Commission), observed that, under full employment, collective bargaining offers for many unions great freedom to exercise their economic power to obtain higher pay and better working conditions.[6] He further noted that tribunal determination of wages 'is usually confined to areas of weak unionism'.[7] These observations are consistent with the incidence of earnings drift as seen in Table 1.1 (at the end of this chapter). During 1969 and 1970 the average quarterly earnings drift was about 1 per cent, suggesting an impetus for wage growth occurring outside the tribunals.[8] During 1971 and 1972, the obverse was however true: there was a negative earnings drift approaching a quarterly average of −1 per cent in 1971, and a smaller negative earnings drift in 1972. These data suggest that the 1971 increase in real hourly earnings was influenced by a (brief) return to tribunal wage determination in a context of weakening labour market conditions. This involved a temporary shift in the focus of momentum in Australian wage formation from decentralized (that is, market) institutions to centralized (that is, arbitral) institutions. Such an interpretation would appear consistent with Isaac's observation that in favourable market circumstances, tribunals 'sought in vain to match [the market] ... by larger award increase for those lagging behind the market'.[9] Tribunal awards were made in the 'name of wage justice' and with an awareness of their significance for the political 'survival' of arbitral institutions.

It may be argued therefore that the 'inflationary bias' of collective bargaining under conditions of full employment is fed by the 'flow-on' influence of tribunals' operations.[10] Under conditions of less-than-full-employment, one may expect a shift of the momentum in wage determination towards centralized determination. Under these conditions, tribunals may act to slow the rate of attrition in wages growth which may be anticipated where there occurs a downturn in labour market conditions. As is later argued in this book (Chapter 5), this implies that the operation of Australian employment tribunals (particularly the Australian Conciliation and Arbitration Commission) influenced a slowing of the rate of market adjustment to changes in economic circumstances. Since market adjustment is integral to the emergence of the upswing in the business cycle[11], it may therefore be argued that the opportunity for shift in the focus of momentum in Australian wage determination has made for a slowing of the market adjustment which is a necessary adjunct to the restoration of the level of market activity towards a 'full employment' trend level of activity. Suggestions along these lines have been made more explicitly by Judith Sloan of the National Institute of Labour Studies (The Flinders University of South Australia) in an address before the 1983 Forum of the Victorian Branch of the Economic Society of Australia, and are further examined later in this book. Although statistics showing the relative importance of arbitral and consent wage determination are not generally available for Australia[12], the evidence is consistent with the suggestion that, during 1971, a swing had occurred giving greater prominence to arbitral wage determination in Australia.

Labor's Proposed Initiatives in Wage-setting as Advertised in the 1972 Election Campaign

It was in the context of this potentiality for shift in the momentum for Australian wages growth between the influence of the market ('decentralized' wages determination) and the influence of arbitral institutions ('centralized' wages determination) that Mr Whitlam advertised the Labor Party's proposed initiatives in the field of industrial relations. What Whitlam proposed was a government policy which would operate to increase the possibility for movement in the institutional focus of wages determination. This would be achieved by the exercise of government support 'in favour of negotiated agreements' ('consent' wage determination), while at the same time having amongst the Party's 'great aims' the reduction of 'government interference and intervention in industrial matters' and the reduction of scope for enforcement of awards by the abolition of penal clauses concerning strike violation of awards.[13]

Thus, Labor's early policy proposals allowed a greater resort to market wage determination in circumstances where this alternative was attractive to labour, along with a reduction in government intervention before tribunals' hearings, as well as a reduction of the machinery for the enforcement of awards. In short, this meant that Labor advertised a programme of reduced federal government control over wages determination in Australia. Such a programme was, in the present author's view, premised upon the assumption that reflationary government policies could, if necessary, sustain an economy at 'full employment'. It may be said that these proposals were but an extension of the practice of Liberal governments in Australia. Nevertheless, Labor's programme did not reckon with fundamental changes that were then emerging (or had emerged) in Australian political economy compared with the conditions that had applied in the Australian economy and society during the greater part of the 1950s and 1960s. The simultaneous experience of inflation and unemployment in which Mr Whitlam advertised his Party's policies suggested that in future 'overall consistency of pay and other income movements to the requirements of full employment and price stability cannot be relied upon to emerge from free sectional collective bargaining'.[14] Especially is this so where arbitral institutions offered (a) in times of favourable market conditions a means of generalizing sectional wage gains, and (b) in times of unfavourable market conditions an alternative means for avoiding real wage attrition. It is the present author's view that the changes in Australian political economy in the late 1960s and the 1970s were themselves in significant part brought about by the economic policy administration of the 1950s and 1960s, but that is a thesis which is not developed in the present work. These changing economic circumstances required a change in government policy purview and practice from a 'passive' and 'accommodating' stance of the past.[15] The critical need was for a searching and empirically-based understanding of the *economic requirements* of national policy objectives. Only on such foundations could policies consistent with actual economic circumstances and requirements be framed and implemented.

A major argument of this book is that the wages policy of the Whitlam Government responded but slowly to the actual requirements of the times. At November 1975 that response was still incomplete. But Labor's wages policy at 1975 nevertheless was markedly different from 1972: it had been 'marked' by the experience of the realities of economic circumstances. A work which attempts an 'economic evaluation' of the wages policy of the Whitlam Government must necessarily try to grapple with the economic realities of the period. The chapters which follow are directed to that purpose.

Resumé of the Book

A survey is provided in Chapter 2 of the shifts in the wages policy of the Whitlam Government from the early policy of 'permissiveness' through to later Government policy, which was understood and articulated in terms of 'wage restraint'.

An outline of the theoretical underpinnings for this research is presented in Chapter 3, and the 'real wage overhang' is explained in outline. The operation of the market distribution of national product is explained and contrasted with an administered distribution through the instrument of wages.

In Chapter 4 evidence of the influence of the Government in wages determination is introduced; and wage variations during the Whitlam period are outlined. There follows an econometric analysis of the significance of increases in wages for male employment. The conclusion of this analysis is that, in terms of the direct effects, the dominant influences on male employment were (a) aggregate activity, and (b) relative wages. The direct influence of change in relative wages upon the 1975 male aggregate hours employment is reckoned as having been almost as significant as the direct impact of change in the level of macroeconomic activity in Australia. Consideration of variation in wages during the Whitlam period is extended to include non-wage labour costs. It is found that the use of a wider measure of labour cost (wage plus non-wage costs) increases the robustness of the results of the econometric analysis introduced in this chapter. Growth in non-wage labour costs is shown to have been substantially more than wage costs (the 1974 increase in non-wage labour costs was more than double the increase in wage costs), and to have had employment-reducing effects similar to increases in wages.

Chapter 5 is devoted to an assessment of the issue of the 'real wage overhang' and this is related to an analysis of movements in wages: profits shares of national income, and to an evaluation of indexation of wages and the Government's successful advocacy of its introduction at 30 April 1975. It is argued that the Government failed to subject the principles of its wages indexation policy to economic scrutiny, and that its successful advocacy of wage indexation should be judged as having contributed to the prolongation of the process of adjustment in the share of national product going to wages.

The questions of 'wages as costs' and 'wages as incomes', and of 'relative wage costs' are examined in Chapter 6. Evidence is presented on the role of government policy for growth in the wedge between labour costs and disposable incomes: between 1973 and 1975 real hourly costs of employment increased by about 20 per cent, but workers' real hourly disposable incomes increased at about half that rate. It is argued that the growth of this wedge worked against containment of increases in labour costs. On the question of relative wage costs, examination of the data reveals that, contrary to Labor policy, there does not appear to have been a compression in wage relativities as between skilled and less-skilled workers. There was, however, a marked increase in the wages of junior relative to adult workers, and the negative employment impact of this is described.

The period of the Whitlam Government saw the completion of the move for equal pay for female workers. An analysis in Chapter 7 of compositional changes in female employment by hours reveals a negative shift in female proportions in the work force, the timing of which suggests a negative employment impact following the implementation of equal pay. The Whitlam Government's contribution to the wider and accelerated implementation of increases in the relative wages of females is thus assessed as having exercised a negative employment influence.

The relationship of wages to the system of public transfer payments is examined in Chapter 8, with a focus upon the labour force participation decisions of junior and of older Australians. The conclusion is that movements of 'wages and welfare' acted to reduce employment both of youth and of older Australians, while at the same time increasing the volume of drawings on the public transfer payments system. It is thus argued that changes during the Whitlam period in 'wages and welfare' acted to reduce the supply of and to increase the demand for market goods and services, and that the impact of these changes was counteractive for the Government's employment objective.

These strands of analysis are drawn together in the concluding chapter, where it is argued that there was a lack of consistency in the formulation and execution of the Whitlam Government's policies. It is argued that adaptation by the Whitlam Government of wages policy to the needs of the time was slow and incomplete, and that the general failure of Labor's wages policy severely impacted upon the achievement of the Government's employment objective.

Table 1.1 Estimates of Earnings Drift

	Average Weekly Earnings per Employed Male Unit		Weighted Average Award Rates for Adult Males			
Quarter	Dollars (a)	Quarterly change (seasonally adjusted), per cent (b)		Weighted average rate lagged one month, dollars (c)	Quarterly change, per cent (d)	Earnings drift [cols (b)–(d)], per cent (e)
1969 Mar.	71.70	4.1	1969 Feb.	49.27	0.8	3.3
June	72.60	1.3	May	49.53	0.5	0.8
Sept.	74.10	2.1	Aug.	49.88	0.7	0.6
Dec.	75.10	1.3	Nov.	50.69	1.6	0.5
1970 Mar.	77.50	3.2	1970 Feb.	51.96	2.5	0.7
June	78.80	1.7	May	52.25	0.6	1.1
Sept.	80.50	2.2	Aug.	52.93	1.3	0.9
Dec.	82.50	2.5	Nov.	53.90	1.8	0.7
1971 Mar.	86.70	5.1	1971 Feb.	57.85	7.3	−1.6
June	88.10	1.6	May	58.27	2.5	−0.9
Sept.	91.30	3.6	Aug.	59.72	2.5	1.1
Dec.	91.70	0.4	Nov.	61.17	2.4	−2.0
1972 Mar.	93.20	1.6	1972 Feb.	61.94	1.3	0.3
June	95.90	2.9	May	63.81	3.2	−0.3
Sept.	98.30	2.5	Aug.	65.50	2.6	−0.1
Dec.	100.30	2.0	Nov.	66.85	2.1	−0.1

Sources: ABS cat. *6302.0*, *6312.0*, & *6314.0*.[16]

Chapter 2
The Wages Policy of the Whitlam Government: An Overview

The purpose of this chapter is to provide an overview of the wages policy of the Whitlam Government, focusing on the Government's overall understanding and policy response concerning the role of wages and wage variation for employment.

Early Government Policy

'Permissiveness' in Wages Policy

It is the Commonwealth's opinion that there is scope in the capacity and the flexibility of the Australian economy for an appreciable rise in wages without undesirable inflationary consequences—and with wage increases being viewed as the appropriate instrument for this redistribution.

(National Wage Case, March 1973)

The principal characteristic of early Whitlam Government wages policy may be described as 'permissiveness' in that the Government acted out an implicit premise that there was room for a redistribution of the national product in favour of those in employment—with wage increases being viewed as the appropriate instrument for this redistribution. This premise was manifested in the 1973 National Wage Case, where Counsel for the Government argued with the unions for a $14 (about 27.5 per cent) increase in the minimum wage. The previous submission by the McMahon Government before the adjournment of the 1972–73 National Wage Case was for only such limited increase in the minimum wage as would not create serious repercussions in the economy. Mr J. B. Sweeney QC, Counsel for the Commonwealth at the reconvened hearing in March 1973, portrayed the

McMahon Government's position as 'one of opposition to wage increases'.[1] Similarly, the Government's permissive response to claims for variation in awards affecting the Public Service is represented in the following extract from a Prime Ministerial Press Statement of 16 August 1973: 'Cabinet decided not to file responses to the present applications to vary determinations covering postal grades and the second and third divisons of the Public Service'.

Increased Relative Wages for 'Lower-paid' Workers

[The Arbitration Commission's decision to increase the minimum wage] completely accords with the Government's objective of greater equality for the disadvantaged ...

(Minister for Labour, Media Statement, 2 May 1974)

In the area of wages for less-advantaged workers, the Government's response was particularly to favour increased relative wages for such workers: 'The Commonwealth's concern is that help should be given to the lower income groups who in our view have been in the past disadvantaged by their relative bargaining weakness'.[2] This premise was manifest in the Government's constantly seeking greater proportional increases in awards for lower-paid workers; in the Government's commitment to plateau wage indexation; and in the Government's commitment to the implementation of equal pay for women.

The Government's submission to the 1972–73 National Wage Case provides a rationale for its views concerning 'the capacity and the flexibility of the Australian economy for an appreciable rise in wages'.[3] The main elements of this rationale were that Australia was in the 'recovery stage of the business cycle' during which 'larger-than-normal productivity gains' were expected[4], and that the new Government's 'comprehensive range of policies' concerning demand management, structural adjustment, and the promotion of competition were such that inflation was 'capable of being suitably controlled'.[5] In addition, Counsel for the Commonwealth emphasized the view that 'it is [the Commonwealth's] responsibility to take account of the effects of any recommendations for change in wage levels and relativities which it may submit to the Commission or indeed [which] the Commission may make'.[6]

With hindsight, one might suggest that this rationale was but a projection of the Government's hopes for the economy and for its economic management. But careful reading of sources would suggest that the most active determinant of wages policy was not the Government's 'hopefulness', but the Whitlam Government's precept about 'wage justice'. Government statements which evidence a characteristic of 'permissiveness', such as those introduced above, show on closer inspection that the active element was an increase in the *minimum* wage, or an increase in wages for what were regarded as *lower* grades of the Public Service. The early thrust of the Whitlam Government's wages policy was one which proceeded from a 'particular concern' for 'considerations of wage justice for low wage earners'.[7]

The notion of 'wage justice' is a difficult one, but it proceeds from a sense that a worker ought fairly to participate in the fruits of his labour. And it further presumes that the appropriate instrument for a fair distribution of labour's contribution to production is wage. The question of what is a *just* wage receives some attention in Chapter 3, and leads to the observation that the notion of a 'just wage' is based on the precept that the appropriate instrument for distribution of labour contribution to production is *wage*. However, the view that wage should be the instrument for achieving a 'just' distribution of goods and services is in conflict with an economic analysis which views wage as a *price* for the contribution of labour factors of production. Economic analysis of this kind separates the question of production from the question of equity in distribution of production between persons. It was the commitment to the precept of 'wage justice' which was the corner-stone of Labor Party wages policy. As is subsequently argued, this precept was fundamentally wanting in economic consistency, or an appreciation of its economic and social implications.

Shifting Government Policy

> The Prime Minister ... welcomed the decision of the Public Service Board to grant no further increase to Public Servants in the clerical, postal and keyboard areas beyond the $16 per week increase which had been announced by the Board on 21 June.
>
> (Media Statement, 13 September 1974)

Within about eighteen months of taking office, there began to emerge a shift on the part of the Government from an attitude of permissiveness towards increases in wages to one of overt resistance. The Government struggled to hold to its notion of 'wage justice' for the disadvantaged, chiefly under the advocacy of the Minister for Labour and Immigration. This advocacy was compromised, however, by the policy of resistance to general wage increases and by what the Government perceived as the political necessities of implementing that resistance.

Government resistance to wage increases was reluctant in its emergence, and was still not firm in the Commonwealth's submission at the 1974 National Wage Case. Counsel for the Commonwealth (the then Mr J. F. Staples QC), on behalf of the Minister for Labour, introduced his March 1974 submission in terms of support for the maintenance of 'the purchasing power of wages fixed by determinations of the Commission'.[8] Reading Mr Staples' submission it is clear, however, that such support was premised upon the Government's desire to influence a shift in wages distribution in favour of lower wage earners. This purpose was clearly manifest in the Government's proposal for the form of automatic quarterly wage adjustment which was being put forward at this time. This 'derived from a reference [to] the movement in the CPI to the minimum wage as distinct from a reference that may otherwise be adopted to the total wage, the average award rate or average weekly earnings'.[9] The lack of firmness in the Government's resistance to a wage increase is evident however in the two qualifications attaching to the Submission to the 1974 National Wage Case: (a) 'If, however, the Commission ... is not persuaded that it should restore automatic cost of living adjustments, then the Government requests the Commission to grant in this case the Australian Council of Trade Unions' claim in respect of the minimum wage and the total wage'[10]; and (b) 'if the Commission does decide to introduce a system of automatic adjustment to operate henceforth, the Government makes no submission as to whether or by what amount the total wage should be increased, except for this: ... that any [indexation] increase that may be awarded should be expressed ... as a flat amount of every award rate'[11]; 'If the Commission introduces a system of automatic adjustment to operate henceforth we make no submission as to whether [the Commission] ought to move the total wage and, if [the Commission] were minded to move it, by how much'.[12]

At this stage the incidence of wage increases, of inflation, and of employment were still largely compartmentalized in Government thinking and policy response. In March 1974 Counsel for the Commonwealth argued that the Commission should not be 'induced to preoccupy itself ... with the problem of ... inflationary pressure in the economy'.[13] The unmistakable message of the Government was that economic considerations were the province and responsibility of the Government: 'The Government unhesitantly accepts responsibility for the economic consequences, if any, that may flow from the adoption of its submissions to [the] Commission'.[14] The responsibility of the Commission in its role in National Wage determinations was concentrated in 'considerations of industrial justice and the need to prevent and settle industrial disputes' and not in the area of management of the economy, which area 'is properly the province of the Government'.[15] Clearly the Government was still clinging to the view of the 'scope in the capacity and flexibility of the Australian economy.'[16]

From mid-1974 one observes a progressive relinquishing by the Government of this view. For example, the comment, 'it is vitally important that wage claims are not made at the expense of fellow-workers' jobs' summed up the message of a speech of 25 August in which Mr Whitlam described the relationship between wage increases and price increases, and the significance of these for industry competitiveness, and thus for employment.[17] Similarly, the statement, 'It is this bloody-mindedness [in aggressive wage demands] on the part of a small section of the trade union movement that is slowly, but surely, pricing thousands of Australian workers out of employment', provided the punch-line for a Media Statement by Mr Cameron of 16 August 1974 concerning the relationship between industrial action and wage increases, and inflation and employment.

During the latter part of 1974 the Government's understanding was moving away from one which compartmentalized wages, inflation, and employment. Ministers made frequent reference to the redistributive effects of wages increases exceeding general price increases, with the 'consequential squeeze on profits' being presented as having 'played a major role in the sharp increase in unemployment over the last few months' (Minister for Labour and Immigration, Speech, 18 November 1974). Mr Cameron, reporting his own Department's contacts, portrayed employer response of labour economization and aligned himself with the

Prime Minister and Treasurer in saying, 'one man's pay increase could mean another man's job' (18 November 1974). The reluctance with which this shift in policy purview was made is clear from Mr Cameron's comments in the same speech, 'I believe that such a redistribution [of wage share] has been welcomed by the unions and is in line with what the Government set out to achieve in its social welfare program. But this redistribution has also brought its problems'.

Although the Government shifted in seeking to halt the progression of this redistribution in favour of employed labour, it nevertheless sought at least to maintain the gains which wage and salary earners had made. In a speech of 18 November 1974, Mr Cameron made the point, 'The Government does not expect trade unionists to suffer reduction in real wages and we haven't asked them to do so'.

There was, however, a shift in that the *wage* was less strongly viewed as the appropriate instrument for achieving the desired distribution of labour's contribution to production. There was a distinct shift in emphasis towards a 'social compact' whereby 'pay-as-you-earn' taxation cuts would operate to maintain (or increase) net disposable employee income. This shift towards increased emphasis on an 'incomes policy package' was chiefly influenced by a heightening awareness that the wage was a *price* and that decisions about factor use were fundamentally influenced by factor prices. This change in perspective was represented by: (a) the Government catch-cry, 'Employees can price themselves out of the market' (Prime Ministerial Statement, 12 November 1974); and by (b) the heightened Government intent that its 'social compact' should operate to ensure that labour costs to employers should not rise. Thus, in his speech of 18 November 1974, Mr Cameron commended in these words the virtue of the 'social compact' intended by the Government to maintain disposable wage incomes, but without increasing labour costs: 'the important thing is that the cost to the employer of this increase in take-home pay is nil'.

By late 1974 the shift from 'permissiveness' was clearly established. Mr Whitlam's statement, 'Let me be frank, inflation costs jobs', appeared under the front-page leader, 'PM blames pay for jump in inflation' in the *Australian* of 22 October 1974, and this message was prominent in newspaper headlines early in 1975.[18] As the following quotations instance, the Government's submission to the April 1975 National Wage hearing forcefully argued for what was represented as 'wage restraint': 'The Government supports [the unions' claim for wage indexation] ... on the condition that wage claims for the next two years are limited in accordance with assurances to be given to the Commission'; (b) 'the Commission is clearly inhibited in what it can award by way of national wage increase'; and (c) 'We will be making it clear wherever possible that money wage restraint is *essential*'.[19]

The increased Government awareness of what economists would call 'factor price substitution'[20] was nevertheless not adequately generalized. Particularly, this is the case with the Government's sustained advocacy for wage decisions in favour of lower-paid workers. In all submissions before the Arbitration Commission, the burden of the Government's case for increases in the minimum wage was 'the Government's objective of greater equality for the disadvantaged' (Cameron, Media Statement, 2 May 1974). Although the growth in unemployment was chiefly concentrated amongst low-paid workers, yet the Government continued to influence a distribution in wage share in favour of these workers (that is, in favour of 'the disadvantaged'). Thus, although the Government statements viewed wage as a price ('Employees can price themselves out of the market'), their commitment to 'wage justice' confused an adequate realization that it was in respect of *the disadvantaged* that such 'pricing out of the market' was most operative. It was the 'low wage earners' enjoying the Government's 'particular concern' who were most subject to being 'priced out of the market'.

Because it could not surrender commitment to the notion of the 'just wage', the Government was unable consistently to free its wages policy to meet its employment objective. This failure clearly to adopt a 'social compact' perspective (where the policy framework was viewed in terms of the matching of instruments and targets) had the effect that wages policy continued to be a 'dilemma'. The Government's submission to the 1974–75 National Wage Case illustrates this conflict. Having argued the need for wage restraint, Counsel for the Commonwealth considered the Commission to be faced 'with the dilemma of [fixing a wage that would be] both equitable in terms of protecting the interests of lower paid workers ... [and which would be] economically responsible in terms of the national economy'.[21] That dilemma was not yet resolved, for the Government (under the declining influence of the Minister for Labour and Immigration) continued to argue for a plateau indexation to 'ensure that those with little bargaining power do not fall behind in wage increases'.[22] The operation of Government policy was thus directed to a narrowing of relative wages between higher-paid and lower-paid workers. As will later be argued, the effect of this policy was to reduce further the employment opportunities for 'low wage earner' workers. That is, the retention of the notion of 'wage justice' in respect of 'low wage earners' operated to increase the incidence of dis-employment borne by low-productivity workers. The partial demise of this bastion of 'wage justice' did not occur as a result of economic reasoning of the kind introduced above, but from political realities which led to the appointment in June 1975 of a less doctrinaire Minister for Labour and Immigration, the Hon. Senator Douglas McClelland.[23]

Late Government Policy

> In [the 1974 National Wage] case, the Government was prepared to give open-ended support to wage indexation whilst in the present case, it put forward a rigorous set of conditions to accompany the application of indexation.
>
> (Commonwealth Conciliation and Arbitration Commission, 'Reasons for Decision', April 1975)

As late as 12 November 1974 the Prime Minister was still presenting plateau indexation as the Government's objective, and his Minister for Labour and Immigration (Mr Cameron) continued vigorously to argue for this policy.[24] When indexation was reintroduced by the Arbitration Commission on 30 April 1975, Mr Cameron hailed it as 'a milestone in the history of Australian wages policy'. But he continued to decry full indexation saying, 'Those in least need ... will get the most benefit. The Government is totally opposed to total indexation ... [which will] still widen the gap between high ... and low incomes'. Five weeks later, Senator McClelland replaced Mr Cameron in his portfolio. By July 1975 the Whitlam Government had responded to union pressure and shifted its support from plateau indexation to full indexation of earnings. This shift finds expression in a speech of 7 July 1975 by the new Minister for Labour and Immigration to the Metal Trades Industry Association, where he said: 'The proposal which I put forward in my recent discussion with the representatives of the metal industry unions would ensure that indexation relates to actual pay, not merely to the award rate'. Nevertheless, this shift was a reluctant one, and Senator McClelland in a speech of 14 September 1975 reveals that even comparative pragmatists within the Government continued to view wage advances favouring the well-placed workers as 'not fair'.

It was this shift in Government policy from an attitude of permissiveness to one of supposed restraint in respect of wage growth to which the Arbitration Commission referred in presenting its introduction of full Consumer Price Index wage indexation for the March quarter of 1975. The Commission commented: 'In [the 1974] case, the Government was prepared to give open-ended support to wage indexation whilst in the present case, it put forward a rigorous set of conditions to accompany the application of indexation'. Mr R. E. McGarvie QC, Counsel for the Commonwealth, summarized the Government's plea before the Commission as requiring a decision for 'those needing work'. The substance of the Counsel for the Commonwealth's argument was the now familiar one which drew links between the increase in wages, and the incidence of inflation, leading to the distribution of income away from profits, and consequent unemployment. In its 'Reasons for Decision', the Commission twice quoted the submission of Counsel for the Minister of Labour and Immigration that 'the prospects for the economy in the immediate future will depend crucially on the behaviour of wages'.

The Arbitration Commission's reasoning in declining the Government's plateau indexation submission and in introducing *full* indexation was 'industrial relations considerations'. It was this political pressure which chiefly influenced the fall in June 1975 of Mr Cameron and his replacement by Senator McClelland. Although the cause of the 'low wage earner' was supported less vocally, the Labor Government's desire to redistribute wage income to the low wage earner remained to the end, and in the 1975 minimum wage application the Government was explicit in making no submission on that part of the claim.

Substantial though the changes were, the adaptation of the wages policy of the Whitlam Government to the facts of the Australian economic environment was still incomplete. The late wages policy of the Whitlam Government was argued as one of wages 'restraint'. But its purpose was to maintain the real wage increases gained by those retaining employment. It may be suggested that the prolonged adjustment and adaptation of the Australian economy and society to the wages policy of the Whitlam years is in the mid-1980s still incomplete.

The Australian Labor Party entered government in 1972 believing that it could direct a major transformation of Australian political economy in accordance with its own designs. During the last year of the Whitlam Government, the emergence of a new pragmatism was in evidence, and one may detect a growth in awareness by the Government of the importance of economic policy being consistent—both in conception and implementation—with economic realities. The documentation and analysis of these 'realities' is the chief interest of this book. The following chapter introduces the economic theory which is employed in this evaluation of the wages policy of the Whitlam Government.

Chapter 3
The Theory of Wages and Employment: An Overview

Introduction

Neoclassical Analysis

Considerable recourse will be made in this study to neoclassical economic analysis. The purpose of this introduction is to set out how the author views that mode of analysis, and how it is to be related to the topic of the book. An understanding of the argument of the subsequent chapters nevertheless does not depend upon a full comprehension of the exposition of this chapter.

In a neoclassical framework, wages are thought of as determined by the forces of supply and demand deriving an equation of the value of the marginal product and marginal factor cost with the value of the marginal product being equal to the marginal physical product of the last factor increment times marginal revenue. Under conditions of perfect competition, each economic agent faces given prices, in both factor ('input') and product ('output') markets. This leads to a cost-minimizing (profit-maximizing) outcome where factor use continues until the marginal cost of the last product increment is equal to factor price, and marginal revenue from the last product increment is equal to product price. The 'given' factor and product prices are derived by a process of price and quantity adjustments which ensure that markets are cleared, so that in product markets inventories are at the levels planned, and in factor markets resources are not involuntarily idle.

Within the neoclassical framework the starting point for valuation of goods and services may conveniently be thought of as a balance between consumer subjective evaluation of desired goods and services and the availability of resources to support the provision of these goods and services. In this framework, valuation is a measure of *scarcity*—in the sense of a measure of the relative preference for, and availability of, certain goods and services. And in such a framework, the 'price system' operates to match supply of and demand for goods and services.

It should be noted that the neoclassical theory of perfect competition contains a normative notion of price—for it comprises voluntary evaluation by users and suppliers, and it also comprises the context of a particular market structure in which transactions take place. In this context, any price so determined takes on a normative significance, and may be described as 'fair', 'free', or 'just', with what is 'just' deriving from a free evaluation of the scarcity of the relevant 'good' under conditions of a perfectly competitive market structure.

Whilst setting aside (for the present) the issue of monopoly restriction of the operation of the market, one should nevertheless not be surprised that the neoclassical purview has not satisfied the full range of personal and social evaluations of a 'just' reward. For the neoclassical framework treats only 'factors of production' and 'products'. In fact, however, one may not be dealing with such neutral terms—for both 'product' and 'factor' could be a person. We restrict the operation of the market to prohibit trade in human 'products'—that is, slavery is outlawed. Personal and social pressure may also operate to restrict the operation of the market in human 'factors' of production—as, for example, occurs where a minimum price for labour services is set in an attempt to derive a wage income (whether monetary, or 'real') at which some socially acceptable 'standard of living' is possible. This restriction of the free operation of the market might arise where a particular type of labour service is in relative abundance and attracts a low scarcity valuation—perhaps a valuation so low that, as argued by Counsel for the Commonwealth during the 1974 National Wage Case, 'our towns and cities [would have] a mass of people ... poorly housed, poorly fed, poorly educated, readily in ill health and otherwise handicapped'.[1]

The introduction of a 'minimum wage' in response to the sort of reasoning suggested above involves further notions of 'justice' from those implicit in neoclassical analysis, and the 'just' price is not simply one which reflects a free evaluation of scarcity. It has been usual in neoclassical analysis to treat such extensions of personal and social interest in factor incomes by separating the normative analysis of the production of goods and services and the normative analysis of the distribution of incomes. Thus it has been possible to sustain an analysis of the opportunities for production of goods and services, where price reflects a free evaluation of *scarcity*. In this context, economists speak of the 'efficiency' of resource use, with the most 'efficient' resource use being that derived where the actions of individual economic agents are constrained only by the structure of a perfectly competitive market in the provision of goods and services.

Sometimes the normative content of the neoclassical analysis of production is left implicit, with the result that the analysis of production 'efficiency' may at times tend to be regarded as 'descriptive'.[2] Usually 'distribution' of command over goods and services has been treated as a more explicitly 'normative' field, and questions such as the progressivity or otherwise of taxes are typically treated as questions of personal and social evaluation of a 'just' outcome, with these evaluations being formed through political and social institutions rather than through the market.

The neoclassical framework may be useful for labour market analysis in much the same way as the *Reports* of the Australian Industries Assistance Commission may be viewed as useful. One wishes to know what are the 'efficiency' costs of extant protection, but one is not necessarily therefore convinced that the most 'efficient' use of resources is the most *desirable* use of resources. Even so, one ought to heed any loss-in-efficiency cost of a decision for protection, for only in so heeding is one making a decision which takes account of the costs (from an economic 'efficiency' viewpoint) of one's choice. That is, it is necessary to assess whether the opportunity cost of alternatives foregone matches the social evaluation (operating through social and political institutions) of gains through the retention of protection.[3] Thus, labour market analysis employing a neoclassical framework (as in the chapters that follow) may usefully indicate the costs of particular aspects of government wages policy (for example, increased relative wages for juniors), and also provide a means by which those costs may be assessed against other non-economic or 'social' objectives of government policy. It is in this sense that the analysis of this book offers 'an economic evaluation of the wages policy of the Whitlam Government'.

Although a dichotomy between 'economic' and 'social' evaluation of protection may have a measure of falsity, it nevertheless underscores a critical point: that 'social' decisions need to be made with a sharp awareness of their 'economic' cost. The boundaries between the categories of 'social' and 'economic' may be very unclear. (An example is where the introduction of a tariff on some particular product—thereby relieving those engaged in a particular industry from the pressures of economic adjustment—is argued on the grounds of protecting the social fabric of a section of Australian society.) But an awareness of economic costs should greatly aid sensible economic and social decision making. Such an awareness also should aid stability in decisions: for thus might 'economic' decisions be made with an adequate assessment of their 'non-economic' costs and consequences; and thus also might 'social' decisions be made with adequate assessment of their 'economic' costs and consequences. And decisions so made may be expected to be less productive of reactionary economic and social consequences. An example might be the introduction on 'egalitarian' grounds of higher relative wages for youths: leading to reduced school participation and to reduced labour market skills; with this in turn generating increased long-term deprivation and increased long-term dependency upon a system of public transfer payments; and with the growth in numbers of people making demands upon market goods and services—whilst not contributing to the provision thereof—giving rise to a reactionary contraction in transfer payment provisions (in 'real' terms) and increased social hostility towards those not engaged in the market provision of goods and services.

It is with this sort of perspective that considerable recourse is made in this work to neoclassical analysis of the operation of the market, and, particularly, to neoclassical analysis of the operation of the labour market.

Theory of Market Distribution of the National Product

On a neoclassical view as described above, the market distribution of factor incomes would be a function of scarcity. If any factor of production was earning more than its opportunity returns (that is, was earning a 'rent'), a free operation of the market would induce the reallocation of resources until returns on alternative resource uses were equalized. So, for example, where a certain category of labour attracted a rent, it should be expected that people would be drawn into that occupational category; and with a consequent reduction of scarcity for that category of labour skills, one should over time expect the elimination of the rent thereon. Similarly with capital: where capital resources directed to a certain productive use earned a rent, one should over time expect a shift in the direction of capital resources towards that use. With the consequent increase in output of the relevant product, and its reduced scarcity and reduced price, one should over time expect the elimination of rents earned on the relevant productive assets. This, of course, assumes that the productive assets are not 'given' or fixed, and that the context is a free market.

This process of redistribution is most important to the consideration of the distribution of 'productivity gains'. On a neoclassical understanding, market distribution of product between factors of production is not simply a function of factor price, where such prices are viewed as given. As was suggested above, the incidence of rents (especially in a growing economy) would be expected to induce a process of change in resource allocation such that relative prices both of factors *and* of products would change. It should be expected that technological change, over time, would operate to reduce the relative price of those products which are more efficiently produced.

It follows from this reasoning that an 'administered' alteration of *factor* prices (such as occurs with alteration of award wages as a result of a National Wage Case determination) is not the only or necessarily the most appropriate means of distributing productivity gains. In his *General Theory*, Lord Keynes concluded the chapter on 'Changes in Money Wages' with an expression of preference for wages rising slowly, rather than prices falling slowly as a result of technical progress, 'on account of the fact that it is easier with an expectation of higher wages in [the] future to keep [up] the actual level of employment'.[4] The seminal work of the Australian economist, Dr W. E. G. Salter, published in his book *Productivity and Technical Change*[5] has influenced a view favouring the granting by wages tribunals of money wage increases in proportion to the increase in national productivity (see, for example, the book *Wages and Productivity*[6] by Dr J. E. Isaac, now Deputy President of the Australian Conciliation and Arbitration Commission). Salter's view, however, was that his research results did not necessarily indicate the appropriateness of such a policy. Salter argued that, 'While the stability of shares in the total product provides some information concerning the overall distribution of productivity gains, *it does not indicate either the means of distribution, or whether it is economically appropriate*'.[7] Productivity gains may also be distributed through the instrument of reduced *product* prices—or, under conditions of inflation, the distribution may be by a *lesser* increase in the general level of product prices than would otherwise occur. As has been argued in Chapter 2, the Whitlam Government saw wage increases as 'the appropriate instrument' for distribution of productivity gains in favour of labour, and this perspective materially influenced the Government's push between December 1972 and mid-1974 for increases in wages.

The Government's outlook contrasts with the neoclassical perspective that productivity growth could, over time, give rise to an increase in the real command over goods and services derived from any given factor price. This leads one to expect that under conditions of free competition and over time, the price system would operate to distribute productivity gains in some degree to *all* factors of production. The distribution of productivity gains amongst factors of production should be expected to be a function of relative factor scarcities after the implementation of the relevant technological innovations. Where—as a result of technological change—certain labour services are less scarce, certain workers may attract a lower monetary wage or a lower real wage. Thus, under free competition, one should expect that the distribution of productivity gains would not be confined to owners of those factors of production wherein the impetus to productivity gain was located, and which, initially, may enjoy some rent from productivity growth. That is, if the impetus to productivity growth were principally located in technological change and if the owners of *capital* factors of production were the active parties in the development and introduction of such change—under a free operation of the price system, and with the necessary time for adjustments—the benefits of those productivity gains would be expected to be distributed in some degree to all factors of production (labour, material, and capital contributors in the production process).[8]

The understanding of economic processes briefly described above, and the conclusions thereby derived, do not appear significantly to have influenced the Whitlam Government's thinking. At least for its early period, one reads nothing to suggest that the Government understood how (if allowed to do so) market processes may be expected to operate to distribute productivity gains. During the first National Wage Case after Labor came into office, the simple *anticipation*[9] of 'larger-than-normal productivity gains'[10] was a key element in the Counsel for the Commonwealth's argument concerning the 'capacity and the flexibility of the Australian economy for an appreciable rise in wages' (National Wage Case 1973). Consideration is later given (Chapters 4 and 5) to the implications of this analysis for the growth of the economy, for the level of economic activity, and for the level of employment at each given level of economic activity. The reasoning of this section is directed to the absence by the Government and those closest to it of an understanding of the role of the *market* in the distribution of productivity gains.

Thus, even apart from the Government's views about the 'just' wage (which would not adequately be represented by the normative views implicit in neoclassical analysis), it may be argued that the Labor Government's inadequate allowance for the operation and the strength of market processes would act to dispose the Government towards a practice of price administration. The irony is that market response to this intervention should be expected to *reduce* what was advertised as the mainplank of Labor policy: *employment*.[11] It is the employment-reducing influence of the Whitlam Government's wages policy which is the focus of investigation in the chapters that follow.

Wages and Employment: Theory in Outline

The theory treated in this section introduces analysis of labour resource use where the level of wages is above a market-clearing level. Other aspects of monopoly restriction of the market are not examined, and the analysis proceeds with reference to a counterfactual of a free operation of the market. No implication is however intended that the model of perfect competition accurately represents market conditions in Australia during the Whitlam era—least of all, labour market conditions during this (or any other) period. The usefulness of the analysis lies in its indication of the expected *direction* of market adjustment to particular government policies as these impinge upon labour market outcomes. The empirical work of this book has been to examine the incidence of labour market adjustment as predicted by neoclassical analysis, and to supply some indication of actual *magnitudes* of

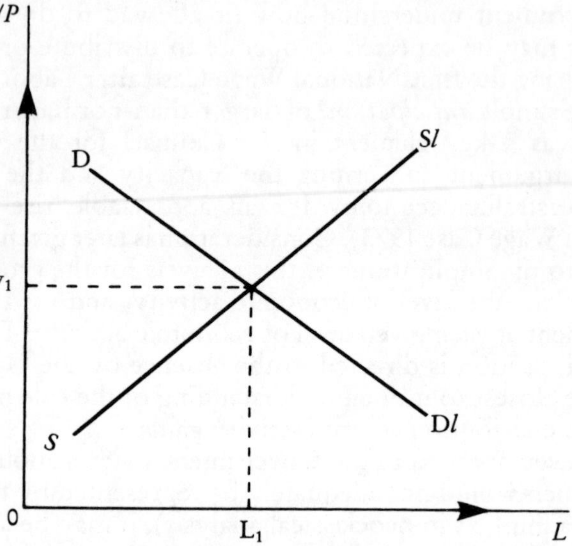

Where, w = monetary wage rate,
P = an index of prices (e.g. CPI), and
L = level of labour employment.

Figure 3.1 Labour Market Equilibrium under Free Competition

labour market responses to various government wages policy initiatives.

As has already been briefly described, in a neoclassical analysis under conditions of free competition both wages and employment are simultaneously determined through the interaction of the forces of supply and demand. In such a context, then, labour resources would not be involuntarily idle, and at equilibrium the real wage would be equal to the marginal value product of labour. Figure 3.1 illustrates this outcome, with ow_1 representing the market clearing wage, and oL_1 the level of 'full' employment of labour resources. SS*l* represents supply of labour services as a function of real wage (w/P), and DD*l* represents real demand for labour services, also as a function of real wage.

On a neoclassical understanding, the incidence of unplanned changes in inventories or of involuntary idleness of resources, would be traced to some failure in price adjustment. Thus, in the context of labour factors of production, labour unemployment would be explained in terms of a failure in price responsiveness to

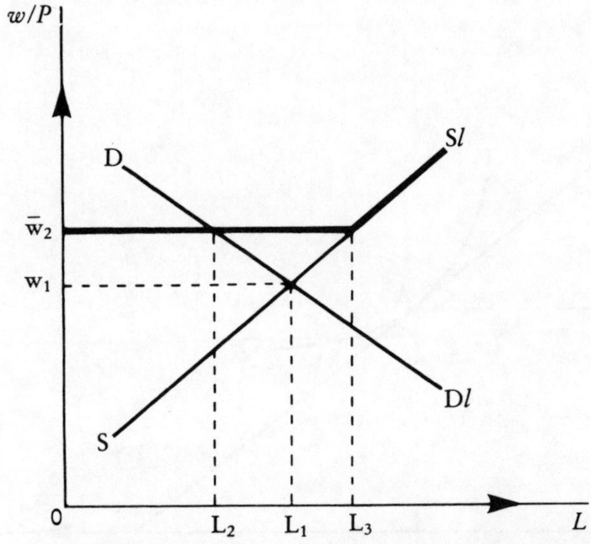

Where $\bar{w}$ indicates some enforced level of real wages.

Figure 3.2 Labour Market Equilibrium with Factor Monopoly: 'Real Wage Overhang' and 'Classical' Unemployment in a Labour Market

current conditions of supply and demand. Such unemployment is commonly referred to as 'classical' unemployment. The usual indicator of a failure in price adjustment and attendant classical unemployment would be the excess of the real wage over the marginal value product of labour at the market-clearing level of employment. This indicator of classical unemployment is now typically termed the 'real wage overhang' (and is treated in Chapter 5).

In Figure 3.2 the distance $\bar{w}_2w_1$ indicates the excess of an enforced real wage level ($o\bar{w}_2$) above the marginal value product of labour at the market-clearing level of employment (that is, above ow_1 at oL_1). Where there is an enforced minimum real wage level (such as $o\bar{w}_2$), the labour supply function would become the heavily-inked kinked function as represented by the line $\bar{w}_2Sl$ of Figure 3.2. The distance L_2L_1 would represent 'classical' unemployment deriving from the incidence of a non-market-clearing price for labour services (namely, $o\bar{w}_2$). Notice that the increase in the real hourly wage of $w_1\bar{w}_2$ leads to an increase in

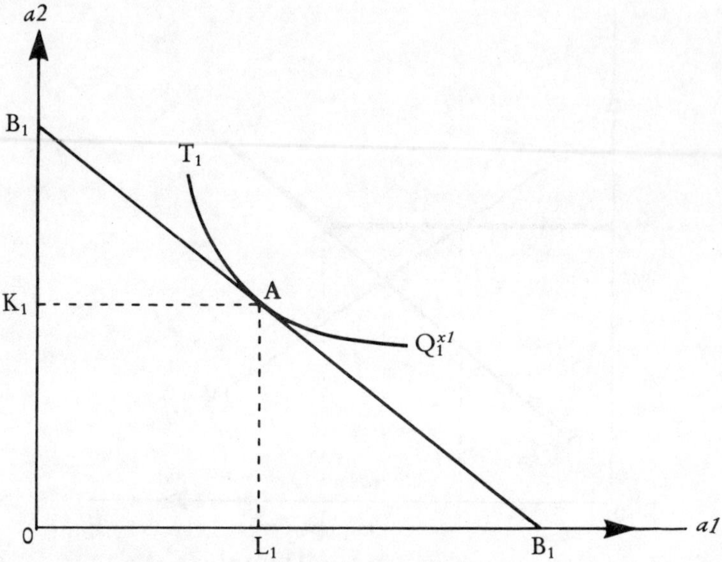

Where, T_1 = the relevant technology of production, and
Q_1 = a level of product output.

Figure 3.3 Neoclassical Model of Factor Choice

market offers of labour services—that is, 'labour force participation' rises as represented by the distance L_1L_3 of Figure 3.2. Thus, the distance L_2L_3 represents 'measured' unemployment (to be further explained) deriving from the incidence of a non-market-clearing price for labour services of $o\bar{w}_2$. The theory therefore predicts an increase in 'measured' unemployment which is greater than the decrease in employment caused by the non-market-clearing wage ($o\bar{w}_2$).

The foregoing Figures (3.1 and 3.2) depict the labour use decision in a short-run context, where capital stock and technology are given. Figures 3.3 and 3.4 above and below extend this theoretical framework and introduce the labour use decision where capital stock is variable (but where technology is constant). This is the framework used in the estimation of Equations (4.1) and (4.2) of Chapter 4.

The abscissa of Figure 3.3 represents hours of labour factor of production (*a1*), and the co-ordinate represents units of capital (*a2*).[12] B_1B_1 is a budget constraint (an 'isocost curve'), repre-

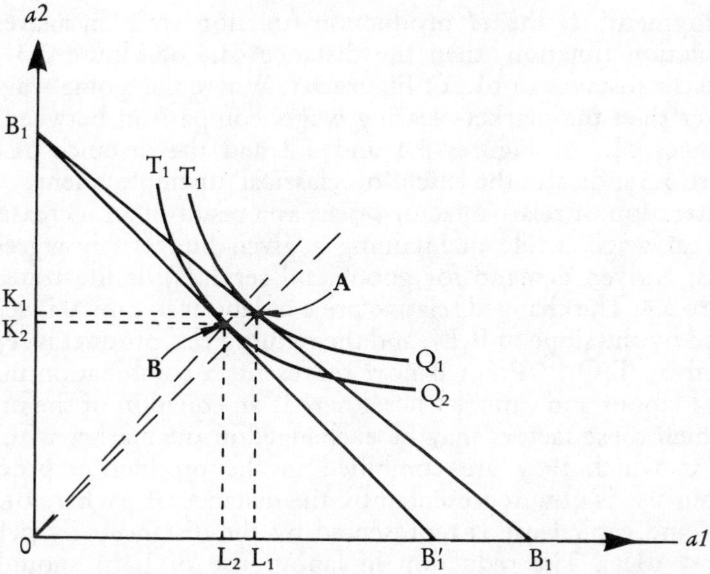

Figure 3.4 Neoclassical Model of Factor Choice with Changed Relative Price

senting the area of real command over the respective factors of production, labour and capital. The importance of B_1B_1 is not principally its position, but its *slope*—this being the relative real price of labour to capital, or the rate at which one factor may be substituted for the other in the market. The concave function T_1Q_1 is an 'isoquant', and shows the combinations of labour and capital factors of production which, with a given technology (T_1), will derive a given output (Q_1) of a given product (*x1*). The slope of the isoquant thus represents the marginal rate of technical substitution of the respective factors (labour and capital) with a given technology.[13] In the production of product *x1*, point A therefore represents a combination in the use of labour and capital where there is an equation of the prices at which these factors may be exchanged in the market (the market marginal rate of factor substitution) with the rate at which factors of production are combined in the production process (the marginal technical rate of substitution). Since this represents the cost-minimizing factor use under the described conditions, labour factor use would be oL_1 hours. Where the real hourly wage is a market-clearing wage (the w_1 of the previous Figures), then oL_1 will also represent 'full employment'. If the *x1* production function were an aggregate production function, then the distance oL_1 of Figure 3.3 will equal the distance of oL_1 of Figure 3.1. Where the 'going wage' is greater than the market-clearing wage, comparison between the distances oL_1 of Figures 3.1 and 3.2 and the distance oL_1 of Figure 3.3 indicates the extent of 'classical' unemployment.

Alteration of relative factor prices as a result of an increases in the real wage, while maintaining a given budget (in aggregate terms, a given demand for goods and services), is illustrated in Figure 3.4. The changed relative price of labour to capital is represented by the slope of B_1B_1', and the reduced real product is represented by T_1Q_2.[14] Point **B** now represents a combination in the use of labour and capital where there is an equation of the prices at which these factors may be exchanged in the market with the rate at which they are combined in the production process. Labour use is now represented by the distance oL_2(where $oL_2 < oL_1$), and capital use is represented by the distance oK_2 (where $oK_2 < oK_1$). The reduction in labour use of L_1L_2 should be noticed to be proportionately more than the reduction in capital use. It is this theory which underlies the estimates of the use of labour services of Chapters 7 and 8 and, more centrally, of Chapter 4, to which attention is now turned.

Chapter 4
The Influence of the Whitlam Government on Wages

Introduction

An outline of the broad movement of the wages policy of the Whitlam Government from one of permissiveness to one of restraint in respect of wage increases was presented in Chapter 2. Some marshalling of direct evidence concerning the Government's influence in wage outcomes is possible. But, with so many other changes simultaneously occurring in Australia (for example: changes in union strategy, and in conditions of demand for and supply of labour services), a definite attribution of the precise significance of the Government's influence in wages determination is not possible. Hence, this precision is not attempted. Circumstantial evidence that the Government's influence was not insignificant is considered in the next section, and the actual magnitude of wage variation is then examined. These data then form the basis for an empirical assessment of the significance for employment of the actual incidence of wage variation during the Whitlam period. This examination is then extended to include non-wage costs of employment. The evidence suggests that the incidence of increases in labour costs during the Whitlam period was of major significance in the decline in hours of employment.

The Influence of the Whitlam Government on Wages

Government Influence in Wage Determination

Because a new Australian Government is in power, with new policies and new priorities, we submit that the Commission should on this occasion take note of the intentions of the Government which bear on the economic considerations relevant to its decision ... The Commonwealth further submits that in present circumstances the Commission ...

should be particularly concerned with considerations of wage justice for low wage earners.

(Mr J. B. Sweeney QC, Counsel for the Commonwealth before the 1972–73 National Wage Case)[1]

We have given [the statement of Counsel for the Commonwealth] due weight in arriving at our decision.

(Arbitration Commission, Reasons for Decision 1972–73)[2]

The 'permissive' stance of the wages policy of the Whitlam Government in its early period was outlined in Chapter 2. In submissions before the Australian Conciliation and Arbitration Commission during the May 1972 National Wage Case, the McMahon Government had declared a general opposition to 'any increase in the total wage', but had 'not opposed' an increase in the minimum wage.[3] The policy of the Whitlam Government meant a shift in the balance of influence in the determinations of the Arbitration Commission. This shift is reflected in the way in May 1973 the Commission links submissions favouring an increase in minimum wage: 'The application to increase the male minimum wage [by 27 per cent] to $65 [per week] received the general support of all organisations representing employees, the Commonwealth Government and the Commonwealth Public Service Board'.[4]

It was argued in Chapter 2 that the most active influence in the Whitlam Government's wages policy was its attempt to increase relative wages for 'lower-paid' workers. The Commission's decision for 'substantial flat money increases ... in minimum wages'[5] appears to reflect the shift in federal Government influence. In its 'reasons' for deciding to 'increase the minimum wage substantially', the Commission specifically cited 'an explanatory provision drafted by the Commonwealth' and agreed to by the Australian Council of Trades Unions that the fixation of the minimum wage 'does not give any reason for any change in rates of pay in [individual awards]'.[6] The Commission's reservations concerning the Government's submission are reflected in its comments that 'it would be unwise to extend this form of increase throughout the wage structure', and '[the Commission is] unconvinced that the social and industrial climate regards wage relativities as unimportant on a long-term basis'.[7] These reservations reflect the Commission's earlier observations that National Wage increases had 'not long prevent[ed] industrial pressure for further increases in award and over-award payments'.[8]

That relative award rates did increase is clear from the data of Table 6.11 which show minimum hourly wages as a percentage of hourly award wages. The relative minimum hourly wage after the May 1974 National Wage decision was about 12 per cent below that achieved by the May 1973 National Wage determination. In announcing the 1973 decision, the Commission had anticipated that its increases in minimum wage would causally influence increases in award wages: 'It is evident of course ... that award wages will generally increase as a result of [the National Wage] decision'.[9] It is also relevant and interesting to notice that, prior to the advent of the Whitlam Government, state-award wages were generally above Commonwealth-award wages. The early period of the Whitlam Government saw federal male awards take the lead in award increases in Australia.[10]

Mr J. F. Staples QC represented the Minister for Labour before the 1974 National Wage bench. The adjustment of the wages of lower-paid workers is again the focus of attention in the Commonwealth's submission, and the application of 'flat sum' increases in minimum and award wages is argued vigorously.[11] Staples' long submission before the Bench on the state of the economy and relevant Government policy[12] is concluded with the statement that, 'The Government unhesitatingly accepts responsibility for the economic consequences, if any, that may flow from the adoption of any of its submissions to this Commission'.[13] The coalition of the Government and the unions was sustained: '[If the Commission is not persuaded by the Commonwealth's submissions] then the Government requests the Commission to grant in this case the ACTU claim in respect of minimum wage and the total wage'.[14] The response of the Deputy President to this submission was to ask Mr Staples,

> Can you really opt out of it in that way, opt out of giving any guidance to the Commission? Because the whole matter of minimum wage and total wage is so closely tied together ... you [Staples] go on to say that if the Commission decided not to introduce the automatic cost of living adjustment system, you support the ACTU claim in full.[15]

As has been suggested in Chapter 2, the latter part of 1974 saw a partial reversal of the Government's 'opting out' of the evaluation of the economic impact of its support for wage growth. During the April 1975 National Wage Case, Counsel for the Australian Government (Mr R. E. McGarvie QC) was arguing that 'Average award rates have leapt ahead of prices dramatically since the beginning of 1974 ... Between the September quarter of 1973 and the September quarter of 1974, the gross operating surplus of companies as a percentage of gross non-farm product at market prices has declined from 15.1 per cent to 9 per cent'.[16] The 1975 argument of Counsel for the Commonwealth, that the Commission was 'clearly inhibited in what it can award by way of national wage increases'[17], marks a sharp turn from the influence of the Commonwealth's intervention before the National Wage cases of 1972 and 1973. In 1975 Counsel for the Commonwealth argued for 'an adjustment of national income back towards profits'.[18] The analysis of Chapter 5 of this book suggests that the Government's successful advocacy in favour of the introduction of wage indexation in 1975 acted to inhibit (rather than to 'facilitate')[19] this adjustment. But clearly the brief period of the Whitlam Government's 'open-ended'[20] wages policy had passed.

Government Response to Wage Claims of Australian Public Service Employees

Ministerial responsibility for the Public Service for the duration of the Whitlam Government was under the Prime Minister (or the Minister Assisting the Prime Minister).[21] Perhaps for this reason, Mr Cameron gives in his apologia a lucid (even objective) account of the influence of the Government's wages policy in the area of Public Service wages and conditions. The Minister for Labour's attempts to influence Public Service wages and conditions of employment extended his sustained commitment to an ideal of higher wages for 'lower-paid workers'.[22]

Mr Cameron portrays himself as arguing throughout 1973 and 1974 that most Public Service grades were 'far ahead of the private sector in pay and perks'.[23] Data on average weekly ordinary-time hourly earnings are available for the 'private sector' and 'all sectors'.[24] The addition of government sector employment ('non-private' employment) differentiates the 'all sectors' earnings series from the 'private sector' series. Differences in the 'composition', or skills profile, between 'private' and 'government' employees make difficult a ready comparison of these series. It is notable, however, that the excess of the ordinary-time earnings series for 'all sectors' over the 'private sector' steadily increases throughout the Whitlam period.[25] While not conclusive, this evidence is consistent with an increase in the wage leadership of federal government employment.

Cameron further argues that his ministerial colleagues did not grasp 'the connection between salary rises in the Public Service, and the wage demands that were to flare up in the private sector from early 1974 onwards'.[26] The Government's response to the August 1973 application of Public Service unions for a 16 per cent across-the-board increase in salaries is described by Cameron as one of 'acquiescence'.[27] A further claim for another 16 per cent increase was lodged in April 1974, this being increased in September to a 33 per cent claim.[28] Cameron recounts that the September 1974 application induced Whitlam to move towards alliance with himself to resist the claim[29], but that their resistance was lost in Cabinet, where fears of opposing a union claim prevailed.[30] This account of Government responses in the area of Public Service pay and conditions suggests the significance for the determination of conditions of employment of the shift in the balance of power in the institutions of political economy which was achieved with the accession of a party having union affiliation.

Wage growth in this study is examined in terms of *hourly* wage. It is therefore also relevant to note the support which government employees received from the Whitlam Government favouring reduced working hours (and, thus, increased hourly wages). On 28 September 1973 the Ministers for the Northern Territory and for Labour made a Press Release stating ministerial 'endorsement of an agreement ... to introduce a 35 hour week to the 39 employees of the Northern Territory Port Authority'. A Media Statement of 16 August 1974 by Mr Cameron announced the Government's intention to intervene to support the union's case in the power union's application for a 35-hour week in their industry. In the last months of the Whitlam Government's office, Mr Cameron's successor (Senator McClelland) 'applauded the initiative of the [Postal Technicians' union in renegotiating] a "productivity package" [introducing a 36¼ hour working week] with the Telecommunications Commission'.[31] As the data for adult male ordinary-time hours show[32], there was during the Whitlam period no dramatic change in award weekly hours. This suggests that the impetus which the Government gave to the reduction in ordinary-time hours per week (and, thus, to the increase of award hourly wage) did not have widespread impact during the Whitlam period. What preconditions this influence provided for the subsequent process leading to reductions in award weekly hours is a subject for further research. One notices, however, that for 1975 there was a small fall in 'all sectors' average ordinary-time hours for adult male employees ('all sectors' represents 'private' plus 'government' employment).[33] It is notable therefore that statistical indication of widespread change in an average measure of award weekly hours first occurs in that measure which includes 'government' employment (but not in the measure for 'private' employment).

It may be argued that the permissive attitude of the Whitlam Government contributed to the 'wage explosion in the Public Service' and that this was instrumental in the more general growth in wages as unions in the private sector attempted to match wage gains in the public sector.[34] The same argument may be applied to the general growth in non-wage labour costs (examined later) where the Australian Public Service exercised a notable leadership in areas including 'superannuation, furlough, sick leave, compassionate leave, transfer allowances, rent allowances, education allowances, etc. etc.'.[35]

Wage Variation During the Period of the Whitlam Government

The story of wage variation during the Whitlam period, it might be said, has been 'oft told'.[36] Because of the variety of measures of wage, and the potential plethora of numbers, only a single table is here given (Table 4.1).[37] This shows the course of earnings for the most frequently quoted measure, and one which for the relevant period is available on a quarterly basis: 'average weekly earnings per employed male unit'. During the three years leading up to the Whitlam period, the average quarterly increase in this measure of average weekly earnings varied between about 2.25 and 3.5 per cent, and for the first year of the Whitlam Government (1973) again recorded an average quarterly increase of about 3.5 per cent. This increase nearly doubled in 1974 to a quarterly average of about 6.5 per cent, with the peak occurring during the September quarter of 1974 when the increase on the previous quarter was 11 per cent (about 26 per cent on the September quarter of the previous year). During 1975, the rate of increase in this measure of average weekly earnings sharply fell to about 3 per cent (that is, within its earlier boundary). The overall 'wage explosion' of the Whitlam period was, therefore, confined to a brief period: the last

Table 4.1 Average Weekly Earnings per Employed Male Unit (current dollars, and current dollars seasonally adjusted)

Year	Quarter	Current Dollars	Seas. Adjusted Dollars	% Gth on Prev. Qtr	% Gth on Prev. Year	Year	Current Dollars	Seas. Adjusted Dollars	% Gth on Prev. Qtr	% Gth on Prev. Year
1969	Mar.	68.50	71.70	4.1	8.3	1975	143.80	151.10	2.0	26.7
	June	72.80	72.60	1.3	8.2		156.40	154.60	2.3	22.0
	Sept.	74.10	74.10	2.1	9.3		157.60	159.40	3.1	13.4
	Dec.	79.00	75.10	1.4	8.9		175.70	167.20	4.9	12.8
1970	Mar.	72.70	77.50	3.2	8.1	1976	165.30	170.10	1.7	12.6
	June	79.40	78.80	1.7	9.9		179.80	179.40	5.5	16.0
	Sept.	80.90	80.50	2.2	8.6		184.80	184.60	2.9	15.8
	Dec.	86.30	82.50	2.5	9.9		195.40	188.10	1.9	12.5
1971	Mar.	82.00	86.70	5.1	11.9	1977	183.80	191.50	2.1	12.6
	June	89.80	88.10	1.6	11.8		198.70	191.10	−0.2	6.5
	Sept.	90.50	91.30	3.6	13.4		204.10	202.40	5.9	9.6
	Dec.	96.50	91.70	4.4	11.2		212.50	206.90	2.2	10.0
1972	Mar.	89.50	93.20	1.6	7.5	1978	205.10	211.40	2.2	10.4
	June	97.20	95.90	2.9	8.9		216.30	216.00	2.2	13.0
	Sept.	97.10	98.30	2.5	7.7		218.90	220.90	2.3	9.1
	Dec.	104.40	100.30	2.0	9.4		228.20	222.20	0.6	7.4
1973	Mar.	97.40	102.30	2.0	9.8	1979	222.80	230.40	3.7	9.0
	June	108.20	107.60	5.2	12.2		232.60	230.90	0.2	6.9
	Sept.	110.60	111.70	3.8	13.6		238.90	239.10	3.6	8.2
	Dec.	120.40	115.40	3.3	15.1		248.90	244.30	2.2	10.0
1974	Mar.	113.30	119.30	3.4	16.6	1980	245.70	250.90	2.7	8.9
	June	128.70	126.70	6.2	17.8		258.20	258.90	3.2	12.1
	Sept.	138.40	140.60	11.0	25.9		268.90	268.70	3.8	12.4
	Dec.	154.40	148.20	5.4	28.4		290.00	278.40	3.6	14.0

Sources: ABS cat. *1311.0*, *6302.0*, and computations on these data.[38]

three quarters of 1974, with the peak occurring in the September quarter of 1974.

Assessment of the Significance for Employment of Wage Increases

Empirical assessment of the significance for employment of wages increases requires separation of the influence for employment of changes in the level of macroeconomic activity, and changes in the structure of the Australian economy. Equation (4.1) specifies an attempt to separate the influence for changes in male hours employment of structural changes in the composition of employment (**S**), changes in the level of macroeconomic activity (**A**), and changes in relative factor price (**W**). There follows an explanation of these variables.

$$\mathbf{E_m}' = f\,(\underset{(-)}{\mathbf{S}'}, \underset{(+)}{\mathbf{A}'}, \underset{(-)}{\mathbf{W}'_{t-1}}) \qquad (4.1)$$

Where $\mathbf{E_m}'$ is the change in male hours of employment for Australia,

S′ is the percentage change in an index of the effects of structural change on Australian female hours of employment (as described below),

A′ is the variation in macroeconomic activity represented by changes in a series for capacity utilization in Australia (as described below), and

W′ is the change in male relative real unit wage cost.

S′ is in percentage change terms. $\mathbf{E_m}'$, **A′** and **W′** are introduced in natural logarithms. It is reasoned (see Chapter 3) that the *relative* wage is the appropriate wage measure where there is sufficient time for variation in the capital intensity of production, and **W′** has been introduced, lagged one year. All data are annual, and cover the period 1967 to 1980.

Changes in the composition of employment, **S′**, are represented by the percentage change in an index of the effects of structural change on female employment by hours. The derivation of **S′** is described elsewhere.[39] The index measures the direct contribution for female hours of employment of change in the sectoral composition of Australian employment. It is therefore anticipated that this variable would have a negative sign where the dependent variable is male hours employment.

Changes in macroeconomic activity, **A′**, are represented by a series derived as follows:

> *a*, real gross non-farm domestic product (RGNFDP), is regressed on time (*t*) and on time squared (*tt*), deriving a trend, *b*.[40] The ratio a/b is calculated. Unity forms a standard, with a ratio greater than unity indicating a level of macroeconomic activity above trend, and a ratio of less than unity indicating a level of activity below the trend level.
>
> In order to capture non-linearity in the relationship, the data are introduced in natural logarithmic form.

Following the Keynesian understanding of labour utilization as a direct function of capacity utilization[41], it is expected that this variable would have a positive sign where the dependent variable is male hours of employment.

Changes in factor prices, **W′**, are represented by a series described as 'change in male relative real unit wage cost'. This is derived as follows:

> Male average weekly earnings are divided by male average weekly hours employed, to obtain an estimate of 'male average hourly earnings' (AHE).
>
> AHE is deflated by an index of the cost of manufactured articles in order to derive an estimate of real wage cost (rather than of 'real wage income') per hour of male employment.
>
> 'Male real hourly wage cost' is divided by an index of productivity per man hour for the Australian non-farm sector, to derive an estimate of 'male real unit wage cost'.
>
> The series of male real unit wage cost is divided by the implicit price deflator index for Australian gross private fixed capital expenditure, equipment.[42]
>
> In an effort to measure 'user cost of capital services', this index was adjusted for the effects of taxation depreciation allowances.[43] The resultant series is described as estimates of 'male *relative* real unit wage cost' for Australia.
>
> At the first point described immediately above, estimates of hourly non-wage labour costs[44] were introduced to obtain a second series where the labour cost includes 'wage *plus* non-wage' costs. Estimations using this second series are reported separately in the last section of this chapter.
>
> Finally, the change in male relative real unit wage cost is derived by taking the series for $t = t\text{-}1$.

In order to capture non-linearity in the relationship, the data are introduced in natural logarithmic form.

Following the neoclassical model of choice in factor combinations (as outlined in Chapter 3), it is anticipated that the **W′** variable would have a negative sign where the dependent variable is male hours of employment.

No theoretical significance is attached to the intercept term, which may be non-significant statistically.

Results of Estimation of Equation (4.1)

The following are the results derived in estimating Equation (4.1):

$$\mathbf{E_m}' = +0.01 \quad -0.01\,\mathbf{S}' \quad +0.52\,\mathbf{A}' \quad -0.07\,\mathbf{W^{4}}'_{t-1}$$
$$(0.54) \quad (2.83) \quad (2.42) \quad (2.27)$$
$$\bar{R}^2 = 0.72 \qquad DW = 1.79 \qquad d.f. = 8$$

(*t* values in brackets)
(Sources are detailed in note 45.)

The Cochrane-Orcutt iterative technique was used to remove the indeterminacy of the estimate for autocorrelation derived under Ordinary Least Squares estimation (the Durbin-Watson statistic of 1.79 satisfies the null hypothesis of serial correlation in residuals at the conventional level of 5 per cent). Movements in explanatory variables represent nearly three-quarters of the variation in hours of employment for Australian males. The coefficients of explanatory variables have the predicted signs and are significant at the 5 per cent level or better. These parameter estimates are elasticities.

Notice that male labour use varies in the same direction by about 50 per cent of the change in the activity variable (**A′**). Male labour use varies in the opposite direction by about 10 per cent of the change in the relative wage cost variable (**W′**). The **S** variable, though statistically significant, shows a small parameter estimate. Removal of **S** from the regressions contributes a significant deterioration in the statistical properties of estimated equations. Its inclusion therefore appears to be important for the efficient estimation of parameters for **A** and **W**.[46] The intercept term is not statistically significant.

An elasticity estimate of approaching 10 per cent on the wage variable falls short of what would be expected where the unitary elasticity of factor substitution of the Cobb-Douglas production function provided a norm for judging the operation of the 'neo-classical mechanism'.[47] The following discussion shows, however, that even a relatively low estimate for the *direct* impact of changes in wages upon employment still gives rise to estimates of substantial direct effects upon employment during the Whitlam period. This statement may be made with greater emphasis when measured as direct effects upon *un*employment during the Whitlam period.

The estimates reproduced above, while sufficiently robust statistically to be given reasonable use, could not be described without qualification as 'robust'. That this should be the case is considered in the discussion of the following chapter which relates changes in wages to changes in national income shares, and changes in national income shares to changes in macroeconomic activity. But the derivation of multiple regression estimates which without qualification would merit the description 'robust' requires as a precondition that explanatory variables should statistically display the property of 'independence'—that is, should be 'independent variables'. It may perhaps be said that the separation of influences achieved through the estimation of Equation (4.1) chiefly serves heuristic purposes. The estimates demonstrate that (apart from any indirect influence which it may have), wage variation exerts a direct influence upon employment. Further, the estimation of Equation (4.1) permits the presentation of orders-of-magnitude estimates for the direct influence of wage variation upon employment.

The results of the econometric estimates reported here are qualitatively consistent with those of other Australian researchers who have used wages in estimating models of Australian labour use.[48]

Orders-of-magnitude Estimates of Direct Influence of Wage Variation upon Australian Male Employment

The 1974 increase of about 40 cents in the male real hourly wage rate represented an increase of about 18 per cent on the 1973 hourly rate of $2.17. This estimate, times the −0.09 elasticity estimate attaching to the real hourly male wage variable,[49] gives a 'back-of-the-envelope' estimate of about −1.6 per cent for the change in the 1974 male hours employment resulting from the direct impact of change in the male real hourly wage.[50] The 'back-of-the-envelope' figure of −1.6 of course estimates the impact of change in **W** with other variables constant: it is therefore a *ceteris paribus* estimate.

The 1974 growth in productivity for the Australian non-farm sector (measured on a man-hour basis) gave rise to a 25 per cent reduction in wage costs when the real hourly male wage rate is converted to an estimate of male real unit wage cost. The 1974 increase in male real unit wage cost of 30 cents on an hourly basis represented an increase of about 17 per cent on the 1973 male real unit wage rate of $1.74 per hour. This estimate, times the −0.09 elasticity estimate attaching to the male real unit wage cost[51], gives a 'back-of-the-envelope' estimate of about −1.5 per cent for change in 1974 male hours of employment as a result of the direct impact of the change in the male real unit wage cost on an hourly basis.[52]

These orders-of-magnitude calculations therefore suggest that, for 1974, increases in Australian hourly labour productivity (*ceteris paribus*) appear to have offset about 7 per cent of the negative impact of the increase in the male hourly wage rate, thus containing the 1974 contraction in male weekly hours of employment for the Australian economy to about 1.5 per cent, or about 2.4 million hours per week, on their 1973 base.[53]

However, as argued in Chapter 3, the introduction of a sufficient time period for the adjustment of capital stocks makes *relative* real unit wage cost assessed on an hourly basis the appropriate wage variable for use in assessing the influence of labour factor price on aggregate employment. During 1974 the implicit price deflator index for Australian gross private capital formation, equipment, increased by about 5.5 per cent, compared with an increase of about 17 per cent in male real unit wage cost.[54] In consequence of this, the 1974 increase in the male relative unit wage cost of about 16 cents represented an increase of about 11 per cent on the 1973 figure of $1.49. This estimate, times the −0.7 elasticity estimate attaching to **W**′ for Equation (4.1), gives a 'back-of-the-envelope' estimate approaching −1 per cent for the change in 1975 of male hours of employment deriving from the direct impact of the *ceteris paribus* change in *lagged* male relative real unit wage cost.[55]

It may therefore be suggested (*ceteris paribus*) that increases in capital equipment prices thereby offset about a third of the employment-reducing effects of the 1974 increases in male real unit wage cost.[56] That is, the increase in 1974 in capital equipment prices would have influenced a containment of the order of about a third in the 1975 contraction of male hours employment deriving from the lagged 1974 change in male relative real unit wage cost.

Applying the sort of 'back-of-the-envelope' arithmetic as introduced above suggests that the lagged change in relative wages *directly* contributed about −1.25 million hours to the aggregate change in Australian male weekly employment during 1975.[57] When it is recalled that during 1975 Australian male 'unemployment' grew by about 71 000 males, the proportional significance of the figure changes markedly: 71 000 times average ordinary-time hours of 38.2 per week gives a figure of about 2.7 million hours per week for which Australian men were not engaged in wage employment.[58] The −1.25 million hours reduction in male employment is derived by what may be regarded as a lower boundary (*ceteris paribus*) estimate of the *direct* impact only of wages growth upon employment. This reduction corresponds to about 46 per cent of the 1975 growth in measured Australian male unemployment.

Non-wage Costs of Employment

The empirical assessment of the impact of wage costs upon employment (as considered in the preceding section) is extended in this section to include non-wage costs of employment.[59] The list of 'non-wage costs of employment' is a long one: a useful survey by Australian Industries Development Association employs more than 17 categories.[60] Non-wage employment costs which were the subject of decision and influence by the Whitlam Government include: workers' compensation benefits, payroll taxation, annual leave provisions (including annual leave loading), long-service leave and superannuation provisions, and hours of employment. The Whitlam Government's influence on hours of employment was noted in the second section of this chapter. Hourly labour cost data are used for the estimates introduced above. The influence of special provisions relating to women is treated in Chapter 7. The following are examples of Government influence on increases in non-wage employment costs:

Workers' compensation benefits:

The Minister for Labour ... announced [the preparation of] a Bill to provide considerably improved compensation benefits for Australian

Government employees ... Mr Cameron said that these amendments were only a first step in a full scale review of workers' compensation ...

(Cameron, Press Statement, 9 January 1973)

Payroll taxation:

Payroll taxation was handed back to the States in August 1971 by the previous federal Government. The Whitlam Government made no efforts to arrest the drift in payroll taxation: illustrated by Victorian payroll taxation increasing from 2.5 per cent (September 1971), to 3.5 per cent (September 1972). In September 1973 Victoria increased this taxation to 4.5 per cent, and in September 1974 to 5 per cent (see also Table 4.2, below) (*Victoria Year Book*, 1979, p. 436).

Annual leave provisions:

The Prime Minister ... said today that the Australian Government will support a claim by Australian Public Service Unions for four weeks annual leave ...

(Whitlam, Press Statement, 20 December 1972)

Annual leave loading:

The Australian Government had decided to introduce legislation to provide for the payment of an annual leave loading to all its employees. The legislation ... will provide for the payment of a loading of an amount equal to average weekly earnings of all adult male wage and salary earners ... the Government ... would raise no objections to an interim settlement in respect of leave accruing on or after 1 January 1973 ...

(Whitlam, Press Statement, 10 December 1973)

Long-service leave and superannuation provisions:

The Prime Minister ... said today Cabinet had decided that the basic qualification period for furlough in Australian Government employment will be reduced from 15 to 10 years ... Furlough will be available to all employees—including part-time employees ...

(Whitlam, Press Statement, 3 April 1973)

The Treasurer ... announced that legislation to give effect to the new superannuation scheme for Australian Government employees would be introduced ... The main points of the new scheme [included] ... post retirement adjustment annually of the government-financed pension in accordance with CPI increases ...

(Crean, Media Statement, 4 December 1974)

Data allowing estimation of non-wage costs of employment are available for (a) payroll taxation, (b) superannuation, (c) workers' compensation insurance, (d) annual leave loading, and (e) annual leave (see Table 4.2, below).[61] The speed of implementation across the economy of the four-weeks annual leave provision is uncertain, so the adjustment for annual leave (column (e) of Table 4.2) is not included in non-wage costs introduced in this re-estimation.[62] The resultant estimates are as follows[63]:

Re-estimation of Equation (4.1) using wage plus non-wage labour cost data:

$$\mathbf{E_m}' = \underset{(0.60)}{+0.01} \quad \underset{(2.80)}{-0.01\,\mathbf{S}'} \quad \underset{(2.32)}{+0.51\,\mathbf{A}'} \quad \underset{(2.21)}{-0.07\mathbf{W}^{5\prime}{}_{t-1}} \qquad (4.2)$$

$\bar{R}^2 = 0.71 \qquad DW = 1.82 \qquad d.f. = 8$

(*t* values in brackets)

(Sources: As given for Equation (4.1) and for Table 4.2.)

It is interesting to note that the use of the more inclusive measure of 'labour cost' (wage plus non-wage costs) in generating a series for relative factor cost improves the statistical qualities of the estimated Equation. The stability of the estimated coefficients may be noticed by comparing these results with those of Equation (4.1), above. It may therefore be concluded that the employment impact of the changes in non-wage costs is approximately proportional to the employment impact of the changes in direct wage costs.

Reference to Table 4.4, below, highlights the significance of these changes. Notice that for 1974 the increase in nominal hourly wage costs was 32 per cent (column (a)), while the estimated increase in non-wage costs per hour of employment was more than double, 71 per cent (column (b)). The 'real' increases were 18 and 53 per cent, respectively (columns (d) & (e)). In terms of real hourly wage costs, the increase in non-wage costs therefore contributed nearly 2 per cent of the 1974 growth of 20 per cent in real hourly labour costs (column (f)). By comparison, the estimated 1974 increase in the cost of capital was at a rate nearer 5 per cent per annum (column (g)). This led to a growth in unit hourly labour cost for 1974 of about 18.7 per cent, and in relative unit hourly labour lost of about 12.6 per cent (columns (h) and (i)).

The sort of 'back-of-the-envelope' calculations applied above to wage costs may therefore be used to indicate the orders of magnitude of the effects of changes in non-wage costs. The described increases in male non-wage labour costs gave rise to a 1974 increase in male relative real unit labour cost (not simply, *wage*) of about 12.6 per cent (compared with the 1974 growth in male relative real unit wage of 10.9 per cent). The additional growth of 1.7 per cent in the estimate of *lagged* relative unit cost, times the −0.7 elasticity estimate attaching to **W** for the re-estimated equation (Equation (4.2)) gives a 'back-of-the-envelope' estimate of about −0.1 per cent for the change in 1975 male hours of employment deriving from the direct impact of the *ceteris paribus* change in the non-wage component of lagged male relative real unit labour cost.[64] This suggests that the lagged change in non-wage labour costs directly contributed about −190 000 hours to the aggregate change in Australian male weekly employment during 1975.[65] That is to say (according to this *ceteris paribus* estimate), about 7.5 per cent of the 1975 decline in hours employment may be attributed to the extraordinary 71 per cent increase in non-wage labour costs of the previous year.

This highlights the significance of non-wage labour costs for Australia's employment experience, and gives emphasis to the 'permissiveness' of the Whitlam Government's influence upon the escalation of employment costs during its early period in government. No sense of the significance of these increases for employment is betrayed by the Government: except in the marked reduction during 1974 in Government initiatives in the area of employment conditions. The deficiency (or even the absence) of economic reasoning in support of more generous employment conditions is particularly notable in the introduction of the 'annual leave loading', which institutionalized an addition of 17.5 per cent to annual leave payments.

The conclusion to be drawn from this research concerning the Whitlam Government's influence on non-wage labour costs, and on the impact of changes therein, is a further firming of a critical judgement on the Government's wages policy. From the viewpoint of non-wage costs, the lack of economic consistency of the Government's wages policy becomes clearer—as also does its contribution to the non-achievement of the Government's stated employment objective. The following chapter extends the evaluation of the Government's wages policy with an examination of the *indirect* influence of wages upon employment operating through

Table 4.2 Non-wage Weekly Costs of Employment for Males (dollars)

Year	Payroll Tax (a)	Super-annuation (b)	Work. Comp. (c)	Leave Loading (d)	**Sub-total**	Annual Leave (e)	**Total**
1967	0.93	1.32	0.79	0.0	3.05	5.96	9.01
1968	0.98	1.41	0.76	0.0	3.15	6.37	9.52
1969	1.07	1.51	0.77	0.0	3.35	6.83	10.18
1970	1.14	1.63	0.82	0.0	3.60	7.38	10.98
1971	1.20	1.83	0.88	0.0	3.92	8.27	12.19
1972	1.85	1.96	1.10	0.0	4.92	8.87	13.79
1973	2.25	2.31	1.43	0.0	5.99	10.44	16.43
1974	3.59	2.97	1.97	1.47	9.99	13.43	23.42
1975	4.53	4.95	2.60	1.63	13.70	14.92	28.62
1976	5.19	5.61	4.19	1.85	16.84	16.92	33.76
1977	5.72	6.20	4.00	2.04	17.96	18.69	36.65
1978	6.12	6.68	3.83	2.20	18.83	20.15	38.98
1979	6.70	7.63	3.43	2.43	20.19	22.26	42.45
1980	7.50	8.56	3.40	2.73	22.19	24.98	47.17

Sources[66]: (a) ABS cat. *5204.0*, *5206.0*, *6304.0*; (b) ABS cat. *6304.0*, *6312.0*, *6319.0*, AIDA, *Understanding Employment*, Melbourne, 1978, and 'The True Cost of Labour', *AIDA Bulletin*, No. 350, 1983, pp. 9–12; (c) ABS cat. *5204.0*, *5620.0*; (d) & (e) ABS cat. *6304.0*, *6312.0*.

Table 4.3 Non-wage Weekly Costs of Employment for Males (dollars (1969 = 1.00))

Year	Deflated Data as per Table 4.2 Sub-total	Total
1967	3.23	9.54
1968	3.23	9.75
1969	3.35	10.18
1970	3.46	10.57
1971	3.61	11.24
1972	4.32	12.11
1973	4.96	13.61
1974	7.42	17.40
1975	8.67	18.10
1976	9.47	18.99
1977	9.12	18.61
1978	8.81	18.23
1979	8.50	17.88
1980	8.07	17.16

Sources: ABS cat. *6412.0* and Table 4.2, and computations on these data.

Table 4.4 Annual Rates of Growth in Cost Data used in Estimation of Equation (4.2) (percentage changes, annual)

Year	MHAWE (a)	MHNWLC (b)	MHLC (c)	MRHAWE (d)	MRHNWC (e)	MRHLC (f)	IMPDF (g)	MRUHLC (h)	MRRULC (i)
1968	6.32	2.80	6.16	2.83	−0.57	2.67	1.14	−1.18	−2.29
1969	6.51	5.62	6.47	3.95	3.08	3.91	2.77	−0.47	−3.15
1970	8.36	7.71	8.33	4.29	3.67	4.26	2.40	1.52	−0.86
1971	12.78	9.65	12.64	8.00	5.00	7.87	5.27	5.44	0.16
1972	8.00	26.39	8.78	2.88	20.40	3.62	6.77	−0.08	−6.42
1973	17.14	21.18	17.34	10.54	14.36	10.73	3.04	6.38	3.24
1974	32.02	71.15	33.98	18.38	53.47	20.15	5.48	18.72	12.55
1975	12.95	39.46	14.65	−3.84	18.73	−2.39	22.22	−4.49	−21.86
1976	13.43	22.92	14.17	0.86	9.30	1.52	14.32	−1.91	−14.20
1977	10.47	6.65	10.15	−0.24	−3.69	−0.53	10.98	−3.61	−13.15
1978	7.54	4.59	7.30	−0.96	−3.68	−1.18	10.31	−1.77	−10.95
1979	9.65	6.45	9.40	−1.25	−4.13	−1.48	10.61	−3.98	−13.19
1980	12.51	10.17	12.32	−2.84	−4.86	−3.00	9.76	−3.00	−11.62

Notes:
(a) MHAWE = male hourly average weekly earnings.
(b) MHNWLC = male hourly non-wage labour costs.
(c) MHLC = male hourly labour costs (wage plus non-wage).
(d) MRHAWE = male real hourly average weekly earnings.
(e) MRHNWC = male real hourly non-wage costs.
(f) MRHLC = male real hourly labour costs (wage plus non-wage).
(g) IMPDF = implicit price deflator for Australian gross private capital formation, equipment, adjusted for the effects of taxation depreciation allowances.
(h) MRUHLC = male real unit hourly labour cost.
(i) MRRULC = male relative real unit labour cost.

Sources: See Chapter 4, note 45. Full details are given in McGavin, 'Wages and Employment', Appendix 4.1.

Table 4.5 Proportional Significance of Non-wage Costs to Wage Costs (per cent)

Year	Male Average Wkly Earnings, (a)	Non-wage Labour Costs attaching to (a) (b)	Column (b) as a proportion of (a) (c)
	Dollars, current		Per cent
1967	64.60	3.05	4.72
1968	69.00	3.15	4.57
1969	74.00	3.35	4.53
1970	80.00	3.60	4.50
1971	89.60	3.92	4.38
1972	96.10	4.92	5.12
1973	113.10	5.99	5.30
1974	145.50	9.99	6.87
1975	161.60	13.70	8.48
1976	183.30	16.84	9.19
1977	202.50	17.96	8.87
1978	218.30	18.83	8.63
1979	241.10	20.19	8.37
1980	270.60	22.19	8.20

Sources: ABS cat. *6304.0*, *6312.0*, and as per Table 4.2.

the influence of wages growth on profits share, and thus on production, on investment, and on employment. The significance of wage indexation for factor shares in national income and for employment is also examined.

Chapter 5
Real Wage Overhang, Wages Share, and Wage Indexation

Introduction

The analysis of the previous chapter focused on the course of changes in male labour costs during the Whitlam period, and on the assessment of the *direct* impact upon male employment of these changes. The direct contribution of increases in labour costs on employment may, however, be 'modest' compared with the effects operating through the reduction in actual and expected business profitability, and the weakening of the incentive to invest, with the consequent contraction in investment significantly accounting for the slowing of growth in demand.[1] As has been noticed in Chapter 2, the Whitlam Government gained some understanding of the direct impact of wages growth for employment ('employees can price themselves out of the market'). During the latter part of 1974 the Government also presented the view that 'The consequential squeeze on company profits has been severe ... [and] has played a major role in the sharp increases in unemployment over the last few months' (Cameron, Speech, 18 November 1974), and, 'Unemployment has jumped to a high level mainly as a result of a severe squeeze on profits' (Whitlam, Premiers Conference, 14 February 1975).

This chapter moves from an examination of the 'real wage overhang', to a consideration of the course of the shares of national income going to 'wages' and to 'profits'. This leads to an analysis of 'wage indexation', and of the role of the Whitlam Government in its introduction. The analysis points to further mis-perceptions and inconsistencies in the Government's wages policy, and to further counteractive influences upon the employment objective.

The 'Real Wage Overhang' and the Wages: Profits Share of National Income

Real Wage Overhang

Much discussion of the employment impact of wage increases has been conducted with reference to the 'real wage overhang'.[2] This concept was first mentioned in Chapter 3 of this book, where it was described as 'the excess of the real wage over the marginal physical product of labour at a market-clearing level of employment'. In practice it will be difficult to specify the level of labour productivity at which there is no involuntary unemployment.[3] While noting the economic significance of productivity *at the margin*, Treasury consider that *average* productivity estimates only can be given 'satisfactory measured form'.[4] Some researchers have suggested the use of a trend value for labour productivity in order to circumvent the difficulty in specifying an appropriate productivity estimate.[5] The choice of the base year (or period) for estimation of trend (or of actual) productivity may, however, remain a matter of contention[6], as also may the choice of an appropriate data base.[7] Treasury present 'real wage overhang' estimates using both actual and linear trend average productivity data, and report 'only slight difference' between estimates of the 'real wage overhang' derived by using actual and trend productivity data. Treasury argue the 'preferred' use of actual productivity estimates for the calculation of the 'real wage overhang', on the grounds that 'employers make their employment decisions on the basis of *actual* costs and productivity'.[8]

The relevant Australian debate has therefore focused on an index of 'real unit labour cost' derived by dividing an index of real wages or of real labour costs by an index of average actual or of trend average national productivity. The excess over 100 in the index so derived has been termed 'real wage overhang'.[9,10] Table 5.1, below, presents the 'preferred' measure of Treasury. The consensus of Australian economic opionion[11] views the emergence of a real wage overhang as contributing to the incidence of a reduction in employment in Australia during 1974–75. Appendix 5.1 offers a critique of a dissenting view.

Table 5.1 Estimates of Real Unit Labour Cost for the Non-farm Market Sector, Based on Actual Average Productivity*
(Base period: 1966–67 to 1972–73 = 100)

Period	Index
1966–67	101
1967–68	99
1968–69	98
1969–70	98
1970–71	101
1971–72	102
1972–73	101
1973–74	105
1974–75	111
1975–76	108
1976–77	107
1977–78	109
1978–79	106
1979–80	106

Notes: * Adjusted for changes in average hours worked by employed persons.
Sources: Treasury, RES, September 1978, p. 24, and October 1983, p. 39.

Wages Profits Share of National Income

It is essential ... that the people of Australia should understand what is happening and why ... The problems of the rapid rise in unemployment and continuing steep rise in prices and costs are interlocked. The rate of wage and salary increases has easily outstripped the rate of increase in prices. The consequential squeeze on profits has been sharp [and in these circumstances] ... greatly increase the risks involved in making new investments. The Government's immediate concern must be to stop and reverse the downturn ... The Government ... intends to take action which strikes at the root cause of the present downturn, the high rate of inflation and the decline in business profitability.

(Whitlam, Ministerial Statement, 12 November 1974)

[It is] the Government's view that ... the Prices Justification Tribunal (PJT) should give particular attention to the problems of sustaining and stimulating an adequate level of private investment and of maintaining rates of return on capital which will induce the new investment required to maintain economic growth and employment.

(Whitlam, Letter to the Chairman of the PJT, 12 November 1974)[12]

The analysis in Chapter 4 focused on the direct influence of wages growth upon employment, and the conclusions there drawn are consistent with the consensus view on the real wage overhang debate. The question of the *indirect* influence of real wage growth requires consideration however. From the latter part of 1974, the Whitlam Government gave prominent attention to the negative influence upon employment of the 'severe squeeze on profits' (Whitlam, Premiers Conference, 14 February 1975). In sourcing the causes of this squeeze, the Government gave considerable prominence to the indirect influence of wage increases operating through the reduction in actual and expected business profitability, to the weakening of incentive to invest, with this contraction of investment significantly accounting for the slowing of growth in overall activity.[13] It is to consideration of aspects of the indirect influence of wage growth on employment that attention is now turned.

The close relationship between the real wage overhang and the share of profits in national income has been clearly shown by Dr S. M. Bonnell.[14] By use of an identity, Bonnell shows that percentage movements in the share of wages, salaries and supplements at factor cost will be equal to the percentage movements in real unit labour cost, provided that the proportional change in hours worked by wage and salary earners does not differ from the proportional change in hours worked by the work force (including employers and self-employed).[15]

Between 1959–60 and 1972–73 there was a remarkable stability in the shares of Gross Domestic Non-farm Product (seasonally adjusted) going to (a) wages, salaries and supplements, and (b) gross corporate operating surpluses. The share going to wages varied between 56 and 59 per cent, around a modal 57 per cent; while the share going to corporate profits varied between 14 and 17 per cent, around a modal 16 per cent of seasonally adjusted Gross Domestic Non-farm Product (GDNFP(sa)) (refer Table 5.2, below). During the first three quarters of 1973–74 one observes a movement towards the previous boundaries—for wages, to the upper boundary of 59 per cent; and for profits, towards the previous lower boundary at 15 per cent of GDNFP(sa). During the June quarter of 1974 the wages share of GDNFP(sa) jumped to 62 per cent, accompanied by a sharp drop in the profits share to 12 per cent. Not until the September quarter 1976 did the wages share fall to 59 per cent (its previous upper boundary), and not until 1978–79 did it fall to its previous modal value of 57 per cent. Except for the June 1974 quarter figure of 14 per cent, the share of profits did not regain a level within its

Table 5.2 Wages and Profits Shares of Gross Domestic Non-farm Product (seasonally adjusted, per cent)

Fiscal Year	Quarter	Wages, Salaries and Supplements	Gross Operating Surplus for Corporate Trading Enterprises
1959–60	Sept.	0.57	0.15
	Dec.	0.57	0.16
	Mar.	0.57	0.16
	June	0.57	0.15
1960–61	Sept.	0.57	0.16
	Dec.	0.57	0.15
	Mar.	0.58	0.14
	June	0.59	0.14
1961–62	Sept.	0.59	0.14
	Dec.	0.58	0.15
	Mar.	0.57	0.16
	June	0.57	0.16
1962–63	Sept.	0.57	0.16
	Dec.	0.57	0.15
	Mar.	0.57	0.16
	June	0.57	0.15
1963–64	Sept.	0.57	0.16
	Dec.	0.57	0.16
	Mar.	0.57	0.16
	June	0.57	0.16
1964–65	Sept.	0.57	0.16
	Dec.	0.57	0.16
	Mar.	0.57	0.16
	June	0.57	0.16
1965–66	Sept.	0.57	0.15
	Dec.	0.57	0.15
	Mar.	0.58	0.15
	June	0.57	0.15
1966–67	Sept.	0.58	0.15
	Dec.	0.58	0.15
	Mar.	0.57	0.16
	June	0.57	0.16
1967–68	Sept.	0.58	0.15
	Dec.	0.57	0.16
	Mar.	0.56	0.16
	June	0.57	0.16

Fiscal Year	Quarter	Wages, Salaries and Supplements	Gross Operating Surplus for Corporate Trading Enterprises
1968–69	Sept.	0.57	0.16
	Dec.	0.57	0.16
	Mar.	0.57	0.16
	June	0.57	0.16
1969–70	Sept.	0.57	0.16
	Dec.	0.56	0.17
	Mar.	0.57	0.16
	June	0.56	0.17
1970–71	Sept.	0.57	0.16
	Dec.	0.57	0.16
	Mar.	0.59	0.15
	June	0.59	0.15
1971–72	Sept.	0.58	0.15
	Dec.	0.57	0.16
	Mar.	0.58	0.15
	June	0.58	0.15
1972–73	Sept.	0.58	0.15
	Dec.	0.57	0.16
	Mar.	0.57	0.16
	June	0.58	0.15
1973–74	Sept.	0.58	0.16
	Dec.	0.59	0.15
	Mar.	0.59	0.15
	June	0.62	0.12
1974–75	Sept.	0.63	0.12
	Dec.	0.63	0.13
	Mar.	0.63	0.12
	June	0.61	0.14
1975–76	Sept.	0.61	0.12
	Dec.	0.60	0.12
	Mar.	0.60	0.12
	June	0.60	0.13
1976–77	Sept.	0.59	0.13
	Dec.	0.59	0.13
	Mar.	0.59	0.12
	June	0.60	0.12

Table 5.2 *(Continued)*

Fiscal Year	Quarter	Wages, Salaries and Supplements	Gross Operating Surplus for Corporate Trading Enterprises
1977–78	Sept.	0.59	0.12
	Dec.	0.60	0.12
	Mar.	0.60	0.12
	June	0.59	0.12
1978–79	Sept.	0.59	0.12
	Dec.	0.57	0.13
	Mar.	0.58	0.12
	June	0.57	0.13
1979–80	Sept.	0.58	0.12
	Dec.	0.58	0.13
	Mar.	0.57	0.12
	June	0.57	0.13

Source: ABS cat. *5207.0*, June 1980, and computations on these data.

previous boundary, and at 1979–80 still stood at between 12 and 13 per cent of GDNFP(sa) (refer Table 5.2).

Massive analytical questions are raised by shifts of this magnitude in shares of national income going to factor groupings, and it could not be said that Australian economists are agreed on the detailed analysis of these issues. However, it can confidently be said that there is a consensus that increases in the wages share during the Whitlam era had a significant negative impact upon the overall level of economic activity and of employment in Australia.[16] The following sections consider the influence of wage indexation in retarding the process of adjustment required by the emergence of a real wage overhang.

Indexation and Wages

[From the September quarter 1973 to the June quarter 1974] the share of national income going to [employed] labour has increased from 58.7 per cent to 64.1 per cent. I believe that such redistribution ... is in line with what the Government set out to achieve in its social welfare programme.

(Minister for Labour and Immigration, Speech, 18 November 1974)

As was suggested in Chapter 2, the Labor Party entered government with the view that there was 'scope in the capacity and the flexibility of the Australian economy for an appreciable rise in wages without undesirable inflationary consequences'.[17] It was consistent with this belief that the Government should support a policy of formulated compensation of wages for price increases ('indexation'), both from the viewpoint of the maintenance of real wages and of the desired real wage gains, and the supposed minimization of 'inflationary consequences'.[18] As was also suggested in Chapter 2, the Labor Party entered government with an objective, actively fostered by the Minister for Labour, of 'greater [wage] equality for the disadvantaged' (Cameron, Media Statement, 2 May 1974).[19] A corollary of 'greater wage equality' is the compression of wage relativities.[20] The Minister for Labour's advocacy of 'plateau' indexation (explained below) was consistent with this position.

At the 1974 National Wage Case, Assisting Counsel for the Minister for Labour, the then Miss M. G. Gaudron, submitted on behalf of the Minister that the Commission should 'increase the *minimum* wage by a flat sum determined by reference to the percentage movement in the CPI between the end of the March quarter 1973 and the latest figures available' and that 'henceforth the minimum wage and the total wage be adjusted quarterly by a *flat sum* derived from a reference of the movement in the CPI to the minimum wage, as distinct from a reference that may otherwise be adopted to the total wage, the average award rate, or average weekly earnings'.[21] The Commission responded defensively to the Government's claim, stating its 'preference ... to keep wage adjustments under its direct control in order to be able to apply the size and form of increase in pay in a flexible way from year to year depending on the circumstances prevailing at the time'.[22]

The Government's submission in favour of indexation before the 1974–75 National Wage hearing involved a shift of ground from adjustment for increase in the CPI applied to the minimum wage[23] to adjustments for increases in the CPI up to the figure of the *average weekly earnings*.[24] Hence the Government's claim for 'plateau' indexation differed from the unions' claims for 'full' indexation, or the application of the percentage change in the CPI to award rates. It was this latter claim which the Australian Conciliation and Arbitration Commission granted.[25] The Minister for Labour and Immigration continued to decry 'full' indexation of award rates on the grounds that it contributed to a 'widen[ing of] the gap between high ... and low incomes'.[26] However, Mr Cameron's replacement in the portfolio in early June 1975 by

Senator D. McClelland quickly led to a further shift in the Government's position in favour of indexation of 'paid rates' or *actual*, and not merely award, wages.[27]

The Australian Conciliation and Arbitration Commission, in determining in favour of indexation (although on neither 'automatic' nor the 'plateau' basis as argued by the Government), pointed to a shift in the Government's position before the Commission from what it saw as 'open-ended support for wage indexation', to what was described as support for wage indexation within the context of 'a rigorous set of conditions'.[28] It will be convenient to assess the Government's commitment to and understanding of indexation within the framework argued before the Commission at the hearings leading to the re-introduction of quarterly CPI adjustment to award wages at 30 April 1975.[29]

Framework in which the Whitlam Government Argued for Indexation

Mr Whitlam's Ministerial Statement of 12 November 1974, which was tendered as an exhibit before the Arbitration Commission, states the Government's perception of the context of its intervention before the Commission:

> The problems of the rapid rise in unemployment and continuing steep rise in prices and costs are interlocked. The rate of wage and salary increases has easily outstripped the rate of increase in prices. The consequent squeeze on profits has been sharp ... The Government's immediate concern must be to stop and reverse the downturn ... The Government has decided to provide a further demand stimulus to the economy ... The Government has decided to reduce further personal income tax ... Changes in the rates of income tax should be regarded by the Commission as compensation for the increase in the cost of living which is expected for the December quarter 1974 ... We will be making it clear wherever possible that money wage restraint is essential.[30]

The Government's submission before the 1974–75 National Wage bench therefore clearly proceeds from a stance which it understood as one of 'wage restraint'. The Commission observed in its discussion of the case: 'indexation loomed as the main issue in this year's national wage proceedings'.[31] The Government's indexation proposals were central to its declared purpose of 'wage restraint'. The plateau form of the Government's indexation proposals—the application of movement in the CPI to the average weekly earnings figure—did not so much represent the view of the Government, as the position of the Minister for Labour and Immigration.[32] Mr Cameron claims that he personally carefully checked the text used by Counsel for the Government[33], and the Commonwealth's submissions before the 1974–75 National Wage bench consistently portray Mr Cameron's purpose: 'The Australian Government strongly supports wage indexation in the form of its system of plateau percentage indexation. It strongly opposes the introduction of full percentage indexation of wages at all levels.'[34] Mr Cameron's purpose was a long-standing one: to narrow the wages gap between high-paid and low-paid sectors of the work force.[35] The Government's argument was that its indexation proposals 'would create the expectation in employees that beyond doubt or contingency they will regularly and automatically receive adjustments in respect of price increases' and that 'by taking prices out of consideration in wage claims, the Government's wage indexation system will stop the spreading of wage increases obtained by the stronger unions'.[36]

The Commission, in deciding in favour of wage indexation, placed emphasis on what it described as the Government's proposal of 'a rigorous set of conditions to accompany the application of indexation'.[37] The main thrust of these conditions were as follows: (a) 'unions seeking an indexation provision in an award rate should give the Commission an assurance undertaking not to seek increases in wages beyond the increases provided for under the Australian Government's wage indexation system': (b) 'wage increases other than on account of prices be limited to changes in national productivity, work value, or other special circumstances'; and (c) wage adjustment for price increases should be on a quarterly basis.[38]

The framework in which the Whitlam Government argued for wage indexation may be summarized as follows:

1 Reflation of the economy was premised upon the containment of real wage increases.
2 The containment of real wage increases was to be achieved by the benefit of automatic adjustment for consumer price increases being generally restricted to workers whose award increases comprised only compensation for price changes and changes in national productivity.
3 Automatic adjustment for consumer price increases was to be applied up to the figure for average weekly earnings.

4 The indexation of wages was to be applied from the first quarter of 1975, on the reasoning that general wage compensation for inflation in the last quarter of 1974 had been achieved by discretionary changes in the rates of income taxation in November 1974.[39]

Critique of the Government's Case for Indexation

Use of Taxation Instrument to Compensate for Income Effects of Inflation

The Prime Minister announced in a Ministerial Statement of 12 November 1974 a further revision of the personal income taxation schedule from that proposed in the 1974–75 Budget. In this statement he presented data comparing the effects of the announced taxation cuts with an increase in gross earnings. The effects of the revision of the taxation schedule were estimated as a reduction of about 24 per cent in taxation payable by an employee with a dependent wife and two children earning $140 per week (which was about the then male average weekly earnings). This was noted to be the equivalent of respective increases of 5.75 and 3.0 per cent in gross and net pay.[40] Mr Whitlam's statement was presented as an exhibit to the 1974–75 National Wage bench by Counsel for the Commonwealth as an argument concerning tax compensation for price increases during the latter part of 1974.[41] During the fourth quarter of 1974 the CPI had increased by about 3.8 per cent; the typical effect of the Government's measures on disposable income for a worker on average weekly earnings was an increase of about 3 per cent.

In this case, the Government argued vigorously that its use of the instrument of fiscal redistribution relieved the Commission of the need to consider the fourth quarter of 1974 inflation in its wage determination. The matching of instruments and targets, and appropriate assignment of instruments would involve a large exercise of public education. Such challenging opportunities for public education concerning the efficiency gains of a policy package combining the matching of instruments and targets, with the appropriate assignment of instruments, were, however, not seriously engaged by the Government. And the argument concerning tax compensation for price increases during the latter part of 1974 stands as a rather isolated example of the Government's appreciation of the way in which the assignment of the redistributive instrument (taxation) to the achievement of the Government's income distribution objective could free the wage instrument for assignment to the target on which it has greatest impact (employment).

Use of 'Plateau Indexation' to Influence a Compression of Wage Relativities

As has been argued in the previous section, the Government perceived the proposed plateau form of indexation as operating to provide proportionately more price compensation to lower-paid than to higher-paid workers. Its effect would therefore be to further influence the compression of wage relativities, an influence clearly understood by the Commission.[42]

The disturbance of wage relativities between different award groups contributed to the emergence of wage push during the late 1960s and early 1970s.[43] In 1974 Dr E. A. Boehm argued, 'If it is decided to introduce wage indexation, its chances of success and even its chance of not aggravating inflation ... would depend partly on the restoration of an acceptable relative wage structure ...'[44] On this line of reasoning, the use of wage indexation to influence a compression of wage relativities would seem ill-advised, and potentially counter-productive.

Additionally, under conditions of a downturn in the business cycle (with the attendant leftward shift of labour factor's 'value of marginal product' function), it may be expected that real wage maintenance for workers having a lower value of marginal product would increase their risk of retrenchment. Where the market for employment of these 'lower-paid' workers has the characteristics of a 'secondary labour market'[45], the likelihood of retrenchment is increased. The effect therefore of a plateau form of wages adjustments for consumer price increases would be to compress wage relativities, and to increase the relative price of lower-paid labour services. This would be expected to contribute further to the share of employment contraction borne by lower-paid workers.[46]

Thus the effect of Mr Cameron's proposals, dictated by his zeal for 'equity'[47], would be to increase the burden of employment adjustment borne by the 'least advantaged' of the work force. In the present author's view, this is a clear case of inappropriate assignment of instrument: the incomes objective should have been met by another policy instrument, thus freeing the use of the wage instrument to accord with the purported argument of the Government for the Commission to deliver 'a decision for those needing work'.[48]

In rejecting the Government's plateau proposal in favour of 'full' indexation, the Commission would not appear to be making strong acknowledgement of the force of market influences upon the wage structure, nor to be responding to the Government's view of 'employment considerations'. It is 'industrial relations considerations' which appear to have been paramount in the Commission's April 1975 decision.[49] Yet it is extremely interesting and instructive that the Commission should also observe that 'real [disposable] income at various levels of pay can be altered by the tax scale and by social service benefits without affecting pay relativities'.[50] This comment, unusual from the Arbitration Commission, is consistent with the policy framework argued in this book. Carried to its conclusion, the argument may also be applied not only to the maintenance of relative income, but also to the maintenance of *real* income.

The 'Policing' of Wage Indexation Provisions

The Government's indexation framework included the containment of real wage increases by the benefit of automatic adjustment for consumer price increases being generally restricted to workers whose award increases comprised only compensation for price changes and changes in national productivity. The question of the appropriateness of *automatic* adjustment for consumer price increases is considered in a separate section below. Before turning to that, the proposed restriction of adjustment to workers formally meeting certain conditions is considered. At least three points require examination:

The degree to which the Commission, or other parties, may enforce formal compliance of the conditions: To the extent that unionists can force costs on their employers greater than the gains reaped by formal compliance, one should anticipate that the maximization of returns to labour would induce a violation of the conditions to accompany the application of indexation[51], and, thus, the generation of wage agreements outside the Commission. (This point is extended below.)

Formal compliance: The phrase 'formal compliance' is significant, for the clause of the 'Principles of wage determination' allowing hearings of 'work value cases' and of 'anomaly cases' gave considerable leeway for generous interpretation of 'compliance'.[52] The Institute of Applied Economic and Social Research (University of Melbourne) estimated 'that by September 1980, 70 per cent of the work force had received increases on work value grounds [Principle 7(a)]'.[53] D. H. Plowman has documented the flow-on (over a four-month period) to twenty-six other awards, following the December 1978 increase of the 'transport workers (oil companies) award' by $7.50 per week as a 'work value' increase.[54] Within such a framework, 'formal compliance' may be achieved, but its achievement is a contrivance.[55]

Agreements outside the Commission: The 'generation of agreements outside the Commission' may be expected where unions are able to exercise a strong strike threat. But a general downturn in economic activity may be expected to reduce the strength of the strike threat. In these circumstances, one might anticipate that, for most workers, the maintenance of real wages through the institution of the Commission may offer *greater* returns to labour than would be the case outside the Commission and under market influences. Under conditions of economic upturn, wage formation shifts towards consent agreements, while in conditions of economic downturn, wage formation shifts towards determinations by employment conditions tribunals.[56] It is thus argued that the tendency to move out of and then into Commission wage formation on a cyclical pattern contributes a 'ratchet effect', and that this effect operates to lift the trend average rate of wages growth. It is reckoned that wages growth in these circumstances is greater than would occur where wage formation is entirely outside the Commission, *and* also greater than would occur where wage determination is confined within the Commission.[57] This sort of analysis therefore implies that the reintroduction of indexation in Australia at April 1975 contributed to the course of average wages being *above* what they would have been in the absence of indexation (since Australia had already entered an economic downturn, which continued until late 1977).[58]

The shift in Government wages policy during the latter part of 1974 to one described as 'wage restraint'[59] may therefore have been more apparent than real. One may expect that the growth in wages during the latter part of the Whitlam Government was less than it would have been in the absence of a shift in government wages policy: in this sense it was a policy of 'wage restraint'. But the Government's 'successful' advocacy of wage indexation and its influence in restoring the role of the Australian Conciliation and Arbitration Commission in Australian wage determination may, however, have created conditions such that real wage outcomes over this and subsequent periods were greater than what would otherwise have been the case. In which event, one may reasonably describe the Government's policy of 'wage restraint' as being more apparent than real.

The generation of an appropriate counterfactual is too involved, and perhaps too speculative, here to be attempted. Three substantial strands of evidence are however consistent with the view that the wages outcomes fostered by the Whitlam Government were higher than what may have been the alternative to the determinations of employment conditions tribunals. First was the incidence of 'work value' and 'anomaly' consent awards as described above.[60] Secondly, the proportion of award wage increases granted by the Commission in National Wage Cases rose sharply following the introduction of indexation late in 1974–75 (refer below, Table 5.3). And, thirdly, the proportion of earnings increases accounted for by National Wage case decisions also rose rapidly following the late 1974–75 introduction of indexation (refer below, Table 5.4).

Table 5.3 Percentage Contribution of National Wage Case Increases to the Total Increases in Average Award Rates*

Year	Per Cent
1968–69	41
1969–70	53
1970–71	51
1971–72	28
1972–73	38
1973–74	19
1974–75	21
1975–76	90
1976–77	97
1977–78	98

Notes: * Average Award Rates = Weighted average award weekly wage rate for males. Refer to note 61.

Source: See note 62.

Table 5.4 Percentage Contribution of National Wage Case Increases to Increase in Average Weekly Earnings

Year	Per Cent
1968–69	25
1969–70	23
1970–71	33
1971–72	23
1972–73	31
1973–74	21
1974–75	15
1975–76	61
1976–77	119
1977–78	98

Sources: ABS cat. *1311.0*, *6302.0*, *6312.0* & *6314.0*, and Howard, 'Australian Trade Unions'.[62]

Appropriateness of Automatic Adjustment of Wages for Price Change

The practice of fixing wages on an index number based on certain groups of retail prices is unsound. A system of machine-made wages ... concentrates the burden through unemployment upon the minority least able to bear it.

(Statement of Australian Economists, June 1930)[63]

Wherever the price level is disturbed for whatever reason, the cost-of-living criterion involves magnifying the disturbance ... [We] reject any suggestion that price increases add to the economy's ability to pay higher wages.

(Vernon Report, 1965)[64]

In a paper published in the *Economic Record* in 1961, Professor R. I. Downing and Dr J. E. Isaac argue, 'In general ... price increases should not provide satisfactory grounds for wage increases'.[65] A summary presentation of their argument provides several cues for a critique of the April 1975 decision in favour of automatic full adjustment of wages for change in the CPI:

Changes in seasonal conditions and import prices: First, it is argued that price increases arising from changes in seasonal conditions and from changes in import prices 'represent changes in the economy's real income ... from which the wage earner cannot be insulated by changes in his monetary wages, except at the expense ... of relatively-fixed income recipients'.[66] The official import price index, all items, increased at a rate of about 8 per cent per annum in the March quarter of 1975, and at a rate of about 43 per cent for 1974–75.[67] These import price data suggest that at least part of the increase in CPI as awarded by the Commission represented the impact of negative 'changes in the economy's real income', and that the attempt to 'insulate' wage earners from this contributed to further inflation. (The point made here of course depends also upon a point subsequently considered, namely, how export prices were changing.)

Price increases deriving from increases in government charges: Secondly, price increases may derive from increases in government charges, and increases in indirect taxes. Downing and Isaac question whether the alleviation of hardship to low-wage earners caused by such price increases 'should be carried out through the clumsy and self-defeating process of general wage increase'.[68] Relevant estimates appended to the *Report* on the 1978 'Inquiry into Principles of Wage Fixation' are reproduced below as Table 5.5. It is estimated that increases in indirect taxes (less subsidies) contributed about 22 per cent of the increase in the Australian CPI during 1974–75 (an increase of about 50 per cent for the inflationary influence of increases in indirect taxes, compared with that influence during the last fiscal year of the McMahon Government, 1971–72). These data suggest the unwisdom of linking wage adjustment to movement in an index of consumer prices.

Table 5.5 Influence of Indirect Taxes on Consumer Expenditure Prices

Year	(a)	(b)	(c)
1970–71	0.6	5.9	10.2
1971–72	0.9	6.2	14.5
1972–73	1.2	5.5	21.8
1973–74	2.4	11.0	21.8
1974–75	3.1	16.0	19.4
1975–76	3.7	14.8	25.0

Notes: (a) Contribution of indirect taxes less subsidies to change in private consumption expenditure prices, Australia, per cent.
(b) Change in implicit price deflator for private consumption expenditure, per cent.
(c) Proportion of (a) to (b), per cent.

Sources: ACAC, *Inquiry into the Principles of Wage Fixation*, AGPS, Canberra, 1978; Australia, *Budget Paper No. 1*, 1975–76, & 1976–77; and ABS cat. *5204.0* (see note 69).

Wage increases already reflecting price increases: Thirdly, under either 'conditions of excess demand', or under conditions of 'differential sectoral increases in demand or in productivity', wage rises may accompany price rises. Under such circumstances, increases in average weekly earnings will already have reflected increases in prices. To further increase wages because of the observed price increases 'would merely aggravate the inflation'.[70]

Increases in export prices and in monopoly power of capital: Finally, prices may increase as a result of higher export prices, or an increase in returns to capital deriving from an increase in monopoly power. If a rise in real wages was deemed justified because of higher export prices it should nevertheless be questioned whether Arbitration Commission determinations are the most appropriate instrument to produce the desired redistribution.[71] A rise in real wages could not be justified because of an increase in monopoly power, because it could not be expected to 'redistribute ... profits back to wage-earners': 'all that would happen would be for the general price level to rise'. This suggests that monopolistic practices must either be tackled directly through means such as restrictive trade practices legislation, or a redistribution achieved through the taxation system.[72]

Use of partial indexation: Additionally, in their argument against automatic adjustment of wages for price changes, Downing and Isaac were critical of adjustment of some *portion* of the wage (for them, the 'award' wage). In the language of the 1975 debate, they were arguing against 'plateau' indexation—whether that plateau be calculated in relation to the 'minimum wage', the 'average award wage', or the 'average weekly earnings'.

Applying their analysis to the adjustment of award wages for price increases, they argued that (in some measure) the market operates to distribute increases in productivity in the form of wages above the 'award rate'. The data they present for the period 1953–54 to 1960–61 are consistent with this view. They show that 'average weekly earnings' increased about 1.7 per cent per annum more than the increase in the 'minimum weekly wage' (5.0 compared with 3.3 per cent per annum).[73] They argued that the 'ratchets which hold up costs and prices' were such that market wage determination will be 'biased in favour of wage increases in excess of productivity increases, with consequent price rises'.[74] Where award rates are adjusted to compensate for these price rises, they argue that the response of unions is such that an increase in award rates would not be absorbed by the 'margins' of those earning above award wages, but that *all* workers would share in the grant of award increases.[75]

Downing and Isaac thus argue that the results (in some measure) already achieved by the market would tend to be duplicated by a central wage institution granting award wage increases in the form described above.[76] Additionally, they argue that such centralized increases of awards would further fuel the inflationary process: 'A national wage policy then becomes a built-in wage-inflationary device'.[77] The data of Table 5.6, below, support the application of this argument to the later period. The difference between growth in award rates and average earnings is less marked than for the period of Downing and Isaac's data. Notice, however, that for the five years 1971–75, adult male average ordinary-time hourly earnings increased at a rate slightly less than did adult male award hourly wage rates; whereas for the five-year period following the introduction of indexation, the reverse was the case, with a measure of male average earnings increasing at an

Table 5.6 Rates of Increase in Australian Adult Male Awards and Earnings*

	Award Hourly Wage Rates		Average Ordinary-time Hourly Earnings	
Year (Oct.)	Dollars, current	Per cent growth on previous year	Dollars, current	Per cent growth on previous year
1971	1.52	14.29	1.98	13.14
1972	1.65	8.55	2.14	8.08
1973	1.91	15.76	2.49	16.36
1974	2.60	36.13	3.31	32.93
1975	2.94	13.07	3.76	13.60
1976	3.30	12.24	4.27	13.56
1977	3.67	11.21	4.72	10.54
1978	3.86	5.18	5.06	7.20
1979	4.18	8.29	5.54	9.49
1980	4.67	11.72	6.23	12.45

Notes: * Award rates are weighted average minimum weekly hourly rates for Australian adult male employees (excluding rural, shipping, etc. workers), and earnings are for full-time male employees (other than managerial staff) in the private sector, including 'qangos'.

Sources: ABS cat. *6312.0* & *6304.0*.

annual average about 1 per cent more than the annual increase in adult male award rates.

It is extraordinary that the arguments examined above do not appear to have qualified the Arbitration Commission's decision. The 30 April 1975 decision of the Commission to introduce wage indexation[78] includes mention of price increases deriving from increases in government charges ('fiscal action which adds to costs and prices will have a direct and rapid effect on wage movements through indexation'[79]). But this consideration apparently did not modify that decision.

There is a lack of attention to these arguments in the submissions of the Government and in ministerial statements concerning indexation proposals. The Government's support for automatic adjustment of wages for price changes should therefore be judged as being inadequately informed by an objective evaluation of the appropriateness of automatic wage indexation.

Indexation and Inflation

> [There] ... has been little attention to the illogicality (on economic grounds) of adjusting wages for wage-induced price increases and thereby unnecessarily multiplying (as general wage indexation under these circumstances would) the size of the price inflation which would inevitably have been initiated by the big wage increases themselves.
>
> (Boehm)[80]

Central to the case for the introduction of wage indexation was the proposition that a programmed system of wage compensation for price increases would reduce the rate of inflation.[81] This proposition, which has been accepted uncritically in some quarters (especially by the then Department of Labour)[82], presumes in the absence of indexation that the wage (w) is determined as follows:

$$w(\mathrm{t}) = \mathrm{A} + \{\mathrm{A}\,[\mu \dot{\mathrm{p}}^{\mathrm{e}}\,(\mathrm{t} - \mathrm{n})]\} \qquad (5.1)$$

where,

t = time period (in quarters),
A = monetary wage at t − 1,
μ = a parameter, where $0 > \mu \leqslant 1$,
$\dot{p}$ = (actual) percentage change in the CPI,
$\dot{p}^e$ = expected percentage change in the CPI, and
n = length of adjustment lag (specified in quarters).

The proposition also implies that full price compensation is achieved ($\mu = 1$) at the end of each quarter ($n = 1$). Thus, where the $\dot{p}$ has been at an increasing rate (as was generally the case between the second quarter of 1972 and the third quarter of 1974), the second term of Equation (5.1) will be increased because expected inflation in the current period will be greater than actual inflation ($\dot{p}^e(t) > \dot{p}(t)$). For example: for the four quarters 1973:3 to 1974:2, $\dot{p}$ averaged 3.4 per cent a quarter, but increased by 50 per cent to 5.1 per cent for 1974:3. If the experience of 1974:3 influenced the price compensation sought for 1974:4, a $\dot{p}^e$ of 7.7 per cent for the quarter would be assumed—a figure almost double $\dot{p}$ for 1974:4.

The validity of the proposition (that a programmed system of wage compensation for price increases would reduce the rate of inflation) depends, however, upon several conditions:

The appropriate 'counterfactual': Evaluation of any policy is against some 'counterfactual'; that is, the circumstances that would have obtained in the absence of the relevant policy implementation. In the case of wage indexation, the relevant counterfactual is not the incidence of inflation *prior* to its introduction, but the likely rate of inflation in the absence of wage indexation. It may be considered that the larger environment of macroeconomic and political circumstances, in significant degree, will determine both the measure of wage compensation for CPI increases which is achieved, and also the speed with which any such compensation is achieved. During 1975–76, there was considerable change in both macroeconomic and political circumstances in Australia. It is principally these and subsequent circumstances (and not earlier circumstances) that should inform the specification of the counterfactual relevant to an evaluation of the implementation of wage indexation. Thus, a clear evaluation of the effect upon inflation of the introduction of wage indexation requires a clear sense of the methodological importance of an appropriate counterfactual. The precise specification of an appropriate counterfactual may be a matter of great practical difficulty, even of contention. The principle of that specification, however, should be clear and uncontentious, and any evaluation not reckoning with this must be considered to be clearly defective.[83]

Dr E. A. Boehm and Professor G. H. Moore[84] indicate the first quarter of 1974 as a peak in the business cycle. With the downturn in the business cycle, one should expect both reduction in the proportion of price compensation achievable (μ), and the prolongation of the lag in adjustment of wages for price change (n). For example, if μ were reduced from 1.0 to 0.5, price compensation achieved at 1974:4, using the formula of Equation (5.1), would be at about the actual rate of $\dot{p}$.

Whether inflation is accelerating, or decelerating: A related question is whether one judges the rate of inflation to be accelerating, or decelerating. As noted above, the business cycle may be reckoned to have peaked at 1974:1, and it may be noticed that trend $\dot{p}$ is decelerating from 1974:4. In which event, at the time of the implementation of wage indexation, it should be expected that recent experience would reduce the augmentation of $\dot{p}^e$ over $\dot{p}$—indeed, could even give rise to $\dot{p}^e < \dot{p}$. What was achieved by indexation was the 'adjust[ment] of wages in the same proportion as lagged increases in the cost of living'.[85] In the circumstances of its introduction, indexation (as was argued above) is likely to have generated a measure of price compensation to wages greater than may be expected otherwise to have occurred. The consequent increased rate of wage inflation would contribute to an augmentation of the rate of inflation for Australia. It may thus be argued that the deceleration of inflation (the 'winding back' of inflation) was slowed by the institutionalization of wage compensation for CPI increases as achieved at 30 April 1975.

The extent to which wage indexation leads to redirection (rather than reduction) of issues in industrial disputation: Also related is the question whether the formulated compensation of wages for price increases leads to a lessening of the role of price expectations in wage bargaining, and to a lessening of their role in industrial disputation. This question, which is one of fact, not of principle, also is not answered by reference to *ex post* data[86], for there arises the question of the appropriate counterfactual as mentioned above. Additionally, there is the question of the degree to which institutionalization of wage compensation for price increases alters measured industrial disputation (that is, alters the 'public profile' of industrial disputation)[87], rather than *per se* reduces the incidence of industrial disputation. An example of this *redirection* of issues in industrial disputation occurs where reduced opportunity for variation of wage relativities which an indexation regime entails[88] results in wage relativity issues assuming a higher profile in industrial disputation.[89]

Direction of causality between changes in prices and wages:

> The Government asks the Commission ... to maintain and protect the purchasing power of wages ... so that purchasing power is not at risk of being diminished in any significant or measurable respect by increases in relevant prices.
>
> (Mr J. F. Staples QC, Counsel for the Commonwealth, 1974)[90]

> [Principle 1 of the wage indexation guidelines] establishes a prima facie link between price and wage movements and ... gives primacy of place in the system to substantial maintenance of real wages.
>
> (Plowman)[91]

Wage indexation proposals as a *genre* proceed from the premise that 'prices' lead 'wages'.[92] If, in fact, the direction of 'causality'[93] has principally been in the reverse direction (with 'wages' leading 'prices'), then the *raison d'être* of wage indexation virtually collapses. The evidence of Boehm's research generally supports a direction of causality for Australia's inflationary experience which runs from 'wages' to 'prices': 'on the basis of [the tests of causality applied] the strength of causation from AWE to CPI appears to have been consistently stronger than from CPI to AWE'.[94]

In the present author's view, the evidence of Boehm and other researchers deals a heavy blow to the economic case in favour of wage indexation.

Relationship of indexation to other policy initiatives: Fifthly, evaluation of the inflationary impact of indexation must be in the context of a 'package'. In speaking to its decision for the introduction of wage indexation, the Arbitration Commission referred to the 'indexation package'.[95] Principally, this 'package' involved the issues of 'compliance' with the 'conditions of indexation' (see the earlier section of this chapter on 'the "policing" of wage indexation provisions').[96] Yet, the 'package' context is not only that of 'compliance' and 'restraint' narrowly conceived. The indexation policy needs also to be seen in the context of the overall framework of economic and social policy formulation. As the Commission noted: 'the success of indexation rests heavily on support mechanisms which are outside the Commission's control'.[97] The policy stance of the Whitlam Government could only be described as one which would fuel 'reflationary expectations': 'Should the need arise, we stand ready during the year to take action on the expenditure side of the Budget to give a quick stimulus to demand and employment' (Whitlam, Ministerial Statement, 12 November 1974).

Initiating disturbance: 'supply', or 'demand'?: Dr J. Carmichael and others have argued that the impact of wage indexation upon inflation is contingent upon the source of the initiating disturbance: whether on the demand, or on the supply side. They summarize as follows:

> The essence of the result is that wage indexation steepens the aggregate supply schedule of the economy. Since demand disturbances ... involve movements along this steeper schedule, they will (*ceteris paribus*) lead to smaller changes in output and larger changes in prices than would occur without indexation. Supply disturbances ... on the other hand, shift the aggregate supply schedule horizontally. In this case, a steeper schedule will (*ceteris paribus*) result in larger changes in both output and the price level: the failure of real wages to adjust to supply shocks causes *employment* to bear the full brunt of adjustment.[98]

The Whitlam Government's support for wage indexation appears not to have been informed by analysis of this kind. The influence of 'supply side shocks' from overseas was not treated in *Wage Indexation for Australia? A Discussion Paper*, issued by the Department of Labour in 1974. As Boehm notes[99], key assumptions in the Departmental *Discussion Paper* were that 'wage increases follow price increases and wage increases help maintain labour's share of national income', and 'in the absence of wage indexation the adjustment of wages for increasing prices occurs after a lapse of time'.[100] Evidence cited above refutes a ready acceptance of these assumptions, and is consistent with the view that wage increases acted as 'supply side shocks'. The analysis of Carmichael, Fahrer and Hawkins suggests that 'wage indexation increases the response of [the] price level to all disturbances'.[101] It should therefore be concluded that the influence of the 1975 introduction of wage indexation (in restricting adjustment of the real wage to supply shocks) 'cause[d] *employment* to bear the full brunt of adjustment'.[102] This conclusion means that the Government's indexation policy should be seen as counteractive, both for its price-stabilization policy and for its employment objectives.

This discussion should not be considered to represent an exhaustive survey of issues relevant to an evaluation of indexation from the viewpoint of its impact upon the course of inflation.[103] It does make clear, however, that any anti-inflationary impact of indexation is a far more open question than the Whitlam Government and its advisers were prepared to concede. Counsel for the Commonwealth argued: 'The Government's system of ... wage indexation would play a substantial part ... in counter-acting inflation, counter-acting business recession, and counter-acting unemployment'.[104] The weight of the evidence would appear to the present author to favour the view that, on balance, the introduction of wage indexation at April 1975 worked to increase, not to decrease, Australia's rate of inflation and unemployment.

Conclusion

The analysis of this chapter leads to a highly critical judgement of the Whitlam Government's wage indexation policy.

The Arbitration Commission, in introducing the indexation 'package', placed considerable stress on the Government's support for indexation 'subject to certain conditions'.[105] It would seem to be special pleading to call the conditions accompanying the application of indexation 'rigorous'.[106] The question of 'compliance' is prominent in the Commission's discussion of its 30 April 1975 decision.[107] The analysis in this chapter suggests that the Commission did not effectively discharge the monitoring function which it clearly advertised as its purpose.[108] In not addressing that failure, the Commission also failed to maintain the view declared in introducing indexation: that, unless wage gains outside the indexation guidelines were 'negligible', indexation 'would have no future' and would be something which the Australian economy 'cannot afford'.[109] Assessment of the Commission's performance is beyond the scope of this study. The Commission, however, faced a great deal of pressure from the Whitlam Government for the introduction of indexation. In terms of rhetoric, the Government's policy fitted the context of a policy of 'wage restraint'. In terms of fact, however, it may reasonably be argued that government policy contributed to a wage outcome above that which would have occurred in the absence of indexation. Combining such a judgement with the analysis of Chapter 4, would suggest that the employment impact of the introduction of indexation was negative. On employment grounds, as argued earlier, the late shift (June 1975) to 'full' indexation would seem advised. But there appears to be no evidence that analysis of employment effects contributed to that policy shift. Rather, it would appear to be an undirected response to the political pressure of the trade union movement.[110]

To someone unsympathetic to the economic stance of this study, the failure to reckon with political influence may seem to evidence a lack of 'reality' in economic analysis. What is here being argued, however, is that political ideology and political influence are not above economic assessment. Economic analysis may inform one's political judgement. Additionally, economic analysis plays a significant educational function. For an economic assessment of a given course of action either strengthens or qualifies one's commitment to that course of action. And an economic analysis of the effects of a certain course of action provides a control function in respect of those who support the proposed action.

The Whitlam Government's ideological commitment to wage indexation is reflected in the failure of the Government and its advisers to subject the principles of its wage indexation policy to critical economic scrutiny. The direction of causality in the inflationary process, and the appropriateness of automatic adjustment of wages for price change essentially remained unexamined. Necessarily, therefore, the Government's contribution to appropriate policy formulation should be considered to be misconceived.

In terms of policy practice, the Whitlam Government's contribution should also be judged to be seriously deficient. For, on the Government's own reckoning, there was a need for adjustment reducing the share of national product going to wages (for example, the Prime Minister's speech at the February 1975 Premiers Conference). Yet the Government's successful advocacy of indexation may be assessed as having contributed to the prolongation of that process of adjustment: 'The ACTU in [its] opening submission indicated ... [the] aim was to ensure that the real wage gains ... were in fact preserved' (Counsel for the ACTU before the 1974–75 National Wage Case).[111] Additionally, such advocacy in a context where compliance with its proposed 'conditions' could not be policed (and could not reasonably be expected to be policed)[112] may be judged to have further inhibited the adjustment of returns to labour.

It may be argued that the slowing of the process of adjustment to economic imbalance in the Australian economy contributed to the reduced competitiveness of the Australian economy, and thus to the prolongation of the decline in the trend level of economic activity.[113] The employment implications of such a judgement are necessarily unfavourable. Moreover, in a context where the queue of those offering labour services at the going wages was increasing, wage indexation should be seen on average as operating to maintain a relative price for labour services above its economic cost (in the sense of 'opportunity cost').[114] As was argued in Chapter 3, a policy contributing to an artificially high return to labour services may be expected to generate a process of factor substitution away from labour use. Because the relevant relative factor price was not in these instances a reliable economic indicator of the relative social cost of resource use, the course of factor substitution so generated cannot be expected to be a socially optimal course. That is, one should expect the process of economization in the use of labour services to give rise to a greater contraction in labour use (in the employed work force) than is socially optimal.[115] Such a view is consistent with the evidence examined in Chapter 4, and leads to the conclusion that the Government's indexation policy ('counted among [its] principal achievements'—Whitlam, Media Statement, 14 September 1975) was counteractive for its stated 'prime responsibility' of employment (Cameron, Media Statement, 16 August 1974).

Chapter 6
Wages as Costs and as Incomes, and Relative Labour Costs

Wages as Costs and Wages as Incomes

[It would appear that some State Premiers hold] ... a view that increases in income tax ... are somehow painless. It is surely now obvious to us all that such a view is mistaken. There is an outdated attitude that income taxes are less inflationary than indirect taxes. Wage earners are conscious of high marginal tax rates, wage claims are made accordingly.

(Whitlam, Premiers Conference, 19 June 1975)

This section outlines the course of wages as *costs* and wages as *incomes* during the Whitlam period with the objective of making clear the growth of the wedge between these series, and the implications of this growth for labour costs and for employment. Chapter 4 dealt with the growth of direct wage costs and of non-wage labour costs. The term 'labour cost' is used to refer to wage plus non-wage costs of labour services. Except where otherwise noted, data are in nominal terms. A variety of considerations may be examined in distinguishing wages as costs and as incomes. The examination undertaken here will be confined to two aspects: (a) the deduction of income taxes to derive labour earnings net of taxation, and (b) the allowance for the differential impact of inflation upon producers [the 'cost' side] and consumers [the 'income' side] by the use of two price deflators; namely, (i) an index of the cost of manufactured articles, for deriving estimates of real labour cost, and (ii) the consumer price index, for deriving estimates of real labour income. As throughout this work, data will be analysed in *hourly* terms.

Changes in Rates of Taxation

Table 6.1 gives an overall picture of the changes in rates of income taxation for individuals with an assessable income at the annual rate for male average weekly earnings. Column (a) shows the gross income tax rate for an employee with a taxable income equal to male average weekly earnings (AWE). This figure is that which an employee could calculate using the data on his pay slip.[1] It is the rate of taxation before allowance for concessions and deductions which are taken into account in deriving the assessed taxation and the refund received by the taxpayer after the end of the fiscal year. The gross taxation rate may be compared with the data of column (b) which gives an estimate of the rate of *net* taxation for a worker on AWE. Calculation of this figure is tedious (and hazardous).[2]

In terms of profile, it is the first figure (*gross* taxation) to which most attention should be paid, since the data for the calculation of this figure confronts a worker every time he sees a pay slip. For the Whitlam period, the most notable figure is for 1973–74, when the annual increase in AWE of about 28 per cent was tied to an annual increase in the rate of gross taxation of more than 18 per cent.[3] Such growth in the relevant rate of gross taxation significantly qualifies the incidence of wage growth in disposable income terms. For workers on AWE, the growth between 1973 and 1974 in earnings after deduction of gross taxation is estimated at 22.5 per cent.[4]

The 1974–75 figure of 24 per cent for the average rate of gross taxation on AWE[5], shows a fall of about 2 per cent on the 1973–74 rate. This approximate maintenance of the rate of average income taxation (at the higher level established in 1973–74) may be expected to have been productive of a wage-push response, unless the expenditure objectives of the Government represented a consensus view of the typical worker: that is, unless the Prime Minister effectively had the 'mandate' which he claimed.[6] It may, however, be questioned whether workers on AWE in fact typically accepted the increase between 1972–73 and 1974–75 of nearly 16 per cent in the rate of gross taxation (refer, Table 6.1). Resistance to these increases was voiced in submissions to the 1974–75 National Wage Case by the Advocate for the ACTU: 'Taxation has been an important consideration for wage earners ... real after tax income for a person on the average weekly earnings barely increased along with productivity. In fact, the increase for the real after-tax earnings on average weekly earnings was 3.4 per cent to the September quarter 1974'.[7]

The 1973–74 increase of 29 per cent in the *net* rate of income

Table 6.1 Income Taxation: Employees (Male) and Companies (percentage rates)

	For Employees on AWE			Company
Fiscal year	Gross rate (a)	Estimated net rate (b)	Marginal gross rate (c)	[Approx.] Average & marginal rate (d)
1966–67	16.87	10.57	29.60	42.50
1967–68	17.73	10.85	29.60	42.50
1968–69	18.74	12.40	32.10	45.00
1969–70	19.94	14.73	35.40	45.00
1970–71	19.53	13.14	31.90	47.50
1971–72	20.90	13.86	34.50	47.50
1972–73	20.70	13.95	35.70	47.50
1973–74	24.48	18.05	39.90	47.50
1974–75	23.96	15.96	48.00	45.00
1975–76	29.33	19.72	35.00	42.50
1976–77	29.21	21.89	35.00	42.50
1977–78	22.39	20.85	33.75	46.00
1978–79	23.10	21.35	33.50	46.00
1979–80	23.92	23.23	33.07	46.00

Notes: (a) Average rate of income taxation before concessions and deductions for an employee with a taxable income equal to male average weekly earnings (AWE).
(b) Average rate of income taxation after concessions and deductions for an employee with a taxable income equal to AWE.
(c) Marginal rate of gross income taxation for an employee with a taxable income equal to AWE.
(d) Marginal and average rates of taxation on corporate income are approximately equal.

Sources: ABS cat. *6304.0* & *6312.0*; and Australia, Commissioner of Taxation, *Annual Reports* & *Taxation Statistics*, various issues; and computations on these data.

taxation for workers on AWE is estimated to have been even steeper than the increase in the rate of *gross* taxation. But the 1974–75 reduction of 11.5 per cent in the estimated rate of net income taxation for these workers meant a lesser increase of about 14 per cent between 1972–73 and 1974–75 in the rate of net taxation for workers on AWE assessable incomes (compared with an increase during this period of about 16 per cent in the rate of gross taxation). The difference between 16 and 14 per cent is not great, and the 14 per cent figure would be less easily estimated by workers. Moreover, there is a long time-lag in the receipt of taxation refunds by workers—and these refunds include neither compensation for earnings foregone, nor for the effects of inflation in reducing the purchasing power of refunds of excess taxation payments. For these reasons, it will be reasonable (and expedient) for subsequent analysis largely to be directed to the *gross* rate of income taxation.

In terms of resistance to cuts in 'take home' pay, the average rate of taxation may be argued as the most pertinent rate. But in terms of each worker's decision about hours of employment (for example, the 'over-time' decision), it is the *marginal* rate of taxation which is the most pertinent rate. The 1973–74 increase in the marginal rate of income taxation on income equal to AWE was nearly 12 per cent.[8] In 1974–75 this increase was over 20 per cent. Thus, in the space of two fiscal years, the marginal rate of income taxation at AWE had increased from about 36 cents to 48 cents in the dollar. For a government with an objective of maintaining employment and influencing wage restraint, the 1974–75 marginal taxation of 48 cents in the dollar at AWE would seem strongly counter-productive.

The 19 August 1975 announcement of the restructuring of rates of income taxation was therefore long overdue. The new tax scale provided a marginal rate of 35 cents in the dollar (which was near to that of the last Snedden budget of 1972–73). But in terms of the average rate of income taxation (both gross and net), this restructuring did not reduce, but increased, the rate of income taxation borne by individuals on AWE assessable income. Thus, the rate of gross taxation on AWE increased in 1975–76 by more than 22 per cent to 29.3 cents in the dollar (an increase of about 42 per cent on the 1972–73 level). Again, therefore, the weakness of the Government's income taxation policy may be noticed, in so far as this policy relates to the Government's supposed objective of wage 'restraint'.

This weakness assumes even greater prominence when comparison is made between the rate of personal income taxation and the rate of taxation of corporate profits. The marginal rate of company taxation for the period 1966–67 to 1972–73 ranged between 133 and 144 per cent of the marginal rate of taxation for individuals having an AWE taxable income (see Table 6.2). At 1973–74, the marginal rate of company taxation was reduced to 119 per cent of the relevant marginal rate of personal income taxation, and in 1974–75 it was reduced to only 94 per cent of the

Table 6.2 Company Taxation Relative to Personal Income Taxation: Ratio of the rate of tax on company profits to personal income taxation

Fiscal Year	Rate of Taxation		
	Gross (a)	Net (b)	Marginal gross (c)
1966–67	2.52	4.02	1.44
1967–68	2.39	3.92	1.44
1968–69	2.40	3.63	1.40
1969–70	2.26	3.05	1.27
1970–71	2.43	3.61	1.49
1971–72	2.27	3.43	1.38
1972–73	2.29	3.41	1.33
1973–74	1.94	2.63	1.19
1974–75	1.88	2.82	0.94
1975–76	1.45	2.16	1.21
1976–77	1.45	1.94	1.21
1977–78	2.05	2.21	1.36
1978–79	1.99	2.15	1.37
1979–80	1.92	1.98	1.39

Notes: Ratio of rate of taxation on corporate profits to:
(a) gross average rate of income taxation for individuals,
(b) estimated net average rate of income taxation for individuals,
(c) marginal rate of gross income taxation for individuals for employees having a taxable income at the level of AWE.

Sources: As for Table 6.1, and computations on these data.

marginal rate of taxation for individuals on the AWE taxable income. In terms of the Government's objective (in the latter part of 1974) of redressing the shift in the distribution of income against corporate earnings, this falling ratio may make sense. But in terms of the wages aspect of industrial relations, the comparison can only rank as invidious, and may therefore be expected to have been productive of a hardening of wage resistance, and thus also to have exercised an influence counteractive to the Government's supposed policy of wage restraint.

The Growing Wedge between Labour Costs and Disposable Wage Incomes

Tables 6.3, 6.5, and 6.7 show the impact of the changes in taxation rates in terms of the growing wedge between labour costs and disposable wage income. Table 6.3 compares: (a) male average weekly earnings, (b) male average weekly labour cost, and [(c) and (d)] estimated weekly income after deduction of income taxation for individuals with a taxable income at the level of AWE. Table 6.4 gives a better at-a-glance picture of this movement. From 1967 to 1973 AWE were about 75 to 80 per cent of male weekly labour cost (for employees with taxable incomes at AWE). During 1974 there occurred a further growth in the wedge between labour cost and disposable wage incomes, and the proportion of disposable wage income (after gross taxation) to labour cost decreased to about 71 per cent (Table 6.4). (This fall was even higher after allowance for income taxation concessions.) The decline in the proportion of disposable *nominal* wage to *nominal* labour costs continued until the last (fiscal) year of the Whitlam Government (1975–76), when the proportion of gross disposable male wage income to labour cost was 65 per cent.

Tables 6.5 and 6.6 reproduce the data of Tables 6.3 and 6.4 in 'real' terms. The 1974 fall in gross disposable male wage as a proportion of labour cost was about 5 per cent in *nominal* terms.[9] In *real* terms the 1974 fall was near to 7 per cent.[10] The experience of such realities concerning the reduced relationship between growth in real wage disposable income and growth in real labour cost can only be expected to have increased 'wage push', and to have increased worker resistance to wage 'restraint'. The ACTU Advocate at the 1974–75 National Wage Case noted: 'Despite the huge increases of money wages in 1974, the year to 1974 showed a small [*sic*] increase in *after tax* income per employee than in the twelve months to the September quarter of 1973'.[11] Additionally, this experience may be expected to have increased worker pressure for a policy of 'indexation' of wages[12]—a policy which in Chapter 5 was argued as being economically deleterious.

Finally, Tables 6.7 and 6.8 introduce the effects of changes in the average hours of male employment per week. In hourly terms the 1974 increase in real male labour costs was about 20 per cent. But in that year (using a figure after deduction of gross income taxation for a worker on AWE) there was a fall of 5.5 per cent in the proportion of real hourly wage disposable income to real hourly male labour cost (see Table 6.8). Thus the 1973–75 growth of about 11 per cent in workers' real hourly disposable income was only about a *half* of the growth in real hourly costs of employment.

The divergence between these two series (wages as *costs*, and wages as *incomes*) should be expected to have contributed both to an increase in wage resistance, *and* to increased attempts at economization in the use of labour resources. Moreover, this divergence should be expected to have contributed to a general reduction in resource use: that is, to have contributed to a reduction in the level of economic activity (refer to the arguments of Chapters 4 and 5). From the perspective of these figures, then, the income taxation policies of the Whitlam Government as they touched upon wages policy, and upon employment policy, must be described as being gravely misconceived:

> The argument has been supported by all the economic witnesses [before the 1974–75 National Wage Case] that taxation has become an important element of the wage claim. All the economic witnesses regard the decline in income tax as a prerequisite for moderation in wage claims.
>
> (ACTU Advocate, 1974–75 National Wage Case)[13]

Table 6.3 Gross and Disposable Income at the Earnings Level of Average Weekly Earnings, Males (dollars, current)

Year	AWE	AWE plus Non-wage Costs	Estimated Weekly Income for Individual on AWE after Deduction of:	
			Gross income taxation	Net income taxation
	(a)	(b)	(c)	(d)
1967	64.60	67.65	53.70	57.77
1968	69.00	72.15	56.77	61.51
1969	74.00	77.35	60.13	64.82
1970-	80.00	83.60	64.05	68.22
1971	89.60	93.52	72.10	77.83
1972	96.10	101.02	76.02	82.78
1973	113.10	119.09	89.69	97.33
1974	145.50	155.49	109.89	119.24
1975	161.60	175.30	122.88	135.81
1976	183.30	200.14	129.46	147.05
1977	202.50	220.46	143.36	158.17
1978	218.30	237.13	169.41	172.78
1979	241.10	261.29	185.41	189.62
1980	270.60	292.79	205.87	207.68

Sources: (a) ABS cat. *6304.0* & *6312.0*; (b) computations on ABS data—see note 14; (c) Australia, Commissioner for Taxation, *Annual Reports*; and (d) Australia, Commissioner for Taxation, *Taxation Statistics*, and computations on these data. (See note 15.)

Table 6.4 Disposable Wage Income Relative to Labour Cost, Males (in nominal terms) (dollars)

	Ratio to Weekly Labour Cost of AWE after deduction of:	
Year	Gross income taxation (a)	Net income taxation (b)
1967	0.79	0.85
1968	0.79	0.85
1969	0.78	0.84
1970	0.77	0.82
1971	0.77	0.83
1972	0.75	0.82
1973	0.75	0.82
1974	0.71	0.77
1975	0.70	0.77
1976	0.65	0.73
1977	0.65	0.72
1978	0.71	0.73
1979	0.71	0.73
1980	0.70	0.71

Notes: Ratio to male weekly labour cost (nominal) of:
(a) estimated nominal weekly income after deduction of *gross* income taxation for an individual with taxable income at the level AWE,
(b) estimated nominal weekly income after deduction of *net* income taxation for an individual with taxable income at the level of AWE.

Sources: As per Table 6.3, and computations on these data.

Relative Wages: Skills, Juniors

Wages for Unskilled Workers Compared with Wages for Skilled Workers

The Decision to increase the minimum wage by $8 per week [as of the first pay period after 23 May 1974] and to further review it in six months' time completely accords with the Government's objective of greater equality for the disadvantaged, and its conviction that there is an urgent need to protect the position of the lower paid worker ...

(Cameron, Media Statement, 2 May 1974)

This section compares minimum wages with wages for workers with 'average' skills, using two measures: average award rates for males, and average ordinary-time male earnings. The comparison

Table 6.5 Real Weekly Gross and Disposable Wage Income at the Earnings Level of Average Weekly Earnings, Males (dollars)

Year	AWE	Real AWE plus Real Non-wage Costs	Estimated Real Weekly Income for Individual on AWE after Deduction of:	
			Gross income taxation	Net income taxation
	(a)	(b)	(c)	(d)
1967	68.43	71.66	56.95	61.26
1968	70.70	73.92	58.23	63.09
1969	74.00	77.35	60.13	64.82
1970	77.00	80.46	62.06	66.10
1971	82.58	86.19	66.70	72.00
1972	84.37	88.69	65.82	71.67
1973	93.70	98.66	73.22	79.45
1974	108.10	115.52	79.46	86.22
1975	102.21	110.88	76.13	84.14
1976	103.09	112.56	71.01	80.66
1977	102.84	111.96	69.09	76.22
1978	102.11	110.91	74.50	75.98
1979	101.56	110.06	75.40	77.11
1980	98.44	106.51	75.99	76.66

Sources: As per Table 6.3, with deflation of columns (a) & (b) using ABS cat. *6412.0*, 1969 = 1.00, and columns (c) & (d) using ABS cat. *6401.0*, 1969 = 1.00—the former use deriving real 'costs', the latter deriving real 'income'.

Table 6.6 Real Disposable Wage Income Relative to Real Labour Cost for Males on Average Weekly Earnings (dollars)

Year	Ratio to Real Weekly Labour Cost of Estimated Real Weekly Income after Deduction of:	
	Gross income taxation	Net income taxation
	(a)	(b)
1967	0.79	0.85
1968	0.79	0.85
1969	0.78	0.84
1970	0.77	0.82
1971	0.77	0.84
1972	0.74	0.81
1973	0.74	0.81
1974	0.69	0.75
1975	0.69	0.76

Table 6.6 *(Continued)*

Year	Ratio to Real Weekly Labour Cost of Estimated Real Weekly Income after Deduction of: Gross income taxation (a)	Net income taxation (b)
1976	0.63	0.72
1977	0.62	0.68
1978	0.67	0.69
1979	0.69	0.70
1980	0.71	0.72

Notes: Ratio to male *real* weekly labour cost of:
(a) estimated *real* weekly income after deduction of *gross* income taxation for an individual with taxable income at the level of AWE,
(b) estimated *real* weekly income after deduction of *net* income taxation for an individual with a taxable income at the level of AWE.

Sources: As per Table 6.5, and computations on these data.

Table 6.7 Real Hourly Gross and Disposable Wage Income for Males on Average Weekly Earnings (dollars)

Year	Real Hourly Earnings at AWE	Real Hourly Earnings at AWE plus Real Hourly Non-wage Costs	Estimated Hourly Real Income after Deduction of:	
			Gross income taxation	Net income taxation
	(a)	(b)	(c)	(d)
1967	1.59	1.66	1.32	1.41
1968	1.63	1.71	1.34	1.46
1969	1.70	1.77	1.38	1.49
1970	1.77	1.85	1.43	1.52
1971	1.91	2.00	1.54	1.67
1972	1.97	2.07	1.54	1.67
1973	2.17	2.29	1.70	1.84
1974	2.57	2.75	1.89	2.05
1975	2.48	2.69	1.84	2.04
1976	2.50	2.73	1.72	1.95
1977	2.49	2.71	1.67	1.85
1978	2.47	2.68	1.80	1.84
1979	2.44	2.64	1.81	1.85
1980	2.37	2.56	1.83	1.84

Sources: As per Table 6.5, and computations on these data.

Table 6.8 Real Disposable Hourly Wage Income Relative to Real Hourly Labour Cost

	Ratio to Real Hourly Labour Cost of Estimated Real Hourly Income after Deduction of:	
Year	Gross income taxation (a)	Net income taxation (b)
1967	0.80	0.86
1968	0.78	0.85
1969	0.78	0.84
1970	0.77	0.82
1971	0.77	0.84
1972	0.74	0.81
1973	0.74	0.80
1974	0.69	0.75
1975	0.68	0.76
1976	0.63	0.71
1977	0.62	0.68
1978	0.67	0.69
1979	0.69	0.70
1980	0.71	0.72

Notes: Ratio to male real hourly labour cost of:
(a) estimated real *hourly* wage after deduction of *gross* income taxation for an individual with taxable income at the level of male average weekly earnings, and
(b) estimated real *hourly* wage after deduction of *net* income taxation for an individual with taxable income at the level of male average weekly earnings.

Sources: As per Table 6.5, and computations on these data.

is used to assess the Government's objectives of 'greater equality' and the protection of the 'lower paid' workers.

The course of changes in minimum weekly wages for adult males (federal award) is shown in Table 6.9.[16,17] The 17.6 per cent increase of $9 in nominal minimum wages at 29 May 1973 is notable (8.7 per cent increase in 'real' terms), and matches the Government's rhetoric. As column (b) of Table 6.9 shows, this real gain in minimum adult wage was approximately maintained throughout the period of the Whitlam Government. This outcome is consistent with the Government's stated objectives.

A corollary of the policy of 'greater equality for the disadvantaged' is a compression of the wages scale so that *relative* wages of the 'disadvantaged' worker are increased—or alternatively, relative wages of 'skilled' workers are decreased. A comparison of minimum wage with award wages and with earnings reveals a different picture. Table 6.10 shows three series: (a) minimum weekly adult male wage data (as per Table 6.9), (b) weekly male award wage rates, and (c) ordinary-time weekly male earnings data. Columns (d) and (e), respectively, show the proportion of minimum weekly wage to award wages, and to male ordinary-time earnings, and provide measures of 'unskilled relative wage'. Up to May 1973 there is an approximate stability in the relative wages of non-award workers compared with award workers and with average male earnings. With the 23 May 1974 observation (the date to which the leading quotation by the Minister of Labour applies), there occurred a notable fall in the relative wages of non-award workers of about 11 per cent compared with award rates, and about 5.7 per cent compared with ordinary-time adult male earnings (see Table 6.10, columns (d) and (e)). It is also notable that for both measures of unskilled relative wage, the level achieved by this adverse movement approximately characterizes the relative position of Arbitration Commission minimum wage determinations throughout the remainder of the Whitlam Government's office.

The picture is slightly modified by the introduction of hours data because there was some tendency to a reduction in award (or ordinary-time) hours, whilst no change from 40 hours occurred for minimum wage workers. Thus, the change at 23 May 1974 in (i) minimum hourly wage relative to award hourly rates was a reduction of 11 per cent from 82 to 73 per cent, and the change in (ii) minimum hourly wage relative to ordinary-time male earnings was a reduction of 5 per cent from 61 to 58 per cent (see Table 6.11, columns (d) and (e)).

The increase in real minimum wages was consistent with the Government's declared objectives. In terms of the theory argued in this book, this increase would be expected to work against the maintenance in employment of workers whose wage was at the minimum level. This expectation is, however, qualified by the outcome (contrary to declared Labour policy) of a reduction in *relative* wages for unskilled employees earning the minimum wage. To the extent that the Australian labour market is divided along the lines of 'primary' and 'secondary' markets[18], the significance of this qualification is reduced.

The above evidence compares minimum wages with wages for

workers of 'average' skills, using two measures of average: namely, average award rates for males, and average ordinary-time male earnings. The 1974 fall in the relative wage for unskilled workers (workers paid at the minimum wage) occurred at a time of high demand for labour skills. This outcome is consistent with the analysis of Dr S. Richardson[19], where evidence is presented showing a rise during 1974 (a year of strong effective demand) in relative wages for skilled metal trades workers compared with average ordinary-time earnings. Richardson[20] observes the consistency of this evidence with the predictions of neoclassical economic analysis. If the minimum wage was set by the market, the

Table 6.9 Minimum Weekly Wages for Adult Males (ACAC award, Melbourne) (dollars)

Date		Nominal Minimum Wage	'Real' Minimum Wage
1967	1 July	37.45	36.97
1968	25 Oct.	38.80	36.71
1969	19 Dec.	42.30	38.91
1971	1 Jan.	46.30	40.61
1972	19 May	51.00	40.96
1973	29 May	60.00	44.54
1974	23 May	68.00	44.13
	30 Sept.	68.00	40.45
1975	1 Jan.	76.00	43.65
	15 May	80.00	44.40
	18 Sept.	82.80	45.59
1976	15 Feb.	88.10	44.63
	1 April	93.10	47.16
	15 May	95.90	47.38
	15 Aug.	98.40	47.56
	22 Nov.	100.60	45.87
1977	31 Mar.	106.30	47.39
	24 May	108.30	47.17
	22 Aug.	110.50	47.20
	12 Dec.	112.20	46.83
1978	28 Feb.	113.90	46.93
	7 June	115.40	46.59
	12 Dec.	120.00	46.48
1979	27 June	123.80	45.92
1980	4 Jan.	129.40	45.55
	14 July	134.80	45.17

Notes: Refer to note 16.
Sources: ABS cat. *6312.0*, *6304.0*, & *6401.0*, and computations on these data.

Table 6.10 Comparison of Minimum Wage with Awards and Earnings (current dollars)

Date		Weekly Wage, Adult Males			Minimum Wage as a percentage of:	
		Minimum wage	Award wage	Average weekly ordinary-time earnings	Award wage	Average weekly ordinary-time earnings
		(a)	(b)	(c)	(d)	(e)
1967	1 July	37.45	43.61	55.70	**86**	**67**
1968	25 Oct.	38.80	46.79	58.80	**83**	**66**
1969	19 Dec.	42.30	51.19*	62.50	**83**	**68**
1971	1 Jan.	46.30	55.48*	67.50	**83**	**69**
1972	19 May	51.00	64.37	82.40	**79**	**62**
1973	29 May	60.00	73.29	94.00	**82**	**64**
1974	23 May	68.00	93.33	113.00	**73**	**60**
	30 Sept.	68.00	102.13	121.00	**67**	**56**
1975	1 Jan.	76.00	105.81	137.50	**72**	**55**
	15 May	80.00	112.40	142.50	**71**	**56**
	18 Sept.	82.80	117.69	144.50	**70**	**57**
1976	15 Feb.	88.10	125.69	150.00	**70**	**59**
	1 Apr.	93.10	128.83	164.50	**72**	**57**
	15 May	95.90	129.49	164.50	**74**	**58**
	15 Aug.	98.40	132.28	169.00	**74**	**58**
	22 Nov.	100.60	135.21	179.00	**74**	**56**
1977	31 Mar.	106.30	141.08	166.50†	**75**	**64**
	24 May	108.30	143.88	181.00	**75**	**60**
	22 Aug.	110.50	146.74	186.00	**75**	**59**
	12 Dec.	112.20	149.08	192.50	**75**	**58**
1978	28 Feb.	113.90	151.37	186.50	**75**	**61**
	7 June	115.40	153.51	198.50	**75**	**58**
	12 Dec.	120.00	161.28	207.50	**74**	**58**
1979	27 June	123.80	166.60	212.00	**74**	**58**
1980	4 Jan.	129.40	176.65	225.00	**73**	**58**
	14 July	134.80	185.52	235.00	**75**	**58**

Notes: Columns (d) & (e), respectively, give column (a) as percentages of columns (b) & (c).
* Indicates estimate derived by arithmetic averaging of observations.
† The downward turn for the March quarter observation 1977 is not evident in the seasonally-adjusted data.[21]

Sources: ABS cat. *1311.0* & *6312.0*, and computations on these data.
Award data are federal, for six state capital cities; earnings data are 'Private Sector'.

Table 6.11 Comparison of Minimum Wage on Hourly Basis with Award Hourly Rates and with Hourly Earnings (Adult Males) (current cents)

Date		Hourly Wage			Minimum Hourly Wage as a percentage of:	
		Minimum	Award	Ordinary-time earnings	Award	Ordinary-time earnings
		(a)	(b)	(c)	(d)	(e)
1967	1 July	93.63	112.40	143.56	83	65
1968	25 Oct.	97.00	120.90	151.94	80	64
1969	19 Dec.	105.75	132.27	161.50	80	65
1971	1 Jan.	115.75	143.73	174.87	81	66
1972	19 May	127.50	160.93	214.03	79	60
1973	29 May	150.00	182.47	245.43	82	61
1974	23 May	170.00	232.65	295.04	73	58
	30 Sept.	170.00	255.20	315.93	67	54
1975	1 Jan.	190.00	263.97	359.01	72	53
	15 May	200.00	280.13	372.06	71	54
	18 Sept.	207.00	293.33	377.28	71	55
1976	15 Feb.	220.25	313.63	391.64	70	56
	1 Apr.	232.75	313.75	429.50	74	54
	15 May	239.75	323.15	429.50	74	56
	15 Aug.	246.00	330.44	441.25	74	56
	22 Nov.	251.50	337.50	467.36	75	54
1977	31 Mar.	265.75	352.23	432.11	75	62
	24 May	270.75	359.23	472.59	75	57
	22 Aug.	276.25	366.36	485.64	75	57
	12 Dec.	280.50	372.44	502.61	75	56
1978	28 Feb.	285.74	378.16	486.95	75	58
	7 June	288.50	383.50	518.28	75	56
	12 Dec.	300.00	403.04	541.78	74	55
1979	27 June	309.50	416.41	553.52	74	56
1980	4 Jan.	323.50	421.98	587.47	77	55
	14 July	337.00	463.66	611.98	73	55

Sources: As per Table 6.10, and computations on these data.

reduction in the unskilled relative wage (as described by the data of Table 6.11) would be similarly anticipated by supply and demand analysis. Minimum wage, however, is set institutionally. In arguments put to the federal institution for minimum wage determination (the Australian Conciliation and Arbitration Commission), Counsel for the Whitlam Government consistently pleaded for decisions in favour of the lower-paid worker.[22] It would appear that the Government's wages policy objectives in this respect were unsuccessful. But this apparent lack of success may have lessened the extent of employment contraction suffered by unskilled workers, and—compared with the case where the relative wage of unskilled workers was higher—may have also reduced unemployment among unskilled workers.

Wages for Juniors Compared with Wages for Adult Workers

The Course of Change in Junior Relative Wages

The congresses of the Australian Council of Trade Unions (ACTU) decided in favour of substantial increases in the percentages of tradesmen's wages payable to apprentices, and in the proportion of award wages payable to apprenticed and non-apprenticed junior workers in 1971 and 1973, respectively.[23] Table 6.12, below, summarizes the movement of ACTU policy concerning the proportion of junior to adult wages. Prior to the 1971 decision, apprentices or juniors commenced at a wage approximating 45–50 per cent of the relevant adult rate. This was lifted to 65 per cent in 1973 (and in 1979 to 70 per cent). The first award to show a sharp compression in junior to adult relativities appears to have been the Federal Metal Industry Award.[24] The September 1972 variation of that award achieved a 27 per cent increase in the proportion of the wage for a commencing apprentice relative to the adult award (refer, Table 6.13, below). As the Bureau of Labour Market Research (BLMR) (and others) argue[25], this variation was in response to the then tight labour market conditions for skilled metal tradesmen, and was secured by agreement outside the Arbitration Commission by the Metal Trades Industry Association and the Amalgamated Metal Workers' and Shipwrights' Union. This agreement then gained Arbitration Commission status as a 'consent award', and the *reasons* for the changes which that award variation brought about do not appear in the Commission's award variation.[26] This example well reflects the generalization of BLMR 'that the available documentation of the reasons for the changes [in junior relative wages] is sparse'.[27]

Similarly 'sparse' is any documentation of Australian Government policy concerning relative wages for juniors. The Minister for Labour in his 1982 book, *Unions in Crisis*, includes a single

Table 6.12 ACTU Policy on Junior/Adult Award Wage Relativities (percentages)

	1967	1969	1971	1973	1975	1977	1979
Year	Apprentices						
First	45	45	55	65	65	65	70
Second	55	55	65	80	80	80	80
Third	65	65	85	90	90	90	90
Fourth	85	85	95	95	95	95	95
Age in Years	Non-Apprentice Juniors						
16 or under	50	50	55	65	65	65	70
17	75	75	75	85	85	85	85
18	100	100	100	100	100	100	100

Source: BLMR, *Youth Wages, Employment and the Labour Force*, Research Report No. 3, AGPS, Canberra, 1983, p. 44, using ACTU sources.

Table 6.13 Compression in Junior/Adult Relativities in the Federal Metal Industry Award (percentage of adult award payable to youths)

Year of Apprenticeship	Prior to September 1972	After September 1972
First	33.00	42.00
Second	47.25	55.00
Third	71.00	75.00
Fourth	85.50	88.00

Source: BLMR, *Youth Wages*, p. 45, using ACAC sources.

(but most revealing) reference to the topic: 'As Minister in charge of wages policy, I pressed the case for higher wage rates for young inexperienced boys and girls'.[28] The active push for increased junior relative wages appears to have come from the union movement. The first influential change appears to have been short-term labour market pressures. The generalization of the change appears to derive from the flow-on influence[29] of the critical September 1972 variation of the Federal Metal Industry Award.

It would appear, then, that the critical market and institutional changes influencing the growth of junior relative wages occurred just prior to the advent of the Whitlam Government. The generalization of that change during the period of the Whitlam Government was achieved in the context of a 'permissive' policy of general sympathy for the change on the part of the Government. The Government's general sympathy for increased relative wages for youth received strong support from Government decisions

Table 6.14 Ordinary-time Hourly Full-time Earnings of Juniors Relative to Adults, Private Sector (per cent)

Year (October)	Junior Males Relative to Adult Males (a)	Junior Females Relative to Adult Females (b)	Junior Female Earnings Relative to Junior Male Earnings (c)
1969	53	68	85
1970	53	66	86
1971	52	66	87
1972	53	66	88
1973	55	66	90
1974	55	65	93
1975	56	67	100
1976	56	68	102
1977	56	67	99
1978	56	67	99
1979	55	66	98
1980	55	65	97

Notes: Adults includes 'other than managerial etc. staff' only.
Private sector includes 'qangos'.

Sources: ABS cat. *6312.0* & *6304.0*, and computations on these data.

concerning youth unemployment benefits. Unemployment benefits for youths aged 16–17 years increased between July 1972 and January 1973 as a proportion of the ABS earnings series for youths aged 16–20 years as follows: (a) for males, from 17 to 44 per cent, and (b) for females, from 20 to 49 per cent (refer, Table 3 of Chapter 8). The proportional increase in relative unemployment benefits for youths aged 16–17 years was about double the relative increase for youths aged 18–20 years.

Estimates of junior relative ordinary-time hourly earnings for full-time employees are shown in Table 6.14. From these data it may be observed that between 1972 and 1975 there was a 5.7 per cent increase in estimated junior male ordinary-time earnings relative to adult male earnings. The point is made in *Research Report No. 3* of the BLMR that the employment-reducing impact of the 1974 economic downturn (and also of increases in junior relative pay) should be expected to have a greater proportional effect upon junior employment. The resulting reduction in junior employment would influence a reduction in the age distribution of employees within the junior category, so that older juniors comprised a larger proportion of junior employment. The BLMR

Table 6.15 BLMR Index of Award Relative Wages of Juniors to Adults

Year	Awards, dollars per week		Ratio of Juniors to Adults	Index of Ratio (1972 = 100.0)
	Juniors	Adults		
1969	33.75	54.25	0.62	100.5
1970	37.07	59.74	0.62	100.3
1971	40.48	65.36	0.62	100.0
1972	45.01	70.93	0.64	102.6
1973	53.47	82.94	0.65	104.2
1974	73.57	109.20	0.67	108.9
1975	83.85	124.86	0.67	108.6
1976	96.08	142.61	0.67	108.9
1977	105.82	156.41	0.68	109.4
1978	113.41	169.94	0.67	107.8
1979	119.97	179.62	0.67	107.9
1980	134.07	200.62	0.67	107.9

Note: Data reported are for 1 January of the following year: for example, 1969 data are for 1.1.1970.

Source: BLMR, *Youth Wages*, p. 51.

argues therefore that this 'composition effect' would inflate average estimates of junior relative wage as presented in Table 6.14.[30] As an alternative, BLMR have used data on 13 awards over the period 1970 to 1982 to generate a series of junior relative awards. This series (reproduced above as Table 6.15) uses as a base the proportion of juniors employed in its constituent awards at May 1981, and therefore is not subject to the influence of changes in age composition within junior employment. The junior relative wage series of the BLMR deals with male and female junior award wages on a weekly basis, and is therefore not strictly commensurable with the hourly estimates of Table 6.14. It is, however, interesting to note that the BLMR junior relative wage data derive a 1972 to 1975 increase of 7.9 per cent in junior relative wage—a figure rather greater than the 5.7 per cent for junior male ordinary-time hourly relative earnings mentioned above. The theoretical point concerning 'composition effects' which BLMR make would suggest a *lower* percentage increase. It may be concluded therefore that, during the period of the Whitlam Government, there was an increase in junior relative wages of about 6 to 8 per cent. According to the BLMR, the proportional increase in junior relative wages over that period for males and for females was about the same (about 8 per cent).[31] (Notice that the increase in female junior relative wage is, however, from a higher base.)[32]

Although the change in junior male wages relative to adult male wages, and in junior female wages relative to adult female wages, may have been of about the same order of magnitude, this was not true for changes in actual rates of junior pay for males and females. For the changes in the actual rates for junior females reflected the effects of the 1969, 1972, and 1975 decisions concerning 'equal pay' (see Chapter 7). Column (c) of Table 6.14, above, shows junior female ordinary-time hourly earnings relative to the same measure of junior male earnings. The indicated 1972 to 1975 increase in junior female wage relative to junior male wage of about 14 per cent is lower than the increase for this period of about 19 per cent which is indicated for adult female wage relative to adult male wage (see Table 7.1). The lesser increase for junior than for adult female relative wages is consistent with the effect of the implementation of equal pay reducing the junior female proportion to the adult rate, so that junior female proportions to the adult rate were brought into line with the lower junior male proportions. The 1.02 figure occurring at 1976 for junior female earnings relative to junior male earnings (Table 6.14, column (c)) may suggest that junior female wage data compared with junior male wage data were more subject to 'composition effect' bias. But the increase of about 14 per cent in junior female wage relative to junior male wage indicates an order of magnitude for change in junior female wages relative to junior male wages. The implications of these changes are considered in the following sub-section.

The Employment Impact of Increase in Junior Relative Wages

There have been two Australian studies of the demand for youth labour services, by Dr W. Merrilees[33], and by the BLMR.[34] The BLMR study included a brief but critical review of the study by Merrilees, and gave a verdict of 'doubtful validity' for his estimated co-efficients.[35] The Bureau's criticisms comprise, (a) the deficiencies of ABS time series average wage data (principally, changing 'composition effects'), (b) the time span of the sample period (1964 to 1978), comprising periods of high and of low labour demand, and (c) the length of Merrilees's adjustment lag. The BLMR *Report* includes a summary of the Bureau's estimation work, undertaken using a combined cross-section time series analysis. Their procedures do not entirely avert the effects of composition bias in data. Additionally, they do not allow for the effects of government junior manpower programmes, which were particularly operative during their sample period (1976 to 1981). Furthermore, the BLMR study deals only with full-time employment, during a period of growth in part-time employment.[36] Table 6.16 summarizes the results of the Merrilees and of the BLMR research.

Both these results reveal a substantially higher negative own price elasticity[37] for a change in the junior female wage than for a change in the junior male wage. The BLMR find this result 'consistent with the presence of the apprenticeship system in the Australian labour market', noting that 'about 40 per cent of male school leavers but only a very small proportion of female school leavers have entered apprenticeships'. Apprenticed junior employment involves both a more stable employment contract, and also a greater provision to employers of future labour skills, than does non-apprentice junior employment.[38]

Table 6.16 Price Elasticity of Demand for Junior Labour Services (estimates of per cent change in demand for junior labour services with a 1 per cent change in junior relative wages)

	Merrilees	BLMR
Males	−0.93	−1.80
Females	−1.70	−4.58

Note: See note 39.
Sources: W. Merrilees, 'Teenage Unemployment: The Role of Wage Rates and Other Factors', 49th ANZAAS Conference, Auckland, NZ, 1979, p. 15 f, and BLMR, *Youth Wages*, pp. 90, 148.

Given the way in which the BLMR use their results, they would appear to be excessively critical of Merrilees's research. The principal use to which the Bureau apply the estimation work contained in their *Report No. 3* is to 'confirm an important qualitative result: that increases in youth wages relative to those of other groups decrease their demand significantly'.[40] The conclusions of BLMR and of Merrilees therefore coincide:

> It seems reasonable that the qualitative result of responsiveness [of labour demand] to relative wages, as suggested by neoclassical theory, can be accepted.
>
> (BLMR)[41]

[These] results would be most pleasing to neo-classical supporters. The evidence presented here suggests that relative employment of both teenage males and females is responsive to relative price changes.

(Merrilees)[42]

These conclusions agree with those of overseas and Australian research as surveyed by Dr P. W. Miller, and which he summarizes saying, 'own-wage elasticity of demand for younger workers exceeds unity'.[43]

Implications and Conclusions

An adequate discussion of demand response to change in junior relative wages would need to include a careful relating of these changes to the growth in part-time employment—particularly to the growth in part-time adult female employment (see the following chapter).[44]

The conclusion can be drawn, however, that junior labour services show a clear substitutability following an increase in price. It may therefore be said that an increase in the price of junior labour services relative to the price of adult labour should be expected to have a negative impact upon the demand for junior labour of a magnitude at least about that of the change in junior relative wages. (That is, the own price elasticity co-efficient would be at least about unity.)

Between 1972 and 1975 there was an increase of 33 per cent in real junior male hourly earnings (see Table 6.17, below). In relative wage terms, the 1972 to 1975 increase in junior male hourly wages was about 5.7 per cent (calculated from Table 6.14, above). With an own price elasticity of demand of about unity, this may be taken (*ceteris paribus*) as signifying a reduction approaching at least 6 per cent in the demand for junior male labour services.

The 1972 to 1975 increase in real junior female hourly wages is estimated at an astounding 50 per cent (see Table 6.17). Relatively to adult females, the 1972 to 1975 increase in junior female hourly wages was about 1.5 per cent (see Table 6.14, column (b)). The evidence examined above suggests a greater substitutability for junior female labour than for junior male labour.

These estimates therefore suggest for the period of the Whitlam Government a reduction (*ceteris paribus*) in junior male employment by about 6 per cent. Using a junior female relative wage elasticity estimate of about −2 (Merrilees's estimate) gives an esti-

Table 6.17 Junior Real Ordinary-time Hourly Earnings (dollars)

Year	Males	Females
1967	0.79	0.67
1968	0.82	0.67
1969	0.85	0.73
1970	0.89	0.76
1971	0.95	0.83
1972	0.99	0.88
1973	1.13	1.01
1974	1.36	1.26
1975	1.32	1.32
1976	1.35	1.37
1977	1.35	1.35
1978	1.32	1.31
1979	1.28	1.26
1980	1.25	1.22

Note: See the notes to Table 6.14.
Sources: ABS cat. *6304.0* & *6412.0* (1969 = 1.00).

mated 4 per cent reduction (*ceteris paribus*) during 1972 to 1975 in junior female employment. The higher BLMR elasticity estimate of about −4.5 would derive a reduction (*ceteris paribus*) in junior female employment of about 7 per cent during 1972 to 1975. During the Whitlam period, the 'other things being constant' condition was clearly not met (there was, for example, wide variation in conditions of demand), so different actual magnitudes of change in fact should be expected.

Employment data by age are available for the 15 to 19 years age group, and in respect of employment, this age group will be referred to as 'junior'. These data for junior males and females, full-time and part-time, are presented in Table 6.18, below. At 1972, junior male full-time hours employment stood at 12 million per week (and at higher levels in 1973 and 1974), falling to about 11.5 m. hours per week in 1975—a fall between 1972 and 1975 of about 3.5 per cent. (The full-time plus part-time hours fall for junior male employment between 1972 and 1975 was less—about 1.6 per cent.) At 1972, junior female full-time hours employment stood at 10.2 m. per week. For reasons probably related (amongst other things) to the growth of adult female employment[45], and particularly adult female part-time employment, junior female full-time hours show a decline in both 1973 and 1974—with a fall

Table 6.18 Junior Aggregate Weekly Hours Employment* (millions)

Year	Full-time Hours		Part-time Hours		Total Hours	
	Males	Females	Males	Females	Males	Females
1967	12.77	11.23	0.56	0.30	13.33	11.53
1968	12.23	10.88	0.47	0.34	12.70	11.22
1969	12.40	10.31	0.46	0.34	12.86	10.65
1970	12.47	10.63	0.48	0.35	12.95	10.98
1971	12.63	10.36	0.42	0.44	13.05	10.80
1972	12.01	10.18	0.44	0.54	12.45	10.72
1973	12.61	9.88	0.55	0.66	13.16	10.54
1974	12.22	9.55	0.60	0.76	12.82	10.31
1975	11.59	9.00	0.66	0.80	12.25	9.80
1976	11.75	8.55	0.62	0.86	12.37	9.41
1977	11.65	8.37	0.74	0.98	12.39	9.35
1978	11.64	8.49	0.90	1.08	12.54	9.57
1979	11.95	8.06	0.91	1.12	12.86	9.18
1980	12.01	8.34	0.98	1.23	12.98	9.57

Note: * Computed on the assumption that average hours worked per week by persons may serve as a measure of average hours worked per week by juniors.

Source: ABS cat. *6204.0*, and computations on these data.

between 1972 and 1975 of about 11.6 per cent. Note that the declines of 1973 and 1974 precede the downturn in economic activity. (The full-time plus part-time hours fall for junior female employment between 1972 and 1975 was less—about 8.6 per cent.)[46]

In summary, then, changes in labour demand and in labour supply derive *ex post* outcomes for junior labour employment which show a 1972 to 1975 fall in full-time hours employment of about 3.5 per cent for males, and of about 11.6 per cent for females. The analysis in this chapter suggests that an important factor contributing to these changes in employment was the influence of the relative price change for labour factor use. The estimated magnitudes of the own price elasticity of demand for junior labour services suggest that language which Mr Cameron applied to himself may fairly be applied to the Whitlam Government in respect of its permissive attitude towards increases in junior wages: 'We have not helped the young by demanding that they not be employed unless paid excessive wages. We have priced them out of the labour market and we deserve no thanks for that.'[47]

Chapter 7
An Economic Evaluation of the Implementation of Equal Pay for Women

Introduction

The Prime Minister ... this afternoon authorized a written application to the Industrial Registrar asking to have the recent hearing on equal pay before the Full Bench of the Arbitration Commission re-opened.

(Whitlam, Press Statement, 6 December 1972)

The Government warmly welcomes the Commission's decision to extend the minimum wage to adult females.
This [decision] represents one of the Government's proudest achievements.

(Cameron, Media Statements, 2 May 1974)

Attention is focused in this chapter on evaluating the implementation of 'equal pay' for women, since this represented the Whitlam Government's major wages policy objective for women. This, however, should be seen in the context of the wide range of Government objectives directed to the conditions of women's employment, and having implications for wages policy. Most of these general objectives would come under the heading of 'non-discrimination' in the workplace. They included the following:

1 The introduction as of 1 January 1973 of 12 weeks paid maternity leave for government employees, plus provision for 40 weeks unpaid leave, and an undertaking for re-employment after 52 weeks absence (Cameron, Press Statement, 9 January 1973).
2 Increased access to Public Service employment for middle-aged and married women was isolated for attention in announcing the Government's abolition of upper age limits applying to government employment (Whitlam, Press Statement, 4 May 1973).

3 Ratification in May 1973 of Convention No. 111 (covering Discrimination) of the International Labour Organization, and the establishment of a Women's Bureau in the federal Department of Labour (Cameron, Press Statement, 6 May 1973).
4 The 'reconcil[iation of] domestic and family responsibilities with a career' was singled out for comment in the Government's announcing the implementation of flexible working hours in the Australian Public Service (Whitlam, Press Statement, 24 July 1973).

Changes such as the above should be reckoned as increasing the non-wage costs of female employment, compared with that of males. Because of the difficulty of estimating in dollar terms the magnitude of female-specific changes in these non-wages costs of employment, estimation of the negative impact of these changes for female employment does not seem feasible. To the extent that the cost of female labour services exceeds that of equivalent male labour services, one should expect, however, that opportunities for female wage employment would require the reinforcement of non-market influences such as are currently being exerted with the growth of 'affirmative action' programmes. Assessment of this wide (and contentious) area for study is not undertaken in this book. Major investigation of Whitlam Government wages policy, as this impinged upon females, is confined to evaluation of the implementation of 'equal pay' for women.

On 2 May 1974 the Australian Conciliation and Arbitration Commission in announcing its decision on the 1974 National Wage Case, determined that by 30 June 1975 adult females should be paid at a rate equal to that determined for adult males. When the Labor Party came into government on 5 December 1972 the 1969 decision of the Arbitration Commission providing 'equal pay for equal work' had been fully implemented by January 1972.[1] This decision provided that women workers under federal awards and performing the same or like work of equal value to men were to be awarded the male rate. Women performing work essentially or usually undertaken by women were not covered by this decision, with the result that this phased implementation between October 1969 and January 1972 of equal pay is estimated to have applied to about 18 per cent, only, of the female work force.[2]

An enlargement of the equal pay principle to the concept of 'equal pay for work of equal value' was introduced in the December 1972 Equal Pay Case judgement.[3] Thereafter, award rates were to be considered without regard to the sex of the employee. Full implementation was to be effected by June 1975 through work value cases aimed at assessing the value of work performed by women, especially women working in female-intensive industries.[4] The significance of the May 1974 decision was in the extension of the minimum adult wage to women.[5] This decision provided that from the first pay period on or after 23 May 1974, women were to receive 85 per cent of the amount payable to adult males. From 30 September 1974, this was to be increased to 90 per cent of the male rate; and from 30 June 1975 to equality with the male rate. As of 30 June 1975, therefore, all adult women employed under federal jurisdiction were to receive the same minimum and award wage as adult males.[6]

The Course of Change in Female Relative Pay

The effects of legislative changes concerning female wages may be seen in the data of Table 7.1 which gives the ratio of adult female to adult male weighted average hourly award wages. Reference to this table locates the period from early-1973 to mid-1975 as marking the most significant change in relativity between female and male hourly award wage rates. During that period the ratio of female to male hourly award rates increased by over 20 per cent, from 78 to 93 per cent of the male rate. This represents a significant shift in relative factor price as between male and female labour services. Drs R. G. Gregory and R. C. Duncan have argued that 'the equal pay decisions of the tribunals did not validate relative pay decisions which already occurred in the market place. The equal pay decisions appear to have been initiated by the institutions ...'[7]

If the initiative for changes in female wages was located with market influences, one should expect that increases in female *relative earnings* would tend to precede increases in female *relative awards*. Conversely, if the initiative for changes in female relative wages was through the decisions of employment conditions tribunals, one should expect a stable relationship between female relative earnings and female relative award wages. Data presented in Table 7.2 are consistent with the view that the initiative for increased female relative wages should be located with the influence of arbitral institutions. Table 7.2 compares the proportion of female relative *award* hourly rates with female relative ordinary-time hourly *earnings*. Running down column (c), one notices a remarkable stability in the ratio of relative measures of female award wages to earnings, with the ratio approximately stable at about 90 per cent. The apparent absence of adjustment in the relationship between relative earnings and relative award rates for females preceding and following the implementation of equal pay is consistent with the view that the causal influence in the change in female relative pay was in the institutions of award determination, and not in the labour market. Some variation in the relationship may be observed (presumably reflecting changing market influences), but this is not large.

The official Commonwealth line—both from Ministers, and from the bureaucracy—has been to locate this institutional influence at the federal level. The 1981 Position Paper prepared in the Women's Bureau of the Department of Employment and Youth Affairs said of the May 1974 Decision that it was 'applied subsequently in all State jurisdictions'.[8] Mr Cameron's hailing the decision as 'one of the Government's proudest achievements' (2 May 1974) might be discounted merely as political rhetoric, but it probably also represents the Government's perception of the significance of the role it played.

During the Whitlam period, federal male awards had moved ahead of state male awards—thus suggesting some leadership from the awards of the Australian Conciliation and Arbitration Commission in male wage rises from 1974 onwards.[9] A comparison of federal and state awards data for females gives a different picture.[10] For females, the lead would appear to come from state awards. Only at April 1974 (before the extension by the Arbitration Commission of the minimum wage to women in May 1974) does one notice a marked closing of the leadership gap that state female awards display over federal female awards. This closing of the gap appears to have been quickly reversed (as also was the closing of the relatively smaller gap between federal and state awards of March–April 1975).[11] This evidence is consistent with the Arbitration Commission's 1969 observation concerning the leading influence of legislation for equal pay in New South Wales, South Australia, Western Australia, and Tasmania.[12] In the decisions of 1969, 1972, and 1975 the Commission placed emphasis on social support in the community for the concept of equal pay for women.[13]

The Arbitration Commission attempted to minimize the role of federal government submissions in its equal pay decisions. The Whitlam Government, however, did place enormous pressure on the Commission in favour of decisions for 'equal pay'. One of the first actions of the new Government was its push of 6 December 1972 for the re-opening of the Commission's hearing on 'equal pay'. The submission of the outgoing McMahon Government had 'not opposed' the concept of equal pay for work of equal value; the submission of the new Whitlam Government 'positively supported' this concept.[14] The second 1972 Commonwealth submission, as made by the Labor Government, sought a speedier implementation of equal pay.[15] Pressure for accelerated implementation of equal pay was sustained by the Government—as was shown by the high profile which the Prime Minister gave to the 1973 decision of his Party to 'endorse the principle of equal pay to all eligible females employed by the Australian Government Service without any phasing-in of the pay increases'. Mr Whitlam announced that 'the Government supported the principle of implementing equal pay without phasing-in' and that '[in] the Government's view, this principle should also be applied generally throughout industry' (Whitlam, Press Statement, 23 July 1973).

Comments by the Commission on its 1974 decision again attempted to give an impartiality to the Commission's decision, and do not isolate the influence of the Australian Government's submission.[16] But the pressure from the Whitlam Government was very considerable, and the length and vigour with which the Government argued the case for the implementation of equal pay is illustrated in the following statement by Counsel for the Commonwealth during the 1974 National Wage Case:

> The Government has put a [priority on removing the distinction between male and female minimum wages] ... [This objective has] a high place in the priorities of a government which won an election upon a programme of vigorous social reform and progress ... The Government has no doubt that the community is prepared to pay for the economic consequences [of a decision for the implementation of equal pay], if, indeed, there are any of note.[17]

The arguments before the Commission by the Assisting Counsel for the Commonwealth (the then Miss M. Gaudron) was strongly against a phasing-in period, on the grounds that this would be in conflict with the Government's intentions for ratification of convention 100 of the International Labour Organization (ILO):

> For its part the Australian Government has taken steps to implement the ratification [of ILO convention 100] and in particular has fully implemented [in respect of Australian Government employees] the convention's decision on equal pay, thereby foregoing the phasing-in period.
> [The Australian Government] considers that at ratification all impediments to [the] implementation [of ILO convention 100] should have been removed [and that the convention] should only be ratified when implementation is immediately possible.[18]

Miss Gaudron summarized the Government's 1974 case before the Arbitration Commission as follows:

> The Government urges this Commission to agree to the submission that the minimum wage should apply to females, principally on the basis of ... domestic [that is, Australian] considerations ... and on the basis of the equity of the proposition itself, [and] also on the ground that its rejection would prejudice ratification of ILO convention 100.[19]

These extracts from submissions by Counsel for the Commonwealth clearly evidence the pressure applied by the Australian Government for the Arbitration Commission to discount practical considerations in its decision for the implementation of equal pay. The Commission, speaking to the decision concerning the timing of the equal pay implementation, made the following observation:

> it would be wise to avoid overloading the costs of ... industries by an immediate full application of [the male adult] wage to adult females. A phasing-in period will give industry time for adjustment, and we have therefore decided to extend the male minimum wage to females in three steps.[20]

In conclusion, there does not appear to be a clear case for attributing the decisions of the Australian Conciliation and Arbitration Commission for the implementation of equal pay for women entirely to the Whitlam Government. It is nevertheless clear that pressure applied by the Government influenced the Commis-

Table 7.1 Relative Award Hourly Wage Rates, Adult Females
Ratio of weighted average award nominal hourly rates for Australian adult female employees (excluding rural, mining, building workers) to weighted average award hourly nominal rates for Australian adult males

	1971	1972	1973	1974	1975	1976	1977	1978	1979	1980
Mar.	0.74	0.78	0.79	0.85	0.90	0.93	0.94	0.94	0.93	0.92
June	0.75	0.78	0.80	0.86	0.93	0.94	0.94	0.94	0.93	0.92
Sept.	0.77	0.78	0.81	0.87	0.93	0.94	0.94	0.94	0.93	0.93
Dec.	0.77	0.78	0.86	0.87	0.93	0.94	0.94	0.93	0.92	0.94

Source: ABS cat. *6312.0*, and computations on these data.

Table 7.2 Ratio of Two Measures of Female Relative Wage
Ratio of female relative award hourly earnings to female relative award hourly rates

Year (Oct.)	Female Relative Ordinary-time Hourly Earnings (a)	Female Relative Award Hourly Wage Rates (b)	Column (a) divided by Column (b) (c)
1971	0.69	0.76	0.91
1972	0.71	0.78	0.91
1973	0.75	0.82	0.91
1974	0.79	0.87	0.91
1975	0.83	0.93	0.89
1976	0.85	0.94	0.90
1977	0.84	0.94	0.89
1978	0.83	0.94	0.89
1979	0.81	0.93	0.87
1980	0.83	0.94	0.88

Notes: These measures are calculated as follows:
(a) Female relative ordinary-time hourly earnings are derived as the ratio of female to male ordinary-time hourly earnings (in cents, current).
(b) Female relative award hourly wage rates are derived as the ratio of female to male award hourly rates (in cents, current).
(c) The ratio of (a)/(b) gives the proportion of female relative *earnings* to female relative *awards*.

Source: Computed from ABS cat. *6312.0*.

sion's decisions and also the timing of their implementation. There is a notable lack of evidence of any substantial appreciation by the Government of the consequences of its policies, or of who would bear the costs of its policies.

Impact of Changes in Female Relative Wage

Most writers on women in the Australian labour market give emphasis to the sexual 'segmentation' of the market, arguing that there is a strong tendency to sexual stereotyping of jobs, so that particular jobs become largely gender-specific.[21] Gregory and Duncan[22], taking as their cue the stability of the ratio of female relative earnings to female relative awards, argue that sexual segmentation of occupations in the labour market has protected women's employment from the effects of change in relative wage, and thus 'substitution responses to relative wage changes appear to be trivial'.[23] A similar line has been argued by Sheehan.[24] This author's challenge to these conclusions involves a clearer comparison of data between government and market sector employment, and the introduction of analysis using *hours* of employment data.[25]

Following the suggestion of Snape[26], the present author's preliminary research using hours employment data involved the attempt to re-estimate the work that Gregory and Duncan had performed with per capita employment data, and which they cited in support of their conclusions. The results of these re-estimations were not encouraging: estimated co-efficients were not statistically significant, and serial correlation was a problem.[27] This line of investigation was therefore not pursued.[28] The alternative line of investigation adopted was to employ a decomposition algorithm in order to separate the effects on female hours of employment of (a) changes in the industry mix of employment, and (b) changes in the proportions of female employment by industry.[29]

The growth in female employment over that of males (the 'additional growth rate of the female work force')[30] was partitioned by means of the decomposition algorithm between (a) the 'effects of industry structure changes on female hours employment' (ESC), and (b) the 'effects of changes in the sexual composition of the work force on female hours employment' (SCW). These ESC and SCW estimates are reproduced below, as Tables 7.3 and 7.4.

As can be calculated from the data of Table 7.3, the effects of structural change on the level of female employment by hours averaged +0.60 per cent per annum for the five years prior to the full implementation of equal pay (1970–74), and +0.95 per cent per annum for the subsequent five-year period (1975–79).

Table 7.3 Estimates of Effect of Industry Structural Changes on Growth in Female Hours Employment

Period	Per Cent
1967	+0.66
1968	−0.81
1969	+0.44
1970	+0.57
1971	+0.71
1972	+0.39
1973	−0.10
1974	+1.41
1975	+0.36
1976	+1.91
1977	+0.77
1978	+1.53
1979	+0.17

Note: For an explanation of computational methods, see P. A. McGavin, 'Equal Pay for Women: A Re-assessment of the Australian Experience', *Australian Economic Papers*, 22(40), (1983), pp. 49–51.

Source: Computed using ABS cat. *6204.0*, various issues. ABS record some discontinuity in their series between 1969 and 1970, and 1977 and 1978.

Change in the Sexual Composition of the Work Force

During the five years prior to the full implementation of equal pay for women (1970–74), the change in the sexual composition of the Australian work force contributed an average +0.92 per cent per annum to the growth in female employment. For the subsequent five-year period (1975–79), the change in the sexual composition of the work force showed a *negative* effect on female employment averaging −0.77 per cent per annum (see Table 7.4). This would not appear to imply a situation where the generation of jobs in segmented markets is 'largely independent of relative factor prices' and does not appear to be consistent with one of the terms of Gregory and Duncan's 'central conclusion' that the 'employment response to the equal pay decision should not be large in terms of substitution away from female workers'.[31]

Although it is contrary to the thrust of their paper, Gregory and Duncan in their conclusion do recognize that the additional growth in female employment was 'until recently' mostly attributable to the change in the sexual composition of the work force.[32] Using *hours* employment data reveals that from the full implementation of equal pay for females in 1975 the effect of changes in the sexual composition of the work force on the level

Table 7.4 Estimates of Effect of Changes in Sexual Composition of the Work Force on Growth in Female Hours Employment

Period	Per Cent
1967	+1.05
1968	+1.31
1969	−1.17
1970	+2.22
1971	+0.73
1972	−0.79
1973	+1.08
1974	+1.37
1975	−0.55
1976	−0.89
1977	+0.49
1978	−0.79
1979	−2.11

Note: For an explanation of computational methods, see McGavin, 'Equal Pay for Women', pp. 49–51.
Source: Computed using ABS *6204.0*, various issues. ABS record some discontinuity in their series between 1969 and 1970, and 1977 and 1978.

of female aggregate weekly hours employment tended to be *negative*; while the effect of changes in the industry mix or structure on the level of female aggregate weekly hours employment continued to be *positive*, even strongly positive. These results underscore the inadequacy of evaluating movements in female employment in aggregate and per capita terms as do Gregory and Duncan, and Sheehan.[33]

The incidence of negative figures for changes in the sexual composition of the work force is the more remarkable given that there are two significant areas in which, in contemporary circumstances, women enjoy a comparative advantage in employment—namely, the general confinement of keyboard skills to women, in circumstances where technological change has emphasized keyboard skills; and the peculiar hours-flexibility of female employment response, in circumstances where expansion in the use of part-time labour services has figured significantly in a general attempt at labour rationing by employers.

Technical change emphasizing keyboard skills has been prominent in the business services sector. It is interesting to note that the proportion of female to total hours worked in the business services sector registers negligible change between the five years prior to and the five years subsequent to the full implementation of equal pay for women: the annual average was about 40 per cent of business services total hours employment for both 1970–74 and 1975–79. Throughout the period, business services has been a growth area for hours employment, representing about 6.5 per cent of aggregate person hours employment for all sectors at 1970 and 7.5 per cent at 1979. The sector is also a competitive one.

Leisure services has been second only to retail and wholesale employment for the growth of part-time hours employment. The substantial growth in female leisure services part-time hours employment (the annual increase for 1975 was 25 per cent) did not offset a downturn in female full-time hours employment in this sector. Full-time hours employment of males in the leisure services sector, however, remained stable, with the result that the proportion of female to total hours employment in this sector fell, 1970–74 to 1975–79, from an annual average of 52 per cent to an annual average of 50 per cent. Leisure services has not during the period been a growth area for hours employment, but neither has it been an area of major decline—the proportion of aggregate person hours employment for this sector was about 5 per cent at 1970, and was still 5 per cent at 1979. This sector, too, is a competitive one.

The results of this work are supported by research highlighting the significance for female hours employment of the growth in part-time employment and of growth in non-market sector employment. Data referred to are reproduced in Table 7.5, below.

Growth in Part-time Employment

Aggregate hours employment grew comparatively steadily for males up to 1973, and for females up to 1974. Were it not for the growth in female part-time employment the subsequent movement in women's aggregate hours employment would not have been so markedly different from the movement in hours employment for males—for without the growth of about 1.4 million hours in female part-time employment during 1974–78, female aggregate weekly hours employment would also have *fallen* (although not as much as male employment).

In male plus female aggregate hours employment, part-time hours as a proportion of total hours increased during 1973–77 by more than a third, from 1.4 to 2.0 per cent of aggregate weekly hours employment.[34] Thus, while male and female aggregate full-time weekly hours employment during 1973–77 *declined* by about 4 million hours, male and female aggregate part-time weekly hours *increased* by 1.3 million hours.[35] That is, without the influence of increase in part-time hours employment, the decrease during 1973–77 in aggregate weekly hours employment would have been 49 per cent greater. Therefore, in terms of *changes* in aggregate hours employment, the expansion of part-time employment figures significantly. In terms of *women's* employment, the expansion of part-time employment is yet more notable: a 44 per cent increase in part-time employment during 1973–77; with part-time employment increasing from 5 per cent to 7 per cent of women's total hours employment. In the two sectors most significant for female employment, wholesale and retail trade, and community services, the role of part-time employment is most marked: female retail part-time employment increased, 1973–77, from 5.3 per cent to 8.6 per cent of female hours retail employment; while female community services part-time employment increased, 1973–77, from 5.1 per cent to 6.6 per cent of female hours community services employment. That is, there was a 53 per cent increase during 1973–77 in female part-time hours employment in the retail sector; and a 68 per cent increase over the same period in community services sector part-time employment of females. In the area most significant for female hours employment and which is also a market sector—namely, wholesale and retail trade sector—the 53 per cent increase in female part-time hours employment was in the face of a 10.5 per cent *decrease* in female full-time retail sector hours employment. These observations give emphasis to the importance of introducing employment by hours in an evaluation of the changing pattern of female employment consequent upon the implementation of equal pay for women.[36]

Growth in Non-market Sector Employment

Not only does the evaluation of the course of female employment in Australia require consideration of employment by hours, but it also requires consideration of the pattern of employment by sectors. The data of Table 7.5 show that, were it not for the influence of growth in comparatively non-market sectors (community services and government services), female employment would not have been so seemingly buoyant.

Sheehan[37], and Gregory and Duncan[38] argue that the use of labour factors of production is not sensitive to relative factor

Table 7.5 Aggregate Weekly Hours Employment of Females, by Industry

Industry	Full-time Hours (000s)			Part-time Hours (000s)			Per Cent Change 1973 to 1977	
	1973	1977	Change 1973 to 1977	1973	1977	Change 1973 to 1977	Full-time hours	Part-time hours
01 Agriculture	1 962	2 027	65	279	305	26	3.3	9.3
02 Forestry	–	–	–	–	–	–	–	–
03 Mining	–	–	–	–	73	73	–	–
04 Manufacturing	11785	9 860	–1925	144	194	50	–16.3	34.7
05 Construction	412	576	164	103	137	34	39.8	33.0
06 Wholesale/Retail	13 124	11 880	–1244	731	1116	385	–9.5	52.7
07 Transport/Storage	1 182	1 140	–42	30	49	19	–3.6	63.3
08 Business Services	5 326	5 670	344	136	231	95	6.5	69.9
09 Community Services	10 789	13 760	2971	582	976	394	27.5	67.7
10 Leisure Services	4 719	4 445	–274	733	830	97	–5.8	13.2
11 Other [Government]	3 570	3 966	396	27	67	40	11.1	148.1

Sources: ABS cat. *6204.0*, information kindly supplied by the ABS, and computations on these data.

prices, and Gregory and Duncan[39] argue that an apparent lack of response to variations in relative wages demonstrates the operation of a *segmented* labour market, wherein jobs are rather rigidly divided between male and female occupations. However, the growth in female employment which Gregory and Duncan present as arising from the *segmentation* of the labour market, has instead occurred mainly in the non-market sector of the economy. This would suggest that the influence most operative for the incidence of overall growth in female employment was not principally labour market segmentation as such, but the comparative absence of *market* adjustment to economic stimuli in the major growth areas for female employment—namely, in government employment.[40, 41]

An examination of data on employment by sector locates the non-distributive services sector as being the growth area for female employment. And during the period of the Whitlam Government and the equal pay implementation, it is readily noticeable that the main areas for growth in female *per capita* employment are community services and other industries.[42] Approximately, these groupings may be described as government employment (which includes federal, state, local, and authorities employment).[43] Since most of the growth in female part-time employment has occurred in non-government employment, the highly skewed pattern of change in female employment is further heightened with the introduction of 'hours' data.

There was a notable concentration of growth in female employment in comparatively non-market areas, with 92 per cent of the net change in female *per capita* employment at 1975 occurring in other ['government'] industries, and 127 per cent occurring in community services ['predominantly government-financed services']; and with these groups adding to 220 per cent of the net increase in female employment at 1975. Reckoned in aggregate *hours* employment, the growth of female employment in these non-market areas (or comparatively non-market areas) for 1975 was +0.9 million hours per week, while the net movement across the economy is estimated at −1.2 million hours per week. For the period 1973–77, increased female employment under these two headings represented 130 per cent of the net increase in female aggregate hours employment over that five-year period. Thus the foregoing observation that the growth in female employment preponderantly occurred in the *non-market* sector of the economy, and should be considered in terms wider than the 'segmented' market reference as emphasized by Gregory and Duncan.[44]

Conclusions Concerning Impact of Equal Pay Implementation

Earlier researchers have given some prominence to the effects of recession in favouring male employment, an influence which some might suggest would virtually explain the negative figure of about 3.85 per cent for the period 1975–79 derived from adding Table 7.4 estimates of the effect on female hours employment of changes in the sexual composition of the work force.[45] However, as Gregory and Duncan in the context of the 'real wage overhang' debate remind us[46], the issue turns on the choice of the appropriate comparison (or 'counterfactual') for movement in the sexual proportions of the Australian work force. For reasons explained below, an appropriate counterfactual is not specified in this book. But clearly an evaluation must reckon with a shift in the trend rate of growth in the female proportions in the work force, from one which was positive for the five years *prior* to the full implementation of equal pay, to one which was negative for the five years *subsequent* to that implementation.

However, even if the trend rate of growth in the female proportions in the work force *after* the full implementation of equal pay were compared with a counterfactual of the trend of female proportions in the work force *before* that implementation (with these trends adjusted for cyclical influence), one would still not derive an adequate basis for comparison. For one would still be adding up the extent of a divergence between two trend lines over a period, and comparing the sum of such divergences with the extent of change in female relative wages. If this divergence in trends of female proportions in the work force did not in one's estimation adequately match the degree of change in female relative wages, one might declare this to be 'hardly consistent with the classical mechanism having been operative'[47], or one might conclude that substitution responses to relative wage changes appear to be 'trivial' or 'very small'.[48] However, the relationship between an increase in relative wages and induced growth in productivity consequent upon new investment should be recalled from the real wage overhang debate. This was argued by Snape as follows:

> One important possibility is that ... investment will increase the productivity of labour until the increased real wage is 'validated'—that is, [until the higher real wage] is consistent with full employment ... It should be noted that this adjustment of the marginal product—[by] a shift in the curve due to the productivity of new investment—is quite different from an adjustment of productivity due to a [movement] along an existing marginal product curve due to a change in employment. It is a means by which classical unemployment may be removed without a reduction in real wages.[49]

That is, the mental framework of the analysis should be one which anticipates shifts of, as well as movements along, marginal productivity functions. Applied to the present debate, this means that *a priori* one would not expect negative estimates of the change in the female proportions in the work force to add up over time to a figure approximating the change in female relative wages. Moreover, one would not presume that the negative direction of change in female proportions of the work force would necessarily continue past the period of estimation used for this book.[50]

For the period 1975–79, the negative estimates of change in the sexual composition of the work force suggest a shift in the trend rate of growth of the proportions of females in the work force larger than that which the cyclical influences of that period would have led one to expect. This especially appears to be the case because the cyclical influences which operated against female employment occurred in a context where the shift towards growth in part-time employment offered a comparative advantage to those persons having a time-flexibility in employment—namely, females. This growth in part-time employment very significantly contributed to the different pattern of change in employment for females compared with males. Furthermore, this growth in part-time employment was principally located in the *market* sectors where the processes of market adjustment to change in relative factor prices was most operative.

It is with this sort of reasoning in mind that one may view the timing of the shift in the pattern of change in female employment as being suggestive of an equal pay influence, and as implying a process of substitution responses induced by changes in relative factor prices. These substitution responses would not, however, be confined to an employment adjustment, but would comprise an adjustment of capital stocks also.[51]

The estimates of the effects of structural change, using hours data, make clearer the dominant role of shifts in Australia's industry mix for increased female employment. The pattern of these shifts is made clearer by the use of hours, rather than per capita, data because the incidence of reduced-hours employment was not even across the economy.

Gregory and Duncan's estimates (using per capita data) of the effects of changes in the sexual composition of the work force suggest that, compared with the effects of structural change, there was some diminution in the relative significance of growth in the proportions of females in the work force for the growth of female employment. But estimates of change in the sexual composition of the work force, based on hours data, derive negative estimates of change in the female composition of the work force, and thus show a tendency to *reduced* female proportions in the Australian work force following the full implementation of equal pay in 1975. The results here reported thus show that relative employment varied in a manner not adequately described in the aggregate and per capita analyses offered by Sheehan, and by Gregory and Duncan. This reduction in female proportions in the Australian work force has a timing suggestive of an equal pay influence.

However, because of other dynamic economic and social influences, it is not possible to give precise figures for the 'equal pay influence' upon female employment. The changes in female employment as summarized in Table 7.5 reflect not only the influence of increases in female relative wage, but also the influence of decreases in the level of domestic protection from overseas competition (tariffs), and in the level of overall activity (cyclical movements). Moreover, the impact of tariff changes and of cyclical factors was not even across sectors of the economy. It nevertheless is significant to notice that between 1973 and 1977 the number of female hours of full-time employment in 'manufacturing' employment declined by over 16 per cent, and in 'wholesale and retail' employment declined by about 10 per cent. In the same period, female hours of full-time employment in 'community services' grew by over 27 per cent. Taking these three major areas of change in female employment: 'community services' employment entailed a growth of about 3 million hours per week in female full-time employment, but the other two areas combined represented a contraction in excess of 3 million hours per week in female full-time wage employment.

Only a slight knowledge of government and manufacturing or retail workplaces is required for one to be aware that between these sectors one is dealing with quite distinct kinds of labour services. That is to say, in terms of their labour market characteristics, one is generally dealing with different types of women as between 'public service or quasi public service' female employees, and 'manufacturing' or 'wholesale and retail' female employees. As has been noted above, changes in the female relative wage coincided with a complex of other changes. This complicates evaluation of the issues. But it ought not to cloud the essential issues concerning the economic and social consequences for women. Except in those areas where there was an offsetting growth in demand for the employment of women, increases in female relative wage tended to deprive certain women of employment. Naturally, those women deprived of employment were the women whose employment was most precarious. And these women may be expected characteristically to have been women whose domestic circumstances were most precarious: women married to unskilled labourers, women married to men who had a higher-than-average incidence of retrenchment.

These overall movements, and the marked emergence of an overall surplus in the market supply of female labour in Australia cast a shade on the 'justice' arguments about 'equal pay' for women.[52, 53] It would seem to the present author to be a strange notion of 'justice' for those whose livelihoods are not at risk to be instrumental in forcing an equalitarian wages policy, the practical effect of which would contribute to depriving those who may be in greatest need from access to wage employment.[54] Some idea of the possible magnitude of this deprivation may be gained by applying the estimates of Table 7.4 to female employment data.

Female hours of employment per week at 1974 were 63.1 million. Applying to this figure the 1975 estimate of −0.55 per cent for the effects of changes in sexual composition of the work force for growth in female employment, derives a 1975 reduction in female hours employment of about −347 000 hours per week. Dividing by average hours worked by women in 1975, gives a reduction in female employment of about 11 350 as a result of reduction in female proportions in the work force. Taking 1975 as a base, and similarly estimating the influence of change in the sexual composition of the work force for 1976 (the year following the full implementation of equal pay) derives an estimated reduction in female employment of about 18 100 women.

These figures cannot be used to attribute precise effects of changes in the female relative wage. They do suggest, however, some orders of magnitude for the equal pay influence on changes in the female proportions in the Australian work force, and the magnitudes suggested do not appear 'small'. If it is correctly argued that this contractionary influence was not even across the economy (as the disaggregated data for changes in the sexual composition of the work force indicate), and if it is correctly argued that the typical labour market characteristics of women facing employment contraction were different from the typical characteristics of women facing expansion of employment; then it follows that the Government's contribution to the wider implementation of increases in the relative wage of females exercised a negative employment influence. It further follows that the burden of this contraction in employment was largely borne by one section of Australia's female work force—by the most vulnerable section. In the present author's view, this makes it questionable whether a Labor Government should rank its contribution in this area as being amongst its 'proudest achievements'.

Chapter 8
Wages and the Social Welfare System

Introduction

The general question of 'wages and the social welfare system' is very large and involved, and the issues engaged more closely below are but illustrative of a wide field for investigation. The next section briefly introduces the perspective used in examining the relationship between wages and the social welfare system. Policy changes in the provision of social security transfers are then outlined. There follows a preliminary examination of the relationship between change in the provision of social security transfers and the labour force participation decision as this applies to 'junior' Australians. This question is then examined from the viewpoint of the labour force participation decision of 'older' Australians. Finally, the last section gives a summary and re-statement of the arguments of this chapter concerning the relevance to wages policy of a clear understanding of its relationship to social welfare provision in the context of the question of 'wages and employment'.

Relationship between Wages and the Social Welfare System

As already noted, the relationship between wages and social security transfers is a large and complex question. This question involves more than the way changes in monetary social security benefits relative to monetary wages alter the labour force participation decisions of individuals. Questions are also raised about taxation, income tests on earnings from part-time employment, eligibility tests for social security benefits and the administrations of rules governing eligibility, access to the public provision of goods and services in kind (such as access to public transport, medical services, government rental housing, etc.). These questions raise a larger agenda than is treated in this chapter, where evaluation of the labour force participation decision of individuals is focused more simply on the ways in which changes in wages and social security provisions have altered the 'opportunity costs' relevant to the labour force participation decision. Even this restricted aspect of investigation in the wide area of 'wages and the social welfare system' does not receive full treatment in this book.

Changes in opportunity costs relevant to the labour force participation decision raises empirical questions of the interface between 'wages and the social welfare system'. As has been suggested in the earlier chapters, the Whitlam Government was a significant actor in influencing the increase in reward for labour services. The following section briefly outlines the main policy changes in the public provision of transfer payments.

Policy Changes in the Provision of Social Security Transfers

We are a Government committed ... to bringing about change in the structure of our society.

(Hayden, Speech, 21 September 1973)

The large changes in the provision of public transfer payments brought about by the Whitlam Government were part of a larger programme to alter the relationship between production and distribution in the Australian economy and society. Prominent in this programme was the Government's commitment in its election platform to raise the basic pension rate to 25 per cent of average weekly earnings.[1] This commitment was sustained by the Hon. W. G. Hayden, Minister for Social Security, in each announcement of pension increases.[2] The commitment was extended with the decision of 9 January 1973 to adopt a common rate for welfare benefits and to make minors eligible for unemployment benefits at the full standard benefits rate. Tables 8.1 and 8.2 outline the course of changes in the major categories of public transfer payments, unemployment benefits and pensions (aged, invalid, and service). Analytical descriptions of changes in these payments occur in the section devoted to an evaluation of these changes as they affected young Australians, and in the subsequent section where attention is directed to older Australians. The data

Table 8.1 Unemployment Benefit Entitlements ('Nominal' and 'Real') (dollars per week)

Year	Junior 16–20 years: Yrs 16–17	Junior 16–20 years: Yrs 18–20		Adult: Single	Adult: Married couple	
	($ current)			($ current)		
1970	4.50	6.00		10.00	17.00	
1971	4.50	6.00		10.00	17.00	
					18.00	(29 Sept.)
1972	7.50	11.00	(25 Feb.)	17.00	25.00	(25 Feb.)
1973	21.50		(16 Mar.)	21.50	37.50	(16 Mar.)
	23.00		(26 Sept.)	23.00	40.50	(26 Sept.)
1974	26.00		(22 Mar.)	26.00	45.50	(22 Mar.)
	31.00		(31 July)	31.00	51.50	(31 July)
1975	36.00		(19 May)	36.00	60.00	(19 May)
				38.75	64.50	(1 Nov.)
(Quarter & Year)	($ constant)			($ constant)		
1:1970	4.10	5.46		9.11	15.48	
2:1970	4.05	5.40		8.99	15.29	
3:1970	4.02	5.36		8.94	15.19	
4:1970	3.95	5.26		8.77	14.91	
1:1971	3.91	5.21		8.68	14.76	
2:1971	3.84	5.11		8.53	14.51	
3:1971	3.77	5.03		8.38	14.24	
4:1971	3.68	4.91		8.18	14.73	
1:1972	4.46	6.22		9.99	16.47	
2:1972	6.02	8.84		13.65	20.08	
3:1972	5.94	8.72		13.47	19.81	
4:1972	5.87	8.61		13.31	19.58	
1:1973	7.53	9.78		13.61	20.77	
2:1973	15.96			15.96	27.84	
3:1973	15.40			15.40	26.86	
4:1973	15.90			15.90	28.00	
1:1974	15.53			15.53	27.35	
2:1974	16.87			16.87	29.53	
3:1974	18.10			18.10	30.56	
4:1974	18.44			18.44	30.64	
1:1975	17.81			17.81	29.59	
2:1975	18.59			18.59	30.94	
3:1975	19.82			19.82	33.04	
4:1975	18.78			19.73	32.86	

Sources: DSS, *Annual Report*, 1978–79; p. 112, ABS cat. *6401.0*; and computations on these data. (1966–67 = 1.00).

Table 8.2 Aged, Invalid, and Service Pension Entitlements ('Nominal' and 'Real') (dollars per week)

Year	Single ($ current)	Married Couple ($ current)
1970	15.50	27.50 (8 Oct.)
1971	16.00	28.50 (8 Apr.)
	17.25	30.50 (7 Oct.)
1972	18.25	32.00 (4 May)
	20.00	34.50 (5 Oct.)
	21.50	37.50 (14 Dec.)
1973	23.00	40.50 (4 Oct.)
1974	26.00	45.50 (4 Apr.)
	31.00	51.50 (8 Aug.)
1975	36.00	60.00 (1 May)
	38.75	64.50 (13 Nov.)
(Quarter & Year)	($ constant)	($ constant)
1:1970	13.66	24.14
2:1970	13.49	23.84
3:1970	13.40	23.68
4:1970	13.60	24.12
1:1971	13.45	23.88
2:1971	13.65	24.32
3:1971	13.40	23.86
4:1971	13.68	24.02
1:1972	13.98	24.72
2:1972	13.79	25.30
3:1972	14.46	25.36
4:1972	15.86	27.40
1:1973	16.49	28.76
2:1973	15.96	27.84
3:1973	15.40	26.86
4:1973	15.91	28.00
1:1974	15.53	27.34
2:1974	16.87	29.52
3:1974	18.10	30.56
4:1974	18.44	30.62
1:1975	17.81	35.58
2:1975	19.05	31.72
3:1975	19.82	33.04
4:1975	19.49	32.60

Sources: DSS, *Annual Report*, 1978–79, p. 108; ABS cat. *6401.0*; and computations on these data. (1966–67 = 1.00).

Table 8.3 Weekly Earnings, Juniors and Average ('Nominal' and 'Real')

Junior Males			AWE		
Year (October)	$ current	Per cent change	Year (fiscal)	$ current	Per cent change
1970	35.50	7.6	1969–70	76.30	8.4
1971	39.90	12.4	1970–71	84.80	11.1
1972	43.60	9.3	1971–72	93.40	10.1
1973	52.30	20.0	1972–73	101.80	9.0
1974	70.90	35.6	1973–74	118.30	16.2
1975	80.80	14.0	1974–75	148.30	25.4
	$ constant	Per cent change		$ constant	Per cent change
1970	31.72	2.0	1969–70	68.62	5.0
1971	33.42	5.4	1970–71	72.35	5.4
1972	34.55	3.4	1971–72	75.02	3.7
1973	37.46	8.4	1972–73	75.56	0.7
1974	43.77	16.8	1973–74	76.77	1.6
1975	44.49	1.6	1974–75	82.30	7.2

Notes: Junior Earnings = average weekly ordinary-time earnings, full-time employees in the private sector, Australia.
AWE = 'average weekly earnings per employed male unit', Australia.
These data are chosen to match the data of Tables 8.4 & 8.5.

Sources: ABS cat. *6304.0*; AES, p. 140; ABS cat. *6401.0*; and computations on these data. (1966–67 = 1.00).

of Table 8.3 provide an indication of the movement in earnings during the Whitlam period, and were used in the computations of Tables 8.4 and 8.5, which respectively show junior unemployment benefits relative to junior earnings, and selected aged and invalid pension replacement rates.

'Junior' Labour Force Participation and Changes in the Provision of Social Security Transfers

The increased unemployment benefits for minors will ... help soften the blow of unemployment for many thousands of school leavers.

(Hayden, Press Statement, 11 January 1973)

Labor entered government with the idea that individuals' access to at least 25 per cent of average weekly earnings was a 'right rather than a privilege'.[3] This view was quickly reflected in the Government's decision announced on 11 January 1973 to raise social security benefits for minors to the standard rate as of 1

March 1973. As the data of Table 8.1 show, almost until the end of its office this view was maintained by the Government. Only the 1 November 1975 decision to increase the standard benefits rate to $38.75 pw did not extend this increase to unemployment benefits for Australians aged 16–20 years.

The growth in junior earnings (males and females) during the Whitlam period was examined in Chapter 6. As may be seen from Table 8.3, junior male earnings increased during 1973 by 20 per cent and in 1974 by 36 per cent in nominal terms. In 'real' terms, these increases were about 8 per cent during 1973, and about 17 per cent during 1974. However, the increases in nominal and in real unemployment benefits for juniors as detailed in Table 8.1 were even greater. As a result, the implementation of the January 1973 decision of the Government led to a substantial leap in junior unemployment benefits relative to junior earnings (see Table 8.4). Public statements of ministers do not reveal an understanding that such increases in unemployment benefits substantially altered the opportunity costs of decisions to remain outside the labour force and engaged in full-time education. Nor is there evidence of a movement away from the arbitrary definition of 'rights' to public transfer payments to which the Government adhered.[4] Some of the effects of these policies for youth employment are considered below.

Movement in the Relative Value of Unemployment Benefits

The increase by the McMahon Government in unemployment benefits for youths aged 16 and 17 years to $7.50 per week as of 25 February 1972 lifted the proportion of unemployment benefits from a level of about 12–13 per cent of the BLMR index of junior award wages, to about 18.5 per cent of junior award rates (and to about 17 per cent of the ABS junior *male* average weekly ordinary-time earnings series).[5] The decision of the Whitlam Government, effective as of 1 March 1973, to increase junior unemployment benefits to a common rate of $21.50 pw for both 16–17-year-olds, and 18–20-year-olds, and the same as for single adults, gave respective weekly increases in unemployment benefits of 187 per cent and 95 per cent for these junior age groups. For 16–17-year-olds unemployment benefits were thereby raised to about 48 per cent of the BLMR index of junior award wages (to about 44 per cent using the ABS junior male series; and to about 48 per cent using the ABS junior female series). As may be seen from Table 8.4, these proportions were approximately maintained, or increased, throughout the Whitlam period.

For youths aged 18, 19, and 20 years, the February 1972 decision lifted the proportion of their unemployment benefits from about 16–17 per cent to about 27 per cent of the BLMR index of junior award wages. Because of the higher base for 18–20-year-old unemployment benefits, the Whitlam Government's increase of junior unemployment benefits to a common rate as of March 1973 had a less dramatic effect on the magnitude of unemployment benefits for older juniors relative to their earnings: their unemployment benefits also increased to about 48 per cent of the BLMR series (44 per cent of ABS junior *male* series), but the percentage jump in the proportion of unemployment benefits to earnings was 'only' about 80 per cent for 18–20-year-olds, compared with a jump of nearly 170 per cent for 16–17-year-olds.

These data therefore show that the youth unemployment benefits policy of the Whitlam Government caused these benefits to rise to something like 45–50 per cent of junior earnings (nearer 50 per cent for junior females). Examination of age-specific earnings data would make the comparison yet more invidious for younger workers (and for females). An indication of this is seen by taking the central tradesman (fitter) award rate at 20 September 1972 of $88.70, and multiplying by the proportion for a first-year apprentice of the tradesman (adult) rate (42 per cent), to derive an estimated award earnings for a 16-year-old in the metal industry of $37.25 at March 1973.[6] The 16–17-year-old unemployment benefits rate at March 1973 of $21.50 therefore represents nearly 58 per cent of expected award earnings for a 16-year-old youth considering leaving school to look for an apprenticeship. This figure throws into sharp relief the short-term opportunity cost of continued schooling, and suggests the influential role (as discussed further below) of social security transfer payments in the youth labour force participation decision.

Estimation of the Relationship between Welfare Transfers and the Labour Force and School Participation Decisions of Australian Youth

The most prominent contribution to the Australian literature on the question of the influence of changes in social security provisions for junior labour force participation was made in a 1980

Table 8.4 Junior Unemployment Benefits Relative to BLMR and ABS Junior Earnings Series

Year & Month	Junior Earnings Series					
	BLMR		ABS			
	Males & females (16–20 years)		Males (16–20 years)		Females (16–20 years)	
	Yrs 16–17	Yrs 18–20	Yrs 16–17	Yrs 18–20	Yrs 16–17	Yrs 18–20
Jan. 1970	0.13	0.18				
July	0.13	0.18				
Oct.			0.13	0.17	0.15	0.20
Jan. 1971	0.12	0.16				
July	0.12	0.16				
Oct.			0.11	0.15	0.13	0.17
Jan. 1972	0.19	0.27				
July	0.18	0.26				
Oct.			0.17	0.25	0.20	0.29
Jan. (a) 1973	0.48					
July (b)	0.46					
Oct.			0.44		0.49	
Jan. (c) 1974	0.49					
July (d)	0.45					
Oct.			0.44		0.47	
Jan. (d) 1975	0.42					
July (e)	0.45					
Oct.			0.45		0.45	

Notes: Using benefits applying: (a) 16 March 1973, (b) 26 September 1973, (c) 22 March 1974, (d) 31 July 1974, & (e) 19 May 1975.

The BLMR junior earnings series is based on thirteen awards selected from the very large number available. The data are expressed as a fraction of the adult earnings series.

Sources: BLMR, *Youth Wages, Employment and the Labour Force*, Research Report No. 3, AGPS, Canberra, 1983, p. 51; ABS cat. *6312.0* & *6304.0*; and DSS, *Annual Report*, 1978–79, p. 112.

article by Gregory and Duncan.[7] These authors estimated a series of multiple regression equations with junior male and female labour force participation rates as dependent variables and junior unemployment benefits included as independent (that is, explanatory) variables. These authors conclude that 'an increase in the level of unemployment benefits increases the labour force participation rate'[8], and use the term 'substantial' in referring to their measurement of the effects of increases in unemployment benefits on the labour force participation of junior Australians.[9] Because of the conclusions drawn, the work of Gregory and Duncan has received considerable scrutiny by Australian economists[10], and in its 1983 *Research Report* the Bureau of Labour Market Research (BLMR) concludes: 'Overall, it appears that neither the increases in unemployment benefits, nor the conditions attached to the receipt of these benefits, have had a substantial impact on teenage labour supply'.[11] A 1984 review essay by Dr B. Hughes gives a critique of Gregory and Duncan's work and examines deficiencies in the specification and estimation of their equations. Hughes considers that the complex questions concerning teenage labour force participation in Australia are 'still largely unresolved', and concludes that Australians 'still await a reasonably satisfactory model of teenage [labour force] participation'.[12] On the question of the effect of increases in unemployment benefits leading to increases in teenage labour force participation, Hughes says: 'I am denying the size rather than the existence of [an unemployment] benefits effect'.[13] This conclusion is in the same tone as that of the BLMR, namely, that increases in junior unemployment benefits have not had a 'substantial' impact on teenage labour supply.

The result of this debate is that at present there is not a confident position from which one may estimate the magnitude of the impact on teenage labour supply deriving from the increases in junior unemployment benefits introduced by the Whitlam Government. What follows should therefore be regarded as an arithmetic exercise which allows an illustrative estimation of the effects of increases in junior unemployment benefits. Because this exercise is but illustrative, it is convenient to adopt the co-efficients estimated in Gregory and Duncan's simple model, their Equations (2a and 2b), rather than to use combined co-efficients derived from their more complex model.[14] The results of the more complex model are in certain respects more satisfactory statistically (particularly with respect to evidence of serial correlation), but as argued by Hughes, the specification of the more complex estimations of Equations (4a, b) and (5a, b) is not more satisfactory. Gregory and Duncan's labour force participation Equations (2a) and (2b) for teenage males and for teenage females include co-efficients for weighted real unemployment benefits paid to teenagers (16 and 17, and 18 and 19, years of age) which are 'positive, statistically significant and approximately the same size for teenage males and teenage females, 0.18 and 0.15 respectively'.[15]

Applying these co-efficients attaching to unemployment benefits, the effect of the 31 July 1974 increase in youth unemployment benefits in 'real' terms of about $5, on a *ceteris paribus* basis, would be expected to increase labour force participation by about 0.90 per cent for males, and 0.75 per cent for females, aged 15–19 years. Using civilian population estimates at August 1974, these magnitudes would, *ceteris paribus*, mean a movement of about 5300 males and about 4400 females into the labour force.[16] Estimates of *ceteris paribus* additions to the labour force of these magnitudes during a period when junior full-time employment reduced by about 3500 for males and by about 6700 for females clearly illustrate the way in which increases in unemployment benefits by the Whitlam Government may have attracted young people into the labour force, and so contributed to the growth of teenage unemployment in Australia.

The figures for reduced junior employment are realized outcomes (that is, they are *ex post*), while the figures for teenage entry into the labour force are derived by using estimates made whilst holding other variables constant (that is, the multiple regression technique derives *ceteris paribus* estimates). Moreover, several Australian economists consider that Gregory and Duncan's estimates of elasticities attaching to unemployment benefits are too high—both for the simple and the complex specifications. Elasticities attaching to unemployment benefits in labour force participation equations of 18 per cent for junior males and 15 per cent for junior females do not to the author seem unrealistically high. But given the state of Australian empirical evidence, the above calculations illustrate, rather than demonstrate, the effects of July 1974 increases in unemployment benefits on junior labour force participation in Australia.

The work of Gregory and Duncan on the labour force participation of junior Australians suggested complementary work undertaken by the present author and published in 1981.[17] The author's work involved the modelling and estimation of the school participation decisions of Australians aged 16 years. This age was chosen because it is the age at which eligibility for unemployment benefits commences, and teenagers of this age have not yet entered into the investment entailed in the additional schooling experience of 17- and 18-year-olds (who may be near to attaining the Higher School Certificate). The author's study has also been criticized by the BLMR as having 'an incomplete theoretical structure and as excluding key variables, in particular a real teenage wage variable'.[18] A fuller criticism appears in a working paper by Ms J. P. Smith issued by the Office of Youth Affairs.[19] Smith's list of the deficiencies of McGavin's study include: the absence of a variable reflecting changes in labour supply and demand balance; the omission of variables to represent explicitly the effects of 'human capital' and 'life cycle' influences; as well as the omission of variables capturing changes attributable to real teenage wage movements; the offsetting effects of the Tertiary Education Assistance Scheme and the Secondary [Education] Assistance Scheme; the general changes in community attitudes to the value of education; and also the higher societal value of education in the presence of significant increases in average living standards. The list is so long and the potential research assignment so large that one might perhaps be excused for thinking that simple insights into the economic factors affecting the school participation are not desirable.

Certainly, McGavin's model of school participation rates is a simple one. Following the lead of Gregory and Duncan (and others), it is postulated that higher unemployment benefits would attract young people away from school and into the full-time work force. In March 1973 the Whitlam Government increased the single person, 16–17 years, unemployment benefits from $7.50 to $21.50—an increase of nearly 200 per cent. As the implications of this huge jump may not have been immediately fully perceived and immediately fully instrumental in changing school participation rates, a dummy variable was introduced by the author at 1973, with the expectation that it would have a sign opposite to that of the co-efficient attaching to unemployment benefits. Gregory and Duncan also observe that 'Higher real wages for adult males will increase the ability of families to support their children at school', and this variable is also included in the model.[20] Data are annual and variables are related to the period nearest school participation data, August. Monetary variables are introduced in 'real' terms (deflated by the CPI). The model was estimated by the author for the same period as Gregory and Duncan's study (1964–78), and the following results were obtained:

$$\mathbf{P_m} = \underset{(1.38)}{9.43} - \underset{(3.65)}{0.66}\,\mathbf{B} + \underset{(6.22)}{0.67}\,\mathbf{W_m} + \underset{(3.00)}{4.52}\,\mathbf{D} \qquad (8.1)$$

$R^2 = 0.94$ $F = 55.18$ $n = 15$

$\bar{R}^2 = 0.93$ $DW = 1.96$ $d.f. = 10$

(*t* values are in brackets)

where, $\mathbf{P_m}$ is school participation rates for 16-year-old males,
B is real unemployment benefits for the 16–17-year age group,
$\mathbf{W_m}$ is real average weekly adult male earnings, September quarter, deflated CPI, 1966 = 100, and
D is a dummy variable for the large change in unemployment benefits at 1973 (zeros, except at 1973, where it is unity).
(See note 21 for sources.)

The Cochrane-Orcutt technique was used to remove the marginal indeterminacy of the estimate for autocorrelation derived under Ordinary Least Squares estimation. Movements in explanatory variables represent 94 per cent of the variation in school participation rates for 16-year-old males. The co-efficients of the explanatory variables have the predicted signs and are all significant at the 1 per cent level. Notice that a dollar increase in real average weekly adult male earnings is estimated to have the same effect on the school participation rate as a dollar decrease in real unemployment benefits; namely, an increase of about 0.67 percentage points.

Because of the well-known divergence in paths for male and female school participation rates[22] during the 1970s one should expect Equation (8.1) to perform very poorly with school participation rates for girls aged 16 years as the dependent variable. One might suggest that school participation decisions for females would have diverged from those of males because labour market conditions for junior females were different from those for junior males. But the evidence of Equation (8.1) suggests that, in aggregate, the schooling decisions of males were not forcefully influenced by job opportunities.[23] Another suggestion which might be made is that changes in social attitudes during the 1970s were more instrumental in schooling decisions for females than for males. But before rejecting the applicability to girls' schooling decisions of the hypothesis tested in Equation (8.1), one should note that the $\mathbf{W_m}$ variable performs two functions in respect of schooling decisions for boys: namely, it measures both (a) family income resources for the support of a boy's schooling, and (b) the future earnings expectations for male children. In respect of (a), it may expected that $\mathbf{W_m}$ should remain an accurate index in schooling decisions for girls. In respect of (b), however, one may not so expect; for the 1970s saw a significant divergence in the paths of real average weekly earnings for males and females. Re-estimation of Equation (8.1), with school participation rates for females aged 16 years ($\mathbf{P_f}$) as the dependent variable, and real average weekly full-time earnings for females replacing $\mathbf{W_m}$ derives the following results:

$$\mathbf{P_f} = \underset{(1.06)}{10.55} - \underset{(-2.09)}{1.15\mathbf{B}} + \underset{(3.51)}{0.97\mathbf{W_f}} + \underset{(2.34)}{8.08\mathbf{D}} \qquad (8.2)$$

$$R^2 = 0.96 \qquad F = 80.96 \qquad n = 15$$
$$\bar{R}^2 = 0.95 \qquad DW = 1.92 \qquad d.f. = 10$$

(*t* values are in brackets)

where, $\mathbf{W_f}$ is real average weekly full-time adult female earnings, October annual survey, deflated CPI, 1966 = 100. (See note 21 for sources.)

The co-efficients for the explanatory variables are significant at 5 per cent, or better. Although these results are not as robust as those derived for Equation (8.1), they do provide significant evidence that the divergence of the path of female school participation rates from that of males would appear to have been in response to perceived differences in the movements of the relevant indicators of expected earnings.[24]

The view of the BLMR is that 'the modelling of youth labour supply is in a seriously under-developed state, both in Australia and overseas'.[25] Clearly, the present author's model is a simple one which in the shadow of these judgements cannot be used with unqualified confidence. Those who are not persuaded about these estimates of the effects of increases in unemployment benefits on the school participation of Australians aged 16 years will view what follows as illustrating, rather than demonstrating, the magnitudes of these effects.

The Impact of Changes in Unemployment Benefits on Labour Force and School Participation of Australian Youth

The increase in youth unemployment benefits at 31 July 1974 from the level adopted at 26 September 1973 is used for discussion for the two reasons. First, as was mentioned in the discussion of Equation (8.1); it may be suggested that there would have been a learning period for response to the unprecedented March 1973 increase in unemployment benefits. Secondly, the movement into recession in the latter part of 1974 led to a huge blow-out of youth unemployment in 1975.

On the basis of Equations (8.1) and (8.2), the 31 July 1974 increase in unemployment benefits for 16- and 17-year-olds (of $8 on the level established at 26 September 1973) may be expected, *ceteris paribus*, to have reduced school participation of 16-year-olds by about 3.30 per cent for males, and by about 5.75 per cent for females.[26] At 1973 the school retention rate for 16-year-olds was about 57 per cent for males, and about 51 per cent for females.[27] The *ceteris paribus* reduction in school participation suggested by these estimates implies an addition to the labour force of about 2100 males, and about 3400 females, aged 16.[28] ABS employment data for August show between 1973 and 1974 a decline in full-time employment for males 15–19 years of 3500, and for females 15–19 years a decline of 6700.[29] The implications of the change in welfare payments policy which these calculations suggest include (a) an estimated addition of about 2100 males aged 16 to the labour force during a period when full-time employment of males, 15–19 years, contracted by about 3400, and (b) an estimated addition of about 3500 females aged 16 during a period when full-time employment of females, 15–19 years, contracted by about 6700. This sort of order-of-magnitude estimate of the effect of the 31 July 1974 increase in youth unemployment benefits shows broad agreement with estimates obtained using co-efficients for 15–19-year-old males and females derived from Gregory and Duncan's 1980 study.

The above estimates suggest that from this analytical perspective, Government policy changes in transfer payments as they affected Australian youth were economically misconceived.[30]

Following the estimates of Equations (8.1) and (8.2), additions to the Australian labour force during 1974 are estimated for youths aged 16 at about 2000 males, and about 3500 females. Following Gregory and Duncan, the figures are about 5300 males and about 4400 females in the 16–19 years age group, added to the Australian labour force. The growth between August 1973 and August 1974 in 15–19-year-old measured employment was 1000 for males and 6200 for females.[31]

In comparing 1973–74 estimates of additions to the Australian labour force as suggested by McGavin and by Gregory and Duncan, it is necessary again to be reminded that the data on unemployment are *ex post* outcomes, and also 'measured' outcomes. The figures for reduced school participation and for increased labour force participation are based on *ceteris paribus* assumptions. The 'other things being constant' condition for these estimates of the influence of change in unemployment benefits is not met. The parents' earnings variables (specified in Equations (8.1) and (8.2)) especially were not constant. As has been noted, coefficients attaching to parents' earnings variables are of approximately the same order as those attaching to youth unemployment benefits. It should therefore be anticipated that changes in the ability of families to support their children's schooling, and changes in the future earnings which young people may expect (especially as these expectional changes apply to girls), would have exercised a positive influence on school retention rates. The net movement between 1973 and 1974 in school retention rates for 16-year-olds was −1.5 per cent for boys, and −0.1 per cent for girls. There remains room for debate about the precise magnitude of the effects of the youth wages and the welfare policies of the Whitlam Government. But in terms of labour market conditions of this period, the Government's welfare policy changes, which acted to increase youth labour force participation, would seem to warrant the judgement ill-considered and ill-advised.

Although Mr Cameron, as Minister for Labour, claims to have 'pressed the case for higher wage rates for young and inexperienced boys and girls'[32], the critical market and institutional changes influencing the growth of junior relative wages occurred just prior to the advent of the Whitlam Government. As was argued in Chapter 6, the generalization of that change during the Whitlam period was achieved in the context of a 'permissive' policy of general sympathy for the change on the part of the Government. The Government's influence upon changes in the provision of public transfer payments to youth was, however, a clearly discretionary policy action, the deleterious effects of which should be attributed to the Whitlam administration.

'Senior' Labour Force Participation and Changes in the Provision of Social Security Transfers

In examining the provision of social security transfer payments as these affect the labour force participation of Australian youth, it was possible to concentrate on the influence of changes in unemployment benefits since this category of public transfers is of predominant significance for youth. For older workers, the situation is complicated by the influence of other public transfers, particularly the influence of aged and invalid pensions. In dealing with changes in the provision of social security transfer payments, the question of attraction into the labour force will be less relevant for older persons. The larger issue is the decision to *withdraw* from labour force participation. Changes in the provision of social security transfers will alter the opportunity costs of the decision to withdraw from participation in the labour force. Changes in welfare provision will also be influential in decisions to shift from full-time to part-time labour force participation. This section will be devoted to examining some of the issues in this very wide field. During the period the influence of structural change favouring women's employment and large increases in married women's engagement in full-time and in part-time employment complicates the picture (see Chapter 7). For these reasons, the discussion is almost exclusively in terms of males[33], and is focused upon men who are at the margin of the decision between engagement in wage employment and in retirement activity: that is, upon men in the 60–64 age group.

Changes in the Opportunity Cost for Older Workers of the Decision to Withdraw from the Labour Force

Table 8.5 reproduces data from a paper by Mr D. W. Kalisch and Dr L. S. Williams[34] which show the proportion of gross and of disposable average weekly earnings to standard [single] and to married aged and invalid pension rates. For the period 1969–70 to 1971–72, the standard and married aged and invalid pensions respectively averaged 19.4 and 34.1 per cent of gross average weekly earnings (and 23.9 and 39.8 of net average weekly earnings, respectively). For the last fiscal year of the Whitlam Government, aged and invalid pensions as a proportion of gross average weekly earnings had increased from these bases by about 25 per cent at the standard rate, and by about 13 per cent at the married rate (respectively, to 24.3 and 38.5 per cent of gross average weekly earnings).[35] As a proportion of net average weekly earnings, these increases, respectively, were: standard, 43 per cent, and married, 26 per cent (to 34.2 and 50.3 per cent, respectively, of net average weekly earnings at 1975–76). When Labor assumed office (December 1972), the standard aged or invalid pension rate was $20.00 pw (married rate, $34.50 pw). The last rate determined by the Whitlam Government (1 May 1975) was $36.00 pw standard rate ($64.50 pw, married rate). These increases (of 80 and 87 per cent, respectively) were greater than the growth in average weekly earnings over that period, with the consequence that at the end of the Whitlam administration, the single aged or invalid pensioner received a benefit of more than a third of net average weekly earnings, while the married aged or invalid pensioner with a dependent spouse received about half net average weekly earnings.[36]

The relationship between returns from engagement in wage employment and retirement activity is more complicated than the simple comparison of wage and pension incomes. Eligibility for pensions (and the administration of eligibility tests) may alter.[37]

Table 8.5 Selected Pension Replacement Rates (per cent)

Fiscal Year	Maximum Standard Rate of Aged Pension as a Proportion of		Maximum Married Rate of Aged Pension as a Proportion of	
	AWE	AWE net of income tax for a single wage earner	AWE	AWE net of income tax for a married man with dependent spouse
1969–70	19.7	24.2	35.3	41.4
1970–71	18.9	23.1	33.3	38.6
1971–72	19.5	24.3	33.2	39.6
1972–73	21.1	26.1	37.4	44.3
1973–74	22.0	28.0	35.2	42.4
1974–75	24.3	31.1	34.8	43.3
1975–76	24.3	34.2	38.5	50.3

Note: AWE = average weekly earnings per employed male unit.
Sources: See note 38.

Moreover, retirement incomes may also include returns from a variety of sources, such as part-time employment, superannuation funds, accumulated assets, etc. Additionally, there is the complex question of taxation liability as incurred in employment and in retirement. It is therefore a considerable simplification to view the relationship in terms of a comparison between returns from engagement in wage employment and in retirement activity. Nevertheless, such a simple comparison remains useful for examining the influence of changes in welfare provision in the decisions of older Australians whether or not to engage in 'labour force' activity. The change in relative returns between occupation in wage and non-wage engagement which these increases in pension levels achieved means that the opportunity cost of a decision to withdraw from wage employment was reduced. One should, therefore, expect that these changes would have acted to draw older workers out of the labour force.[39]

As remarked, a decision to withdraw from wage employment is, however, also influenced by income sources besides welfare transfer payments. Prominent amongst other income sources may be income from part-time employment. A decision to engage in part-time employment calls for reference to the 'free area', which is the maximum income that a pensioner may accrue and still receive the maximum pension. For the duration of the Whitlam Government, the means test on aged and invalid pensioners remained unchanged from the monetary amounts established by the McMahon Government effective as of 5 October 1972.[40] The influence of inflation meant therefore that the 'real' value of the 'free area' was subject to continuous decline during the Whitlam period. Data for the 'free area' in 1966–67 prices are reported in Table 8.6, and indicate the exent of this fall. Compared with their level at the advent of the Whitlam Government, the real value of the 'free area' at December 1975 had fallen by almost a third for both single and married-couple pensioners: from about \$16 to about \$11 for a single person, and from about \$27 to about \$19 for a married couple (1966–67 prices). This means that during the Whitlam era, older Australians making a decision to leave the employed work force would more frequently have made that decision with the expectation of greater reliance on pension income as a proportion of total income (or else face the prospect of reduced pension benefits). Similarly, older Australians who had already left the work force would be induced to reduce the significance of

Table 8.6 'Free Area' in Constant 1966–67 Prices (dollars)

Year	Single Person	Married Couple
1970	9	15
1971	8	14
1972	16	27
1973	13	23
1974	11	21
1975	11	19

Notes: The 'free area' is defined as the amount of income a pensioner can earn and still receive the maximum benefits. Data are rounded to the nearest dollar.

Sources: Derived from BLMR, *Retired, Unemployed or at Risk*, Research Report No. 4, AGPS, Canberra, 1983, p. 52, using ABS cat. *1311.0*, and unpublished data provided by the Department of Social Security.

other income sources. It should be expected that the effect of this real change in 'free area' would be to reduce the incidence of effort by older Australians to maintain or to seek a part-time labour force participation. Thus, it should be expected that those who withdrew from full-time employment would have a greater tendency to withdraw from employment altogether, and those already outside full-time employment and in receipt of an aged or invalid pension would be less likely to seek (or to maintain) part-time labour force engagement. The conclusion which this analysis therefore suggests is that changes in aged and invalid pension provisions during the Whitlam period appear to have given encouragment to a withdrawal of older Australians from the work force (rather than to have encouraged a change from full-time to part-time employment).

The Consequent Withdrawal of Older Australians from Labour Force Participation

The expectations raised in the previous section are consistent with the outcomes described in the data of Table 8.7, below, where it may be noticed that for Australian males aged 60–64, the proportion in full-time employment fell from 71.1 per cent in 1972 to 60.5 per cent in 1975—a fall of almost 15 per cent in the proportion of the 60–64 male age group in full-time employment. Notice also that between 1971 and 1972 the fall in the proportion of males aged 60–64 in full-time employment of 0.8 per cent was entirely matched by an 0.8 per cent increase in the proportion of males aged 60–64 in part-time employment. But the continuous

Table 8.7 Income Status of Males Aged 60–64 (per cent)

	Employed			Welfare Recipients					
Year*	Full-time	Part-time	Total	Service pension	Invalid pension	UBs	Total	Other†	Total
1971	71.9	4.0	75.9	3.9	(7.5)	0.4	11.8	12.3	100.0
1972	71.1	4.8	75.8	4.3	8.4	0.7	13.5	10.7	100.0
1973	69.4	4.2	73.6	5.9	9.5	0.6	16.0	10.4	100.0
1974	65.9	4.4	70.2	7.0	10.2	0.6	17.9	11.9	100.0
1975	60.5	4.2	64.7	8.0	11.0	1.6	20.6	14.7	100.0

Note: See notes to Table 8.8
Sources: BLMR, *Retired ... or at Risk*, p. 42, using data from the Departments of Social Security and Veterans' Affairs, and ABS cat. *6203.0*.

fall between 1972 and 1975 in the proportion of males aged 60–64 in full-time employment (a fall in proportion adding to 15 per cent over that period) was also accompanied by a continuous fall in the proportion of males aged 60–64 engaged in part-time employment. Further, notice that the clear fall in the proportion of men aged 60–64 engaged in full-time employment also *precedes* the late-1974 change in statistics showing a deterioration in employment prospects. Between 1973 and 1974 there was a decline of about 5 per cent in the proportion of men aged 60–64 years in full-time employment.

An escalation in the rate of decline of older males in full-time employment occurred with the deterioration of the labour market: between 1974 and 1975 the decline in the proportion of men aged 60–64 in full-time employment was 8 per cent.[41] This trend may also be noticed in the data for males 65 years and over (see Table 8.8, where it may be noticed that employment of men of 65 years and over, 'part-time' plus 'full-time'[42], fell by over a quarter, from 21.7 per cent of the age group population in 1972 to 15.9 per cent in 1975). From the viewpoint of the relationship between wages and aged and invalid welfare provisions, the emergence of that decline *before* the downturn in male employment is notable.

These observations remain true when the discussion is in terms of 'labour force participation' for males aged 60–64 years (that is, adding 'employed full-time' + 'employed part-time' + 'unemployment benefit recipients'). Between 1971 and 1972, there was a slight increase for these men in labour force participation—from 76.3 to 76.5 per cent. Then from 1972 to 1975 the proportion of men aged 60–64 engaged in the 'labour force' fell by about 13 per cent, from 76.5 to 66.3 per cent. Notice again that the emergence

Table 8.8 Income Status of Males Aged 65 and Over (per cent)

	Employed			Welfare Recipients					
Year*	Full-time	Part-time	Total	Service pension	Invalid pension	Aged pension	Total	Other†	Total
1971	15.6	5.7	21.4	9.3	(0.7)	52.7	62.6	16.0	100.0
1972	15.7	6.0	21.7	9.0	0.7	53.4	63.1	15.2	100.0
1973	14.0	6.7	20.6	9.5	0.6	64.6	69.6	9.8	100.0
1974	12.1	5.7	17.8	10.3	0.5	65.0	75.8	6.4	100.0
1975	10.7	5.2	15.9	10.5	1.3	70.0	80.8	3.3	100.0

Notes: *Numbers employed are at August; beneficiary and population numbers are as at June; unemployment benefits recipients are the nearest estimate to June.
†'Other' is a net residual item equal to the proportion who are neither employed nor receiving welfare, less the proportion who are both working and receiving welfare. Numbers in brackets are BLMR estimates only.

Sources: BLMR, *Retired ... or at Risk*, p. 43, using data from the Departments of Social Security and Veterans' Affairs, and ABS cat. *6203.0*.

of this continuous fall in labour force participation of older men *precedes* the late-1974 deterioration of the labour market associated with the recession, and continues throughout the 1970s to a low at 1980 (when older male labour force participation is 50 per cent, compared with over 75 per cent at the opening of the decade).[43]

This withdrawal of older men from labour force involvement on grounds, as here argued, significantly related to changes in welfare transfer provisions will naturally be witnessed by the growth of persons in receipt of government pensions. The data of Table 8.7 show a strong growth between 1971 and 1973 in the proportion of men, 60–64 years, in receipt of service and invalid pensions (a growth of 35 per cent from 11.4 to 15.4 per cent of the age group).[44] For men of aged pension entitlement (see Table 8.8), there is a growth between 1972 and 1973 of about 21 per cent (from 53.4 to 64.6 per cent) in the proportion of men of 65 years and over in receipt of an aged pension (a growth which continues through to a 1978 peak of 75.2 per cent of men in that age group in receipt of an aged pension). Referring to service pensions, the data of Table 8.9 show for men aged both 60–64 years, and 65 years and over, a growth between 1972 and 1973 in the the proportion of eligible men drawing these pensions[45] (an acceleration in service pension uptake which continued through to 1980).[46]

The foregoing argument gives a different perspective on the in-

Table 8.9 Proportion of Eligible Males Receiving the Service Pension, by Age (per cent)

	Age Group	
Year	60–64	64+
1971	16.7	48.9
1972	18.0	47.6
1973	23.9	51.6
1974	26.9	57.5
1975	29.3	60.6

Source: BLMR, *Retired ... or at Risk*, p. 43, using unpublished data provided by the ABS and the Department of Veterans' Affairs.

creasing tendency of older Australians to withdraw from labour market involvement from that given in 1981 by Drs P. Stricker and P. Sheehan who stress the influence of the decline in economic performance in Australia. These authors undertake multiple regression estimation of service and invalid pension usage rates for men aged 60–64 years (using data for 1966 to 1979). For service pension usage, the explanatory variables are time, the ratio of the basic pension rate to male average weekly earnings, the ratio of the 'free' income level to male average weekly earnings, and the duration of recorded unemployment for males 25 years and over lagged one period. For invalid pension usage, the explanatory variables are a composite variable derived by weighting the ratios of pensions and 'free' income levels to male average weekly earnings, the composite variable lagged one period, and the duration of recorded unemployment for males 25 years and over.[47] The specification and the results of these estimates are uncertain—as may be seen from the statistical tests for these equations.

The impact of the recession is estimated by holding the duration of unemployment constant after 1974 at a level equal to the 1972–74 average (namely, ten weeks), thereby deriving pension usage rates which are reckoned to estimate what pension usage would have been had unemployment duration remained at the pre-recession level.[48] Stricker and Sheehan thus find a 'very heavy recession-induced resort to invalid and service pensions'.[49]

Those on 'other' income sources are defined by Stricker and Sheehan as 'the difference between the total population and the sum of the number of persons working and the number receiving benefits'.[50] Estimates of 'the recession-induced component of benefit usage, plus half the increase in "other" income sources' give a 1979 estimate of hidden unemployment among men aged 60–64 years of about 37 000.[51] The linear trend between 1966 and 1973 for labour force participation of males aged 60–64 years is projected to 1979, and this is compared with the actual labour force participation rate.[52] This enables the calculation of the 'labour force gap' at 1979.[53] Stricker and Sheehan seem surprised that their estimate of hidden unemployment for 1979 'represents less than 70 per cent of the labour force gap at that time'. Presumably, they anticipated that 'voluntary'[54] factors should account for less than 30 per cent of the divergence from their trend of labour force participation of males aged 60–64 years. They thus conclude: 'Clearly, as with so many issues raised in [their] book, further investigations are needed here'.[55]

Further Australian investigation is provided by Mrs Y. Dunlop and Dr L. S. Williams.[56] The Bureau of Labour Market Research, using the results of its researchers (Dunlop and Williams), partition the reduction from 1973 to 1979 of about 53 000 in labour force participation of males aged 60–64 years between that attributed to 'voluntary' decision, and that attributed to 'involuntary' decision. The work of Dunlop and Williams employs a Generalized Least Squares autoregressive model of labour force participation for older age groups. The magnitudes reported by these authors may be converted into labour force participation elasticities with respect to the various explanatory variables, including 'prime age male unemployment rate', 'real average weekly earnings per employed male unit', and 'real maximum value of government pensions'. Reductions in labour force participation which is 'involuntary' is that derived from the elasticity attaching to unemployment; while 'voluntary' reduction is derived as a residual. In the equation for males aged 60–64 years, the magnitude attaching to government pensions does not meet the conventional test of statistical significance.[57] In consequence, the partitioning by the Bureau of Labour Market Research of the reduction in labour force participation for males aged 60–64 years should not be regarded as a precision *ceteris paribus* estimate. It is, however, suggestive of the relative significance for labour force participation which may be attributed to the discouragement of increased unemployment ('involuntary' retirement), and to the attraction of increased government pensions ('voluntary' retirement).

For males aged 60–64 years, 10 per cent of the 1973–79 reduction in labour force participation for this age group is attributed to the influence of reduced employment opportunity, and the remaining 90 per cent is viewed 'as reflecting the contribution of voluntary factors' (for males 65 years and over, 15 per cent of reduced labour force participation is attributed to the 'discouragement' influence of labour market conditions, and 85 per cent is attributed to 'voluntary' decision).[58] On this evidence, changes in welfare under Whitlam therefore induced a reduction in contributions to the supply of market goods and services, while also increasing demand for market goods and services, and thus contributed to the Australian experience of inflation and reduced employment. Appendix 8.1 presents 'first-estimates' which illustrate this argument.

The marshalling of data in this chapter tracing the effects of changes in welfare provision is consistent with the results of recent Australian econometric research[59] showing the withdrawal of older workers[60] from the labour market principally to have been a 'voluntary' withdrawal, and not principally an 'involuntary' (or 'discouraged worker') response. This conclusion agrees with the findings of numerous studies of the US, Canadian and UK experiences of increases in the provision of social security and reductions in labour force participation.[61]

Wages, Welfare and Employment: Conclusions

The conclusions of the analysis of this chapter include the following:

1 Increases in real wages contributed to an increase in the labour force participation rate for all age groups.

2 Increases in unemployment benefits, particularly the increase in unemployment benefits as a proportion of potential or of actual wage income, increased the participation rate for all age groups in the 'labour force', but especially the full-time labour force involvement of Australian youth.

3 Increases in pensions, particularly the increase in pensions as a proportion of potential or of actual wage income, decreased the participation rate for all eligible age groups. This decrease most applies for those at or approaching the margin where choice is made between 'wage employment' or 'retirement activity'.

4 The reduction in the 'real' value of the 'free area' for recipients of public transfer payments also contributed to a reduction in the labour force participation, and particularly of part-time labour force participation (and, more particularly, of the part-time labour force involvement of older males, and of older unmarried females).

These conclusions mean that the interaction of 'wages and welfare' under the Whitlam Government operated to increase wages, and to counteract any tendency towards reduction in wages or in the rate of growth of wages. In terms of youth labour force experience, this meant an increase in labour force participation *and* a reduction in employment: an increase in the 'labour force' together with a reduction in the 'work force'[62], compared with what otherwise would have occurred. For older Australians, this meant a reduction in labour force participation. The reduction in labour supply that this entailed may be expected to have contributed to wages being higher than they would otherwise have been. A consequence of this was reduced employment for any given demand for labour services.

While the movement of 'wages and welfare' acted to reduce the employment both of youth and of older Australians, there was at the same time an increase in the volume of 'welfare' drawings on the public transfer payments system. Changes in 'wages and welfare' thus acted simultaneously to *reduce* the use of labour services and (*ceteris paribus*) to reduce the supply of goods and services for any nominal level of aggregate activity, and also to *increase* for those drawing on wage and on welfare incomes the demand for goods and services occurring at any nominal level of aggregate activity.

As has been noted at various points in this chapter, the estimates here presented may be considered as illustrations, rather than demonstrations, of the magnitudes of the effects being considered. The question of precise magnitudes remains open to debate, but the direction of influence of changes in wages and welfare policies during the Whitlam period seems clear.

In summary, the changes during the Whitlam period in 'wages and welfare' (as these impinged upon younger and older Australians) acted to reduce the supply of and to increase the demand for market goods and services. Thus, these changes acted to influence both a reduction in the level of real aggregate activity, together with an increase in the rate of change of prices (the rate of 'inflation'). That is, the 'wages' and 'welfare' policies of the Whitlam Government contributed to the increased Australian experience of 'stagflation'. As a consequence, one should conclude that the interaction of the Whitlam Government's 'wages and welfare' policies was counteractive for the Government's 'first priority': the employment objective.[63]

Chapter 9

Wages and Employment: An Economic Evaluation of the Whitlam Government's Wages Policy

Lady Bracknell (to Jack): What number in Belgrave Square?
Jack: 149.
Lady Bracknell (shaking her head): The unfashionable side ... However, that could easily be altered.
Jack: Do you mean the fashion, or the side?
Lady Bracknell (sternly): Both, if necessary, I presume.
(Oscar Wilde, *The Importance of Being Earnest*, Act 1)

Investigation of the wages policy of the Whitlam Government and its implications, in particular, the relationship between wages and employment in its varied aspects is the focus of this study. The conclusions to be drawn from the analysis of the wages policy of the Whitlam Government have been stated at the end of each of the major sections of this book. The purpose of this concluding chapter is to draw together and briefly to restate these findings.

It is clear from the major shifts in government policy as portrayed in Chapter 2 that the Government itself found reason to question its economic perceptions, policy formulation, and policy implementation, with respect to wages. It is not usual for governments to admit their failings, nor to find it necessary to do so after so short a period of time. Yet the Whitlam Government's presentation of the case for the wages policy of its last year in office in significant respects amounted to a retraction of its earlier policies. For example:

> [The] present severe squeeze on profits, and resultant unemployment, has arisen partly from the relative success of the measures we have taken to restrain the growth in prices, in the face of a continued acceleration in wages.
>
> (Whitlam, Premiers Conference, 14 February 1975)

What we submit is that the Australian Government system of plateau percentage indexation is a positive and constructive contribution towards setting Australia firmly on the path to economic recovery ... The system will help to counteract the business recession and is complementary to the extensive initiative taken by the Australian Government by providing assurance to employers about the future wage bills they have to meet ... and by facilitating and contributing to an adjustment of national income back towards profits.

(Counsel for the Commonwealth, National Wage Case, 1974–75)[1]

The research reported in this book supports the judgement implicit in the above quotations: that the wages policy of the Whitlam Government was counteractive for the stated employment objective, the 'first priority' of the Labor Party.[2] But the work of this study has not been merely to confirm a verdict on the Government's wages policy already made by the Government itself, and—by contemporary political standards—clearly made.[3] The conclusions of this book are stronger: that the late wages policy of the Whitlam Government during the third and final year of its office did not reverse the misperceptions of its earlier policy, and did not contribute to correcting the damaging influence of its earlier wages policy.

The late policy of the Whitlam Government was marketed as one of wages 'restraint'.[4] Yet it was not. Its purpose was to retain the real wage increases gained by those retaining employment.[5] The effect of the Government's policy of restricting real wage adjustment was to force a concentration upon quantity adjustment in labour use. The effect of this policy was to concentrate the burden of adjustment upon a minority: upon those not retaining employment, and upon those entering the labour force. Moreover, the late wages policy of the Whitlam Government, with its emphasis on wage indexation, provided the framework for wages policy formation for the following six years. The continuity of this general framework for wages policy may be supposed to have occurred because it suited the majority, the 'employed'.[6] But the minority who bore the burden of quantity adjustment, the 'unemployed', largely seem not themselves to have made the causal link between wages and employment.[7]

In researching the Whitlam Government's wages policy it has seemed to the author that the Government treated the economic environment as something determined by command, or, more particularly, determined by its command. The familiar picture of the imperious 'Gough' of the newspaper cartoons prompted the leading quotations of this chapter. To fill in the picture, the Prime Minister is decked out as 'Lady Bracknell', while 'Jack' appears as a public servant. The caption reads, *Whatever is necessary!* Interpreted, this means, 'Change—as is necessary—the "street" or the "side": government is by command'.[8] The burden of this study has been to demonstrate that an economy is not made subject to the desires of governments. For government economic policy to be effectual requires its consistency with economic phenomena, and a keen recognition that 'economic realities' are not altered by 'command'. That is, both in conception and in implementation, economic policy must be soundly grounded in empirical reality.

The reality of government-induced redistribution in the share of national income towards labour by the instrument of wage is that this contributes to reduced capital formation and to reduced employment and to productivity growth lower than should otherwise be expected. The research reported in this book suggests that for 1975 the lagged change in relative wages contributed about −1.25 million hours to the aggregate change in Australian male weekly employment. This reduction in employment is derived by what may be regarded as a lower boundary *ceteris paribus* estimate of the direct impact only of wages growth upon employment. The estimate corresponds to about 46 per cent of the 1975 growth in measured Australian male unemployment.

The reality of government-induced restriction of market price adjustment in respect of labour rewards is that this increases the measure in which adjustment has to occur in terms of quantities (rather than prices). In consequence, the time-span of reduced employment is therefore increased. Additionally, because the readjustment in factor shares in national income is prolonged, the experience of inflation is prolonged.

The reality of increased direct taxation is that this induces wage increases directed to restore disposable wage incomes (except, of course, where there is widespread consent to the increased taxation). Additionally, the widening of the wedge between gross and disposable wage incomes accelerates the incidence of wages as costs—and this accelerates the attrition of the work force, or the rate of inflation, or both.

The reality of arbitrary increases of relative wages for 'lower-paid' workers—whether less-skilled, junior, or female—is that, in the absence of offsetting increases in demand for the services of these workers, these act to reduce their employment and to increase their 'unemployment'. This reality has predominantly been felt by 'marginal' Australian workers, by Australian youth generally, and by Australian women unable to move into part-time or into tertiary industry employment. It has been widely claimed that 'equal pay for women' increased the wage income of Australian women.[9] But it has not been widely recognized that the increase in wage income of some Australian women has involved a reduction in wage income of other Australian women.

The reality of the increases in the level of benefits payable under the public transfer payments system is—for those contemplating seeking employment—an increased rate of labour force participation, but without an increase of employment; and, for those contemplating withdrawal from employment or the search for employment, a decrease in employment. Increases in unemployment benefits payable to Australian youths as introduced by the Whitlam Government are judged to have increased junior labour force participation at a time of marked contraction in junior employment. The withdrawal of older Australians from market contribution to the production of goods and services is assessed as being predominantly a voluntary response to increases by the Whitlam Government in pension and invalid benefits. Changes in wages and welfare (as these impinged upon younger and older Australians) are thus seen as having acted to sustain aggregate demand for, and to reduce aggregate supply of, market goods and services. Thus, these changes should be seen as having acted to influence a reduction in the resultant level of real aggregate activity, together with an increase in the rate of inflation: that is, to have contributed to the Australian experience of 'stagflation'.

The analysis of this study emphasizes the disemployment effects of the various components of the Whitlam Government's wages policy, and leads to the conclusion that it was the 'least advantaged' Australians (for whom the Whitlam Government voiced its 'particular concern')[10] who have chiefly borne the costs of the Government's wages policy. It may further be argued that it was the 'least advantaged' who continued (and perhaps continue) to bear the costs of the wages policy initiatives of the Whitlam Government. These policies were substantially active in generating the serious imbalances in the Australian economy—and in the Australian labour market in particular—which were evident at the close of the Whitlam period.[11]

The introduction of wage indexation was the last major objective of wages policy secured by the Whitlam Government, and it was hailed as 'a milestone in the history of Australian wages policy' (Cameron, Press Release, 30 April 1975). The analysis of this study reveals, however, that wage indexation provided the conditions for major inhibition of the process of restoration of overall economic balance and of labour market adjustment in the Australian economy. Subsequent analysis may reveal the introduction of wage indexation in 1975 to have been not a 'milestone', but a 'mill stone'—and a mill stone the weight of which was borne chiefly by Australians for whom the market valuation of their labour product was less than the wage determined (and maintained) through government and arbitral influence exercised without substantial reference to the economic conditions for the wage employment of these Australians.

Although the research involved in documenting and analysing these 'realities' has involved a great deal of original work, the methods and the conclusions are not in themselves 'new'—they simply apply well-known tools of economic analysis that are part of the 'common stock' of economic knowledge gained by the profession through years of grounding in the realities of economic phenomena.

To someone unsympathetic with the economic stance of this study, the failure to allow for political and industrial relations influences may seem to evidence a lack of 'reality' in economic analysis. What has been argued, however, is that political ideology and political and industrial influences are not above economic assessment: economic analysis may inform one's political judgement. Additionally, economic analysis plays a significant educational function. For economic assessment of a given course of action either strengthens or qualifies one's commitment to that course of action. Thus it has been argued that economic analysis of certain economic policy positions provides a control function in respect of those who support the proposed policy positions. This 'control function' is exercised where economic analysis indicates the sorts of responses that are likely to ensue from the pursuit of some given economic policy. It is also exercised where economic assessment gives orders of magnitude to the costs of the implementation of particular policies, and also indicates the likely distribution of those costs within the society. In the area of wages policy, economic evaluation therefore suggests likely consequences of particular policy stances, and gives a sense of the costs of particular policy stances, and an indication of which groups in the society are likely to 'pay' those costs.

The message of this book is neither a counsel of despair, nor of economic determinism. Economic outcomes are in this author's view no more determined than are military outcomes. In warfare, physical circumstances of relative numbers and of comparative technology are highly relevant. Also relevant is the rhetoric of the military commanders. Yet military history has often demonstrated how critical to the outcome is widespread identification of individual combatants with the military objectives of their leaders. Mr Whitlam and his Government understood their programmes as having the 'mandate' of the Australian people. The many and varied choices of individual Australians which pervasively acted to frustrate government policy made clear that the choices which the Whitlam Government purposed did not attract, in the everyday and detailed exercise of their preferences, the widespread identification of individual Australians. Had the contrary been the case, market influences may be expected to have acted to confirm, rather than to frustrate, the purposes of Government policy: and the findings of this study may be expected to have been contrariwise.

Appendixes

The appendixes provide additional information to chapters 1, 5, and 8 respectively

Appendix 1.1
An Outline of Australian Institutions of Wages Determination

It was noted in Chapter 1 that the Whitlam Government 'did not "happen" in a vacuum'. The evaluation of the policies of the Labour Government needs to be made within the context of the economic situation which was inherited. In respect of wages policy, the most critical 'inheritance' was the complex of institutions and principles of wages determination which operated in Australia. It was in the context of these that the formulation and the execution of government wages policy occurred. This Appendix provides a brief outline of the institutional context of wage-setting in Australia.

Participants in the Wage-setting Process

The principal parties in Australian wage determination are:

(a) the employees and the employers directly engaged in the employment contract;

(b) labour unions representing employees, and industry or employer associations representing employers;

(c) peak councils of unions (principally, the Australian Council of Trade Unions (ACTU)), and peak councils of employer associations (notably, the Confederation of Australian Industry);

(d) 'judicial' authorities concerned with settlement and determination of conditions of employment, including wages: the federal 'authority' being the Australian Conciliation and Arbitration Commission, and numerous state authorities (for example, in Victoria, State Wages Boards)—collectively these

may be referred to as tribunals or as arbitral institutions[1]; and
(e) federal and state governments in their roles both as major employers, and as 'interveners' before authorities settling or determining conditions of employment.

The 'Language' of Wages

Throughout this work, wherever the term 'wage' is used, it refers to the general category of 'reward for market labour services'. Within this general category fall a variety of more specific uses of the term. These are outlined below.

Award Wages: Award wage refers to the minimum amount per week payable to employees of particular categories, working in areas defined by the Arbitration Commission or a state tribunal as falling within a certain 'industry' for which a certain *award* applies. (Employers conducting business in more than one state will usually be subject to the awards of the federal tribunal.) For workers falling under a particular 'award', the relevant 'award wage' sets the *minimum* legal wage at which they may be employed in the relevant occupational and industrial setting. The term 'award wages' will be used when speaking of this category, as the term 'minimum wage' is reserved for a different category (to be described below). Unless otherwise stated, award wage data will be referred to on a *weekly* basis for 'full-time' employees, and in *nominal* terms. *Hourly* wage will mean monetary labour reward on a per hour basis. *Real* wage will mean monetary labour reward expressed in some constant dollar terms (for example, 1966 = 1.00).

Collective Bargaining, *Over-award Payments*, and the *Earnings Drift*: Where an agreement on employment conditions between employees and employers (or their representatives) is achieved outside a judical context, the process of achieving that agreement is termed *collective bargaining*. The determination of wages by tribunals therefore tends to be a more centralized process than that occurring under collective bargaining. Thus collective bargaining is sometimes described as 'decentralized wage fixation', and gets contrasted with 'centralized wage fixation' (of tribunals).

Any excess between the wage agreed between employees and employers (or their representatives) and the award wage is termed *over-award payments*. When over-award payments are expressed as a proportion of award wages, they may be referred to as the *earnings drift*. Thus, the earning drift indicates the tendency for wage earnings to be gained outside the sphere of judicial processes.

Determinations and *Consent Awards*: The minimum legal wage may be derived either by *determination* or by *registration* with the Arbitration Commission or a state tribunal. In the former case, 'employees' and 'employers' (or their representatives) are the 'parties' bringing a case before an employment conditions tribunal. Tribunals may authorize other bodies or their representatives who have an interest in the outcome also to put their case before the tribunal: any body so authorized is termed an 'intervener'. Except in its capacity as an employer, the influence of the federal government upon award wage determination will chiefly be through the exercise of 'intervention' in award cases. In the case of a *determination*, the award wage is 'determined' by a tribunal after it has weighed the cases put to it by the parties and interveners (if any).

In the case of a *registration*, the parties will have brought before a tribunal an agreement on employment conditions, seeking to have this agreement achieve the legal status of an 'award'. A tribunal grants this status by 'registering' the 'consent agreement'. An award of this type is termed a *consent award*.

Earnings, Average Weekly Earnings, and *Average Award Wages*: The term *earnings* means 'paid wage rates': that is, the wages actually paid. As earnings data will usually be available as averages of aggregate data, the standard data series used is *average weekly earnings*. Most reference in this book is to adult male average weekly earnings, or to adult female average weekly earnings. Unless otherwise indicated, where simply 'AWE' is used, the reference is to an ABS index which weights earnings for male and female, and for adult and junior components of the work force: ABS describe this index as 'average weekly earnings per employed male unit' (AWE).

It will at times be appropriate to compare average weekly earnings with award wages, and for this purpose, reference will be made to series published by the ABS of 'weighted average minimum weekly rates payable for a full week's work' (cat. *6312.0*). Because, as explained below, the term 'mimimum wage' is reserved for another use, these series will henceforth be described as *average award rates*. The average award rates for adult males will be termed 'male average award rates', and for adult females 'female average award rates'.

Junior Wages: For the general purposes of Australian labour law, an 'adult' is 21 years of age and over. However, many awards specify payment of the adult rate at 18 years of age. Most 'junior' wage data are for persons aged 16–20 years and, unless otherwise stated, this should be read as the relevant age group for 'junior' wage data used in this book.

Minimum Wage: The term *minimum wage* is reserved in this book for reference to that weekly rate determined by the various tribunals payable to employees falling within their jurisdiction, but who are not covered by a specific award category. The 'minimum wage' is therefore the minimum wage at which an adult may be employed in the Australian labour market. From 30 June 1975 there has been a common minimun wage for men and women. (Usually, the terms 'males' and 'females' are used to cover both 'juniors' [boys and girls] and 'adults' [men and women]. Strictly, the terms 'men' and 'women' apply to adults only, but sometimes they have been used simply because they read more 'humanly' than do 'males' and 'females'.)

Ordinary-time and *Over-time*: The minimum wage applies to the standard work week (for example, 40 hours over 5 days); awards may specify a different hours duration of the work week. Work performed outside the specified time profile for work is termed *over-time* and would usually be paid at higher rates. For much wage discussion it will therefore be important to distinguish over-time earnings from standard earnings: these latter are called *ordinary-time earnings*.

Appendix 5.1 Real Wage Overhang and Employment: A Critique of Dissent

Significant amongst those dissenting from the Australian consensus view of the role of the emergence of the 'real wage overhang'

Table A5.1-1 Growth of Labour Productivity, Non-farm Market Sector (per cent)

Period	Per Person Worked	Per Hour
1966–67 to 1973–74	3.0	3.3
1973–74 to 1974–75	1.1	3.5
1974–75 to 1977–78	1.6	2.9

Source: R. G. Gregory and R. C. Duncan, 'The Labour Market in the 1970s', in W. E. Norton (ed.), Conference in Applied Economic Research, Reserve Bank of Australia, Sydney, 1980, p. 283, using 1974–75 constant prices (p. 286).

for employment have been Drs R. G. Gregory of the Australian National University and R. C. Duncan [then] of the Industries Assistance Commission. Gregory and Duncan's view has been that the poor employment record of 1975–79 has primarily been determined by low levels of output growth[1], and that there is little evidence that real wage increases substantially depressed employment.[2] In interpreting the evidence of the influence of real wage increases on depressed employment, Gregory and Duncan point[3] to estimates showing a deceleration of labour productivity per person employed from 3 per cent per annum for 1966–67 to 1973–74 to 1.1 per cent per annum for 1973–74 to 1974–75 (refer to Table A5.1-1, above). This indicated movement is contrary to that explained in Chapter 3. Gregory and Duncan, however, tend to avoid the contrary evidence for labour productivity per hour worked (as shown in their Table 1, the relevant part of which is reproduced above in Table A5.1-1).

Dr C. I. Higgins of the Australian Treasury introduces fuller and revised[4] estimates of labour productivity per hour worked which are reproduced below as Table A5.1-2. Higgins does not attempt to dispute that there was some downturn in productivity trend after 1972–73 (further discussed below). But the estimates which he introduces indicate that for the period 1974–75 to 1977–78 the annual rate of growth in productivity (on a per man-hour-worked basis) for the non-farm market sector is more than the annual rate of growth per annum in output for that sector (whereas, formerly and latterly, the obverse was true—with the annual growth rate in productivity per man-hour worked being less than the annual growth rate of output).[5]

However, Gregory and Duncan further argue that any correct inference should be against the counterfactual of 'productivity

Table A5.1-2 Percentage Growth Rates of Output and Productivity for the Non-farm Market Sector (per annum†)

	Productivity (on hours worked basis) (a)	Output (b)
1967–68	3.1	6.0
1968–69	5.4	7.6
1969–70	2.8	6.6
1970–71	1.7	4.7
1971–72	1.5	2.3
1972–73	4.8	4.9
1973–74	3.4	7.3
1974–75	3.4*	0.2
1975–76	3.2*	0.6
1976–77	3.4*	2.4
1977–78	1.2	1.4

Notes: *(a) more than (b) in these years only.
†Average of four quarters.
Source: C. I. Higgins, 'Comment', in Norton, *Conference*, p. 353.[6]

growth ... relative to past trends and relationships'.[7] As was earlier noted, the majority view of respondents to Gregory and Duncan's argument is that productivity growth had indeed slowed following the downturn of 1974, but that the shedding of and substitution against labour in response to untimely real wage increases had resulted in higher productivity growth estimates than would otherwise have been the case.[8] Treasury estimates[9] show a downturn in the growth of the average labour productivity index from June 1973. But for the fiscal year 1974–75, the year after the 'wage explosion', productivity growth is estimated at a high 7.1 per cent. The four-quarter moving averages[10] of these data give a still comparatively high 4.2 per cent estimate of productivity growth for 1974–75.

Professor F. H. Gruen attempts to marshal evidence that productivity growth was higher than should be expected following the large wage increases of 1974. His method is to regress quarterly data for hourly non-farm labour productivity for 1965:3 to 1973:3 on the following variables: time, the growth in gross non-farm product, the proportion of government consumption to gross national expenditure, and seasonal dummy variables. The co-efficient attaching to growth in gross non-farm product stands out for its size and statistical significance.[11] Gruen then adopts the following procedure:

(a) Take the estimated actual values for non-farm labour productivity.
(b) Deduct the projection values for the regressed trend of non-farm labour productivity (adopting this as an appropriate 'counterfactual').
(c) The difference ('error') indicates the relationship of the actual incidence of productivity change compared with trend productivity change.

Thus, positive 'errors in projections' indicate the actual values of productivity change in excess of what may have been expected in terms of the explanatory regressors for the base estimation period—that is, in excess of the 'counterfactual'. Table A5.1-3 lists the average annual 'errors in projections' so derived. On this evidence, then, hourly productivity performance since 1974 has tended to be above its trend 'counterfactual'.

Gruen initially directs this evidence to argue that for 1975 to 1978 the actual levels of productivity were above the levels which one would expect from the projections, and that this excess was of the order of between 0.9 and 2.4 percentage points (Equation (3)).[12] The 1978 estimates falls to 0.5 per cent once adjustment is made for the influence of public holidays on hours in the first-quarter survey period, so the peak 'error' in productivity growth projection using Equation (3) occurs in 1976 at 1.4 per cent.[13]

Gregory and Duncan appear to have taken Gruen's 'residuals' (as they call them) as cumulative, for they use Gruen's 1978 projection error 'spread over five years' and proceed to argue that 'productivity change is, therefore, trivially small'.[14] This comment would appear to be misplaced. And as Gregory and Duncan's own estimate of annual growth in hourly non-farm labour productivity for 1974–75 to 1977–78 was of the order of 2 to 3 per cent[15], a positive difference from a trend counterfactual of 0.9 to 1.4 per cent per annum cannot reasonably be described as 'not important'.[16]

The larger problem with Gruen's evidence[17] is that the regression estimates are uncorrected for evident serial correlation.[18] Only for Equation (4) does Gruen correct for first-order autocorrelation, and this equation is not strictly comparable with Equation (3) because the proportion of government consumption to gross national expenditure is not included as an explanatory variable. The co-efficients attaching to the remaining explanators of

Table A5.1-3 Growth in Non-farm Hourly Labour Productivity Errors in Projection (per cent), annual averages

Calendar Year	Equation 3	Equation 4
1974	−1.26	−0.21
1975	0.92	0.13
1976	1.43	0.52
1977	1.10	−0.36
1978	2.43 (0.54)*	0.57

Note: * Figure in brackets shows Equation (3) 1978 estimate after adjustment for peculiar influence of public holidays.
Source: F. H. Gruen, 'Comment', in Norton, *Conference*, p. 335.

Equation (4) show a similar size and statistical significance to those estimated in Equation (3). However, with the appearance of a negative figure at 1977, the signs of 'errors in projections' lose consistency, and the size of the positive 'errors' is much reduced (refer to the second column of Table A5.1-3, above). Even so, a positive 'residual' of 0.5 per cent for 1976, when compared with an actual hourly labour productivity growth estimate of 2–3 per cent, represents an actual experience of productivity growth above the level of the counterfactual of between 20 and 33 per cent.

On this evidence, then, one may reasonably consider as being somewhat forced the argument of Gregory and Duncan that Gruen's results 'fully support' their contention that labour productivity behaviour was of 'little significance' as an explanation of the rise in unemployment (but note that Gregory and Duncan focus their remarks on 1974–75).[19] It would seem more reasonable to say that Gruen's econometric evidence of the significance of labour productivity behaviour for the rise in unemployment is not incontrovertible. Nevertheless, by simply employing the revised estimates for growth in hourly labour productivity for the non-farm market sector as reported by Gregory and Duncan[20], one may point out, as does Professor R. H. Snape, that hourly labour productivity growth estimates of about 3.0 per cent for 1973–74 to 1977–8 (compared with 3.3 per cent for 1965–66 to 1973–74) do not seem to represent as significant a recession decline in productivity growth[21] as the implication of Okun's 'law' would lead one to expect.[22]

Critics of the nexus between real wage overhang and unemployment have further argued that evidence of an increase in real unit labour costs does not constitute evidence of inducement for producers to substitute against labour (as part of the generation of reduced employment). This is because the relevant movement is the real unit cost of labour compared with the real unit cost of capital—that is, the movement of *relative* real unit labour cost.[23] The measurement of real unit capital cost is an involved question.[24] Gregory and Duncan's analysis of changes in relative real unit labour cost appears to this author to be deficient. Their treatment of the proffered evidence may be criticized as follows:

(a) Dr R. G. Hawkins[25] is cited as showing that tax incentives to capital dominate the relative movement in prices.[26] But, as shown below in Table A5.1-4, these incentives were not significant until 1975–76—that is, *after* the jump in real wages and after the emergence of the profits squeeze which from late 1974 was the subject of much political comment.[27]

(b) Reference to Table A5.1-4, below, does not support Gregory and Duncan's subscription to Hawkins's viewpoint that negative movements in *post-tax* real unit capital costs were the principal cause of an upward shift in relative real unit factor prices. This is because the proportional significance of taxation subsidies to capital was, in aggregate, not great (being of the order of about 4.5 per cent).[28]

(c) As Higgins points out[29], the Treasury estimates displayed in Gregory and Duncan's Figure 11 present 'real' cost of capital, while their Figure 10 presents nominal cost of capital. This difference is advertised only in the Gregory and Duncan's headings to the Figures, and is quite ignored in the use of the data in their text.[30] Higgins further points out that Gregory and Duncan fail to note that the Treasury estimates only are 'de-trended'.[31] That is, Gregory and Duncan deal in incommensurable estimates of relative real unit factor price. Moreover, they fail to give cognizance to the qualifications with which Treasury's estimates were introduced in their quoted source.[32] And, yet further, in speaking to the approximate constancy of trend in the data of Johnston (and others)[33], they pass over the clearly illustrated widening of movements about the estimated trend occurring during the 1970s.[34]

(d) The significance of Gregory and Duncan's point is thus diminished. The argument that in the longer term it is relative real unit factor cost which is important to factor use is not controverted. But in the short run (with capital stock given) it is not relative factor prices that are relevant. The then Minister for Labour and

Table A5.1-4 Estimated New Capital Expenditure by Private Business, All Industries

Fiscal Year	(a)	(b)	(c)	(d)
1973–74	1874	2709	n.a.	n.a.
1974–75	1734	2814	35	1.24
1975–76	1775	3465	75	2.16
1976–77	1771	4068	100	2.46
1977–78	1963	5029	225	4.47
1978–79	2224	6448	300	4.65

n.a. = not applicable

Notes: (a) New Buildings and Structures, $ millions*
(b) Other New Capital Equipment, $ millions*
(c) Estimated Federal Taxation Revenue Loss on Equipment Investment Allowances, $ millions†
(d) (c) as a proportion of (b), per cent

Sources: * ABS cat. *5626.0*, computed from various issues.
† Australia, *Budget Speech and Statements*, various issues.[35]

Immigration, in referring to his Department's contacts with employers, correctly refers to the real unit price of labour, and not to its relative price.[36]

The argument of Gregory and Duncan may therefore be criticized on four grounds: (a) taxation incentives to capital do not assume significance until 1975–76; (b) the magnitude of taxation incentives to capital appears to be over-stated; (c) confusion exists as between the use of real and nominal estimates of capital cost, and between actual and trend estimates of capital cost; and (d) it may be argued that in the short run, the relevant variable for labour use is real unit labour factor cost (this being the variable used in real wage overhang estimates).

In summary, four shortcomings may be noted of the dissenting view concerning the contributory role of the 'real wage overhang' for reduced employment in Australia during the latter part of the 1970s:

1 Reference to Gregory and Duncan's estimates of growth in productivity *per hour worked* (Table A5.1-1) do not evidence a decline during the recession years in productivity growth.
2 Reference to Higgins's estimates of growth rates of output and productivity (Table A5.1-2) isolates the years 1974–75 to 1976–77 as periods during which hourly productivity growth *exceeded* output growth.
3 Four criticisms of Gregory and Duncan's argument concerning the significance of *relative* 'real unit labour cost' have been

considered, and it has been argued that in the short run 'real unit labour cost' is the relevant indicator for the influence of labour costs upon employment.

4 The basis for Gregory and Duncan's judgement concerning the relevant productivity counterfactual has been questioned, with the conclusion that actual productivity growth was above trend productivity growth by somewhere between a fifth and a third.

Appendix 8.1
The Contribution of Changes in Welfare to Stagflation: An Illustrative First-Estimate

This Appendix reports first-estimates used to give orders-of-magnitude data in support of part of the argument of Chapter 8 that the influence of the Whitlam Government in the areas of wages and welfare contributed to the incidence of stagflation in Australia. Use is made of the results of econometric estimation by Mrs Y. Dunlop and Dr L. S. Williams[1] of the labour force participation decision for males, 60–64 years, and 65 years and over.

Dunlop and Williams introduce the dependent variables (the labour force participation rates) as 'inverse logistic transforms', and the estimated co-efficients on the explanatory variables are 'monotonic transformations of the relevant elasticities'.[2] It is, nevertheless, useful to notice the reported magnitudes in order to observe their relative sizes. For both groups of older males the negative co-efficient attaching to the prime-age (25–44 years) male unemployment rate (the variable assumed to reflect the state of the labour market) was significant at the 5 per cent level. In neither case, however, was the size of the co-efficient large (about 0.10). By contrast, the real average weekly earnings variable has a positive co-efficient of about unity for both age groups (significant at the 5 per cent level). Co-efficients attaching to the real maximum value of government pensions are in both cases negative, with respective values for males of 60–64 years, and 65 years and over, of −0.30 and −0.55 (only the latter is significant at the 5 per cent level). For the 60–64 years male group, the proportion of the population eligible for service pensions has the expected nega-

Table A8.1-1 Estimates of Elasticities of Male Labour Force Participation Rates (with respect to unemployment, wages, and government pensions)

Age Group	$\eta_{\lambda,u}$	$\eta_{\lambda,wa}$	$\eta_{\lambda,g}$
60 − 64	−0.03	0.29	−0.09*
65+	−0.09	1.03	−0.45

Where,

$\eta_{\lambda,u}$ is the elasticity of the participation rate with respect to the prime age male unemployment rate,

$\eta_{\lambda,wa}$ is the elasticity of the participation rate with respect to real average weekly earnings per employed male unit, and

$\eta_{\lambda,g}$ is the elasticity of the participation rate with respect to the real maximum value of government pensions.

Notes: * This elasticity is based on a co-efficient which is not significant at the 5 per cent level. Refer also to note 3.

Source: Y. Dunlop and L. S. Williams, 'Declining Labour Force Participation Rates at Older Ages', Conference Paper No. 24, BLMR, Canberra, 1983, pp. 10, 13, and computations on these data.

tive sign, and for males aged 65 and over, the real value of the married 'free area' also has the expected negative sign (both variables being significant at the 5 per cent level).

The magnitudes reported by Dunlop and Williams may be converted into labour force participation rate elasticities through multiplication by $(1 - \bar{\lambda})$, where $\bar{\lambda}$ is the mean labour force participation rate over the sample period. Table A8.1-1 gives these results for selected variables.

For each of the years 1973 to 1975 there was an increase in the real maximum value of government pensions (married rate), **G**. Third-quarter increases in **G** on the previous year were 5.9 per cent in 1973, 13.8 per cent in 1974, and 8.1 per cent in 1975 (computed from Table 8.2, below). Applying the elasticities of labour force participation with respect to **G** (that is, the $\eta_{\lambda,g}$) derives changes in male labour force participation rates as reported in Table A8.1-2.

Table A8.1-3 reports (for the period 1973 to 1975) *ceteris paribus* estimates of the reduction in the male (60–64 years) labour force. These are derived by applying the estimates of changes in participation rates for males 60–64 years (reported in Table A8.1-2) to estimates for these years of the male population aged 60–64.

The data of Table A8.1-3 suggest that during the Whitlam era about 6000 males aged 60–64 years may have left the labour force

Table A8.1-2 Changes in Labour Force Participation Rates* for Males Aged 60–64 years (as a result of increases in government pensions)

1973	−0.004
1974	−0.011
1975	−0.008

Notes: The method of computation (briefly explained in the text) is explained in note 4.
*The $\eta_{\lambda,g}$ used in deriving these estimates is significant at the 10 per cent level.

Sources: Computed using Dunlop and Williams, 'Declining Participation', and ABS cat. *6204.0*.

Table A8.1-3 Males Aged 60–64 Years Withdrawing from the Labour Force (as a result of the attraction of increases in real government pensions)

1973	1 100
1974	3 000
1975	2 200

Sources: Computed using data of Table A8.1-2 and ABS cat. *6204.0*, and computations on these data as explained in note 5.

in response to the 'attraction' of real increases in pension benefits. It is possible to compute roughly *ceteris paribus* estimates of the added cost to the welfare bill as a result of men leaving the labour force in response to discretionary changes in welfare provision. Estimates of the annual addition to the welfare bill, using a four-quarter average for **G**, are reported in Table A8.1-4. For the fiscal year 1974–75 it may be suggested that the welfare bill of the government was about $4.6m greater than would have been the case had the levels of **G** been held at their third-quarter 1973 level. Also reported in Table A8.1-4 are estimates of the annual real minimum wages (for males). These may be used to give some orders-of-magnitude lower-boundary estimates of the foregone contribution to gross domestic product of males 60–64 years who left the labour force in response to real increases in **G**. For the year 1974–75 it may be suggested that the contribution to GDP thereby foregone was over $7m.

It may therefore be suggested that changes during 1974 in welfare provisions enabled Australian men (with their wives) in the 60–64-year age group who were induced to leave the labour force by these welfare changes to exercise command over market goods and services of about $4.6m over the subsequent year, whilst at

Table A8.1-4 Additions to Welfare Payments and Reductions in GDP (in consequence of the withdrawal from the labour force of males aged 60–64 years)

	Men (a)	Annual G (b)	Annual Real Minimum Wage (c)	Additions to Welfare (d)	Reductions in GDP (e)
1973	1 100	$1 449	$2 235	$1.6m	$2.5m
1974	3 000	$1 535	$2 388	$4.6m	$7.2m
1975	2 200	$1 728	$2 371	$3.5m	$5.2m

Notes and Sources: See note 6.

the same time reducing their contributions to the provision of market goods and services by about $7.2m. These very rough *ceteris paribus* estimates serve to illustrate the arguments of Chapter 8 concerning the contribution to the Australian experience of stagflation of discretionary changes in welfare provisions during the Whitlam period.

Notes and References

The following abbreviations are used throughout the notes:

ABS	Australian Bureau of Statistics
ACAC	Australian Conciliation and Arbitration Commission
ACTU	Australian Council of Trade Unions
AES	W. E. Norton and P. M. Garmston (eds), *Australian Economic Statistics, 1949–50 to 1982–83: Tables*, Reserve Bank of Australia, Sydney, 1984
AGD	*Australian Government Digest* (replaced 1975 with AGWD)
AGPS	Australian Government Publishing Service
AGWD	*Australian Government Weekly Digest*
AIDA	Australian Industries Development Association
ALP	Australian Labor Party
BLMR	Bureau of Labour Market Research
CAR	*Commonwealth Arbitration Reports*
CES	Commonwealth Employment Service
DSS	Department of Social Security (Commonwealth)
Edited TGS	Edited volume of TGS
OECD	Organization for Economic Co-operation and Development
RES	*Round-up of Economic Statistics* (Treasury)
TGS	Transcripts of Government Submissions, National Wage Cases, Australian Conciliation and Arbitration Commission
Transcript	Transcript of Proceedings, National Wage Cases, Australian Conciliation and Arbitration Commission

Chapter 1: Introduction

1 This emphasis is made because, to the author, it seems important that value-laden terms such as 'employment' should be read according to their technical denotative content: common connotative content is not necessarily embraced by the author. So, for example, movement from non-market to market labour engagement involves a change of status. But the author does not share the fashionable assumption that such change involves an *increase* in status. Whether or not a change from non-market labour engagement to market labour engagement (to 'employment') involves an increase or a decrease in status will depend upon the specific circumstances of each case, and will depend upon the relevant social valuations of labour activity. The author subscribes to the view that market valuation is neither final nor complete as a reference of social valuation.

2 It was the highest unemployment rate recorded since ABS collections commenced in 1966. Data from 1950 published by CES (which are not strictly comparable with ABS data) indicate an unemployment rate of 2.6 per cent at June 1961.

3 'It's Time' was the 1972 election jingle of the Labor Party. It occurs on the cover of *Policy Speech 1972*, and provides a refrain in the opening paragraph of Mr Whitlam's speech.

4 This judgement would appear to be in agreement with F. H. Gruen, 'What Went Wrong? Some Personal Reflections on Economic Policies under Labor', *Australian Quarterly*, December 1976, pp. 15–32. Professor Gruen's paper (pp. 15 ff) usefully surveys the economic situation leading up to the Whitlam period and gives greater attention to macroeconomic issues than is here provided.

5 The research of E. A. Boehm and G. H. Moore reported in 'New Economic Indicators for Australia, 1949–84', *Australian Economic Review*, 4th Quarter 1984, pp. 34–56, indicates a growth recovery to have been taking place from March 1972. By contrast, from July 1974 to October 1977, Australia experienced a classical recession (p. 42).

6 J. E. Isaac, 'Compulsory Arbitration and Collective Bargaining Reconsidered', *Journal of Industrial Relations*, 16(1), March 1974, p. 3.

7 ibid., p. 2.

8 See also Gruen, 'What Went Wrong?', p. 23: 'Australia's system of wage settlements was in a period of transition towards considerably greater emphasis on collective bargaining'.

9 Isaac, 'Compulsory Arbitration', p. 2.

10 ibid., p. 9.

11 Refer to E. A. Boehm's Research Paper No. 93, Department of Economics, University of Melbourne, May 1983, where the business cycle is portrayed as a process of adaptation to changes in technology and in relative prices.

12 Isaac, 'Compulsory Arbitration', p. 3.
13 ALP, *Policy Speech 1972*, Canberra, p. 32 f, and D. Yerbury, 'Collective Negotiations, Wage Indexation and the Return to Arbitration: Some Institutional and Legal Developments during the Whitlam Era', in G. W. Ford and others, *Australian Labour Relations: Readings*, 3rd edn, Macmillan, Melbourne, 1980, p. 462.
14 Isaac, 'Compulsory Arbitration', p. 10.
15 The adjectives 'accommodating' and 'passive', interestingly, are applied by Isaac (ibid., pp. 3, 6) to the wages policy of the Gorton (1968–71) and McMahon (1971–72) Governments.
16 Calculated using the method found in the Australian Government submissions to the National Wage Case, May 1980, Vol. II, Exhibit S33, p. 136. For a discussion on the measurement of 'earnings drift', see the *Report of the Committee of Economic Inquiry* ('Vernon Report'), Government Printer, Canberra, 1965, Vol. I, p. 129 f & Vol. II, pp. 606–9. The method employed for Table 1.1 is suitable for the purposes for which the results are used.

Chapter 2: The Wages Policy of the Whitlam Government: An Overview

1 TGS, 1972–73, Vol. II, p. 192.
2 ibid., p. 194.
3 ibid., p. 192.
4 ibid., p. 206.
5 ibid., p. 221.
6 ibid., p. 191.
7 ibid., p. 221.
8 TGS, 1974, Vol. II, p. 344.
9 ibid.
10 ibid., p. 345.
11 ibid.
12 ibid., p. 542.
13 ibid., p. 382.
14 ibid., p. 374.
15 ibid., p. 382.
16 TGS, 1972–73, Vol. II, p. 192.
17 J. P. Nieuwenhuysen and J. Sloan, 'Wages Policy', in F. H. Gruen (ed.), *Surveys of Australian Economics*, Vol. I, Allen & Unwin, Sydney, 1978, p. 115, and also B. Hughes, *Exit Full Employment*, Angus & Robertson, Sydney, 1980, p. 110 f argue that this shift was clear by June 1974. The present author, however, has been unable to verify Nieuwenhuysen and Sloan's citation from the *Age* (either for 15 or 17 June). Hughes's 29 June quotation of the Prime Minister is undocumented as to its precise source.

18 For example, *Australian*, 25 January 1975, p. 1; *Canberra Times*, 27 January 1975, p. 1, & 6 February 1975, p. 1; *Australian*, 24 February 1975, p. 1.
19 Edited TGS, 1974–75, pp. 11, 28, 44, emphasis added.
20 For instance: 'Some retailers responded to the very large increases in wages obtained by shop assistants around the middle of 1974 by applying more stringent tests to their staffing requirements' (ibid., p. 146).
21 ibid., p. 28.
22 ibid., p. 58.
23 The 'political realities' which led to Mr Cameron's demise of course included economic considerations, but these economic considerations do not appear to have been directed by economic reasoning of the kind introduced above.
24 For example, Mr Cameron's Ministerial Statement of 12 November 1973, where he said, 'the [tripartite Conference] parties asked the [Arbitration] Commission to reintroduce a system of wage indexation similar to the previous automatic adjustment of the basic wage'.

Chapter 3: The Theory of Wages and Employment: An Overview

1 TGS, 1974, Vol. II, p. 346.
2 The following is an example of an author making 'descriptive' use of 'efficiency' criteria: '... it must be stressed that although a particular distribution of income between labour and capital ... may be judged to be an economically efficient one, such a judgement is not intended to have any normative connotation' (J. E. Isaac, *Wages and Productivity*, Cheshire, Melbourne, 1967, p. 6).
3 The discussion sidesteps the question that a neoclassical assessment of the costs of protection may be 'static', whereas a 'dynamic' assessment may be more appropriate.
4 J. M. Keynes, *The General Theory of Employment, Interest, and Money*, Macmillan, London, 1964 edn, p. 271.
5 W. E. G. Salter, *Productivity and Technical Change*, Cambridge University Press, Cambridge, 1966.
6 Isaac, *Wages and Productivity*, pp. 60, 71.
7 Salter, *Productivity and Technical Change*, p. 161, emphasis added.
8 This analysis agrees with the findings of Salter (ibid.).
9 The significance of *prospective*, rather than past, productivity gains for assessing non-inflationary wage increases was highlighted in the 'Vernon Report' (Chapter 1, note 16), Vol. I, paras. 7.101, 111, 114. But that Report also pleaded that wage increases should be regular and small (para. 7.111), and emphasized that analysis of productivity should be of productivity trends (para. 7.101). For example: 'In the

assessment of future productivity, long-term rather than short-term changes are the most valuable evidence' (para. 7.114). This view was repeated in the November 1975 *Report of the Working Party on the Measurement of Labour Productivity* (AGPS, Canberra, 1976) in the following terms: 'There has been general agreement ... that productivity estimates used for wage-fixation purposes should be based on the longer term trend ... in productivity' (p. 34).

10 TGS, 1972–73, Vol. II, p. 206.

11 ALP, *Policy Speech 1972*, Canberra, p. 10.

12 Notice that, because labour use is measured along a single axis, the formal exposition treats only the general case where labour is treated as a homogeneous factor of production. The assumption of homogeneity of factors of production is perhaps more difficult with respect to capital (where a unique physical 'unit' is unclear). In practice, the choice involves a scaling in 'real' dollars (using estimates of 'real' hourly cost of labour factor of production, and estimates of 'real' cost of capital factor of production). But in a theoretical treatment (as is illustrated in Figure 3.3), the axes are scaled in 'physical units', because scaling in 'dollars' would require re-scaling each time there was a change in prices. It will be noticed that the text—which serves to introduce the empirical work of Chapter 4—moves to discussion of 'real' prices.

13 An extension of this analysis under conditions of technological change is found in the author's University of Melbourne doctoral thesis, 'Wages and Employment: An Economic Evaluation of the Wages Policy of the Whitlam Government', Department of Economics, University of Melbourne, 1984, pp. 57–60.

14 Note that (following the alteration of relative factor prices as a result of an increase in the real wage) the price line swings on B1 where the price of *a2* is unchanged relative to the price of the product (*x1*).

Chapter 4: The Influence of the Whitlam Government on Wages

1 TGS, 1972–73, Vol. II, p. 221.

2 149 CAR 81.

3 143 CAR 297.

4 149 CAR 78.

5 149 CAR 81.

6 149 CAR 84.

7 149 CAR 81.

8 143 CAR 306, 307.

9 149 CAR 84.

10 See McGavin, 'Wages and Employment: An Economic Evaluation of the Wages Policy of the Whitlam Government', Department of

Economics, University of Melbourne,' 1984: Table 11 of Appendix 4.3 reproduces the awards data, and shows federal awards taking the lead at May 1973, briefly reversed during late 1973 and early 1974, and re-asserting a lead at April 1974. In making comparison between series for federal and state award earnings it needs to be recalled that the skills (and thus the relative wage) composition of workers may differ between the two series.

11 TGS, 1974, Vol. II, p. 344 f.
12 ibid., pp. 349–63.
13 ibid., p. 362.
14 ibid., p. 345.
15 Isaac DP, ibid., p. 542.
16 TGS, 1974–75, Vol. II, p. 533 f.
17 ibid., p. 542.
18 Edited TGS, 1974–75, p. 129.
19 The argument of Counsel for the Commonwealth was that the introduction of indexation would 'facilitate' the process of adjustment to economic balance in Australia (ibid., p. 129).
20 167 CAR 30.
21 See C. R. Cameron, *Unions in Crisis*, Hill of Content, Melbourne, 1982, pp. 277, 281.
22 For example, ibid., pp. 278, 282, 284, 291.
23 ibid., p. 289.
24 See McGavin, 'Wages and Employment', Tables 7a, b of Appendix 4.3.
25 ibid., Table 8.
26 Cameron, *Unions in Crisis*, p. 276.
27 ibid., p. 278.
28 ibid., pp. 284, 289.
29 ibid., pp. 279, 290.
30 ibid., p. 292.
31 Ministerial Letter, 16 October 1975.
32 See McGavin, 'Wages and Employment', Table 6 of Appendix 4.3.
33 ibid., Table 6a.
34 Cameron, *Unions in Crisis*, p. 278.
35 ibid., and Gruen, 'What Went Wrong? Some Personal Reflections on Economic Policies under Labor', *Australian Quarterly*, December 1976, p. 29, n. 20.
36 For example, see Hughes, *Exit Full Employment*, Angus & Robertson, Sydney, 1980; Treasury, RES, 1974; and *Australian* (6 August 1974, p. 1 & 22 October 1974, p. 1).
37 Other relevant wage and employment data may be found in McGavin, 'Wages and Employment', Appendix 4.3.
38 Prior to September 1981, particulars of wages and salaries paid are not available for males and females separately on a quarterly basis.

The derivation of Australian civilian employee 'male units' as used above is briefly described on the face page of ABS cat. *6302.0*. Earnings used in this series encompass both part-time and full-time, as well as adult and junior employees.

39 See P. A. McGavin, 'Equal Pay for Women: A Re-assessment of the Australian Experience', *Australian Economic Papers*, 22(40), (1983); pp. 48–59.

40 This form was chosen because the non-linearity of the time trend for RGNFDP was better captured using a polynomial function.

41 Keynes, *The General Theory of Employment, Interest, and Money*, Macmillan, London, 1946 edn, Ch. 20.

42 The implicit price deflator index for Australian gross private capital formation, equipment, was adopted after unsuccessful use of a series of two-year government bond yields (derived from the Reserve Bank, *Statistical Bulletin*). The statistically unsatisfactory outcome of estimates using data for the rate of return on securities suggests that the 'going rate of interest' is an efficient measure of the equilibrium 'price of capital' only.

43 Details of this adjustment are found in McGavin, 'Wages and Employment', p. 96.

44 These are detailed in ibid., Appendix 4.2.

45 Sources: ABS cat. *5204.0, 6204.0, 6214.0, 6304.0, 6312.0*, various issues, and data kindly supplied by the Bureau; Australia, *Budget Speech & Statements*, various issues; Australia, National Economic Summit Conference, *Information Paper on the Economy*, AGPS, Canberra, April 1983; and computations on these data.

46 The relatively small mean value of the S co-efficient, with a relatively large explanatory power suggests that the effects of structural change are operating indirectly: that is, that the inclusion of a structural change variable enhances the explanatory power of the other variables. That this is so was noticeable in the higher *t* value attaching to the lagged relative wage variable as between two estimations (see Equations (9) and (12) of McGavin, 'Wages and Employment', Table A4.1-1). But that multicollinearity is not a significant problem is evidenced by the stability of the lagged wage co-efficient, which shows a value between 0.07 and 0.11, which in order of magnitude agrees with the value estimated in earlier equations between 0.06 and 0.09.

47 It is not clear that the Cobb-Douglas function provides such a norm—although some Australian researchers appear to imply this: for example, R. G. Gregory and R. C. Duncan, 'Segmented Labour Market Theories and the Australian Experience of Equal Pay for Women', *Journal of Post-Keynesian Economics*, Spring 1981, pp. 403–28 at p. 426.

48 See P. D. Jonson and J. C. Taylor, 'Inflation and Economic Stability in a Small Open Economy: A Systems Approach', in K. Brunner and

A. H. Meltzer (eds), *The Problem of Inflation*, Carnegie Rochester Conference Series on Public Policy (supplementary series to *Journal of Monetary Economics*), No. 8, (1978), pp. 289–323; H. N. Johnston, R. B. Campbell and R. M. Simes, 'The Impact of Wages and Prices on Unemployment', *Economic Papers*, No. 60, (1978), pp. 18–37; J. D. Pitchford, 'Wage Policy and Distribution Theory', *Economica*, xxxiv, (1967), pp. 167–80; and P. K. Trivedi and G. M. Baker, 'Equilibrium Unemployment in Australia: Concepts and Measurement', Discussion Paper No. 59, Centre for Economic Policy Research, Australian National University, Canberra, 1982 (a revised and edited version published in *Economic Record*, 61(174), 1985). Mention should also be made of D. Pope, 'Wage Regulation and Unemployment in Australia: 1900–30', *Australian Economic History Review*, 22(2), (1982), pp. 103–26.

49 McGavin, 'Wages and Employment', Table A4.1-1, Equation (4).

50 The derivation is found in ibid., p. 87, n. 9.

51 ibid., Table A4.1-1, Equation (5).

52 ibid., p. 87, n. 11.

53 ibid., p. 88, n. 12.

54 ibid., Table A4.1-4, columns (b) and (f).

55 ibid., p. 88, n. 14.

56 ibid., n. 15.

57 ibid., n. 16.

58 Source: ABS cat. *6304.0*.

59 Earlier attempts to estimate non-wage costs of employment as made by AIDA in *Understanding Unemployment*, Melbourne, 1978, and by D. Worland, 'Survey of Wage Rates and their Effect on Employment', Working Paper No. 40, National Institute of Labour Studies, Flinders University of South Australia, 1980, derive higher estimates of these costs than are obtained here. (AIDA introduced four weeks annual leave from 1974, and Worland's results are derived from a survey of a small number of companies.)

60 These include: annual leave, annual leave loading, public holidays, long service leave, sick leave, compassionate leave, other paid work absences and benefits, allowances, non-productive paid time, superannuation, workers' compensation insurance, payroll taxation, employee amenities, employee health, uniforms, safety, and other oncosts of employment (AIDA, *Understanding Unemployment*, p. 10).

61 Descriptions of the computations of these estimates appear in McGavin, 'Wages and Employment', Appendix 4.2.

62 Moreover, three weeks annual leave is assumed in computing the adjustment for annual leave loading (Table 4.2, column (d)).

63 Fuller details of estimations are found in McGavin, 'Wages and Employment', Table A4.2-3.

64 ibid., p. 88, n. 23.

65 ibid., n. 24.
66 The computations are explained in ibid., p. 98 f.

Chapter 5: Real Wage Overhang, Wages Share, and Wage Indexation

1 See C. I. Higgins, 'Comment', pp. 340–57, in W. E. Norton (ed.), *Conference in Applied Economic Research*, Reserve Bank of Australia, Sydney, 1980, p. 346 f, 351.
2 See, for example, contributors in Norton (ibid.), and W. M. Corden, 'Wages and Unemployment in Australia', *Economic Record*, 55(148), (1979), pp. 1–19.
3 Compare S. M. Bonnell, 'The "Real Wage Overhang" and the Wage Share of Output', *Australian Bulletin of Labour*, 5(4), (1979), pp. 27–47, and P. Sheehan, B. Derody and P. Rosendale, 'An Assessment of Recent Empirical Work Relevant to Macroeconomic Policy in Australia', *Australian Economic Review*, 1st Quarter 1979, pp. 33–61.
4 [Australian] Treasury, 'The Measurement of Real Unit Cost', Supplement to RES, AGPS, Canberra, September 1978, pp. 15–26 at p. 22; also, 'Factor Shares and Real Unit Labour Costs', Supplement to RES, AGPS, Canberra, October 1983, pp. 27–46.
5 See various contributors in Norton, *Conference*: R. J. Blandy, 'Comment', pp. 326–32 at p. 329; R. G. Gregory and R. C. Duncan, 'Authors' Reply', pp. 370–9 at p. 374; F. H. Gruen, 'Comment', pp. 332–9 at p. 335; Higgins, 'Comment', p. 350; and P. J. Sheehan, 'Real Wages and Unemployment: An Alternate View', in M. R. Fisher and others (eds), 'Real Wages and Unemployment', CAER Paper No. 4, Centre for Applied Economic Research, University of New South Wales, Sydney, March 1978, pp. 19–49, at p. 29; and, D. W. Stammer, 'Real Wages and Unemployment', ibid., pp. 1–18, at p. 15; Sheehan and others, 'Recent Empirical Work', p. 39.
6 Bonnell, 'Real Wage Overhang', pp. 37–42; Gregory and Duncan, 'Authors' Reply', p. 374; Sheehan, 'An Alternate View', p. 31.
7 Bonnell, 'Real Wage Overhang', pp. 38–43; Sheehan and others, 'Recent Empirical Work', p. 39 f.
8 Treasury, RES, (1978), p. 22 f, emphasis added.
9 This is indicated by the distance $\overline{w}_2w_1$ of Figure 3.2 (Chapter 3). The distance L_2L_1 would represent 'classical unemployment', and the distance L_2L_3 would represent 'measured unemployment'.
10 There is disagreement on the precise estimation of 'real wage overhang' and on the course of its demise. Bonnell, 'Real Wage Overhang', provides an excellent survey of the issues in estimating the 'overhang'. Alternative measures have been presented by the National Institute of Labour Studies, editorial comment in the

Australian Bulletin of Labour, (1977), p. 10, and (1978), p. 2; Sheehan and others, 'Recent Empirical Work', p. 39; Bonnell, 'Real Wage Overhang',; and W. E. Norton, *The Deterioration in Economic Performance*, Occasional Paper No. 9, Reserve Bank of Australia, Sydney, 1982.

11 Compare E. A. Boehm, 'Distortions in Relative Wages: The Inflationary Consequences and Policy Implications', *Australian Economic Review*, 4th Quarter 1974, pp. 39–50, at p. 49; Blandy, 'Comment', p. 329; Corden, 'Wages and Unemployment', pp. 6–10; Gruen, 'Comment', pp. 333, 338; Higgins, 'Comment', pp. 348, 351 f; R. H. Snape, 'Comment', pp. 359–67, in Norton, *Conference*, p. 362 f. It is interesting to note that the significance of the real wage overhang may first have been raised by Boehm, ibid., pp. 46 ff, in his discussion of the 'emergence of a significant price-gap'. Popular attention to the concept dates from the discussion in OECD, *Economic Outlook*, No. 21, (1977), pp. 54–64.

12 Reprinted in the Tribunal's *Annual Report*, 1974–75, p. 47.

13 See Higgins (an officer of the Treasury), 'Comment', p. 346 f; Treasury, RES, (1978), pp. 33–7, and (1983), p. 27 f.

14 Bonnell, 'Real Wage Overhang', and also Norton, 'Deterioration in Performance', pp. 72, 129, and Treasury, RES, (1983), pp. 27, 34 f. An ordinary least squares regression of (a) the profits share of seasonally adjusted gross domestic non-farm product on (b) an index of real unit labour cost, derives an $\bar{R}^2$ of 0.81. (Data used are seasonally adjusted quarterly 1969 to 1977 (inclusive) from ABS cat. *5207.0*, and Treasury, (1978), p. 25, and computations on these data.).

15 Bonnell's identity is as follows:

$$\frac{W}{Y} \equiv \frac{w}{y} \times \frac{e}{E}$$

where,

W = wages, salaries and supplements at current prices,
Y = gross domestic product at factor cost at current prices,
e = hours worked by wage and salary earners,
E = hours worked by the labour force inclusive of employers and the self-employed,
P = the implicit price deflator of expenditure on gross domestic product,
w = real labour cost per hour for employed wage and salary earners

$= \frac{1}{P}\left(\frac{W}{e}\right)$, and

y = real output per hour of labour employed

$$= \frac{1}{P}\left(\frac{Y}{E}\right).$$

Thus, real unit labour cost = $\frac{w}{y}$. (See Bonnell, 'Real Wage Overhang', p. 27 f.)

16 See, for example, the discussion in Norton, *Conference*.
17 Counsel for the Commonwealth, National Wage Case, March 1973, 149 CAR 81.
18 C. R. Cameron, *Unions in Crisis*, Hill of Content, Melbourne, 1982, pp. 253, 255.
19 ibid., p. 257.
20 For example AGD 1:2:620, 1:3:1152, 2:2:394, AGWD 1975:141, and Cameron, *Unions in Crisis*, p. 257.
21 TGS, 1974, Vol. II, p. 344 f, emphasis added.
22 157 CAR 305.
23 157 CAR 298.
24 167 CAR 34 and Edited TGS, 1974–75, p. 78. Refer also, AGD 2:4:1257, and Cameron, *Unions in Crisis*, p. 256 f.
25 167 CAR 37.
26 AGWD 1975:141, and Cameron, *Unions in Crisis*, p. 274.
27 AGWD 1975:532.
28 167 CAR 30 and Edited TGS, 1974–75, pp. 11, 91. Compare also, Cameron, *Unions in Crisis*, p. 257.
29 An excellent summary of events, from Mr Cameron's viewpoint, is to be found in his 1976 recollection, Note to Mr Whitlam, reproduced in full in Cameron, *Unions in Crisis*, pp. 267–74.
30 TGS, 1974–75, Vol. II, pp. 556 ff.
31 167 CAR 27.
32 Cameron, *Unions in Crisis*, pp. 246, 254 f, 273.
33 ibid., p. 252.
34 Edited TGS, 1974–75, p. 57.
35 Cameron, *Unions in Crisis*, p. 248, referring to the Platform of the Australian Labor Party issuing from the Party's 1973 Conference.
36 Edited TGS, 1974–75, p. 59.
37 167 CAR 30.
38 Edited TGS, 1974–75, p. 91. Subsidiary components of the Government's proposals for the implementation of indexation were: (e) adjustment should be applied to award rates; (f) the first adjustment should be for the March quarter of 1975; and (g) the form of indexation should be reviewed after two years (ibid.).
39 ibid., pp. 44, 91.
40 AGD 2:4:1256 f and *Budget Paper No. 1*, 1974–75, p. 86 f.

41 Edited TGS, 1974–75, pp. 41–55, and 167 CAR 40 f.
42 167 CAR 34.
43 Boehm, 'Distortions in Relative Wages', pp. 42 ff.
44 ibid., p. 49.
45 The 'secondary labour market' is characterized by jobs requiring comparatively low skills, and having high turnover of personnel, and low wages (see P. B. Doeringer and H. J. Piere, *Internal Labour Markets and Manpower Analysis*, Heath, Lexington, Mass., 1971).
46 The partial indexation decisions granted by the Arbitration Commission during the period of the Fraser Government (see D. H. Plowman, *Wage Indexation: A Study of Australian Wage Issues, 1975–80*, Allen & Unwin, Sydney, 1981) may be expected to have influenced a compression of wages. Dr P. Scherer ('Insubstantial Compliance: Changes in Composition and Distribution of Earnings under Wage Indexation, 1975–80', Tenth Conference of Economists, Australian National University, Canberra, August 1981) examines this question and concludes that, 'The relative distribution of earnings is the same in 1979 as in 1975' (p. 22). This evidence, then, brings into question whether Mr Cameron's plateau indexation proposal, if implemented, would have been effective.
47 See B. Hughes, *Exit Full Employment*, Angus & Robertson, Sydney, 1980, p. 112.
48 1975 National Wage Case, 167 CAR 24.
49 Compare ACAC, 167 CAR 34.
50 167 CAR 34. This comment closely parallels one by R. I. Downing and J. E. Isaac, 'The 1961 Basic Wage Judgement and Wage Policy' *Economic Record*, 37(80), (1961), pp. 480–94 at p. 488.
51 See 167 CAR 30.
52 See 167 CAR 37.
53 See 'Prospects for the Economy in 1981', *Australian Economic Review*, 4th Quarter 1980, p. 10.
54 Plowman, *Wage Indexation*, p. 42 f.
55 ibid., pp. 123, 169.
56 For a formalization of this argument, see J. Sloan, 'Decentralized versus Centralized Wage Fixation', *Economic Papers*, 2(2), (1983), pp. 8–13.
57 Interestingly, this analysis would appear to be consistent with Mr Cameron's comment; '... it is only the high level of unemployment that has so far saved the Commission's restrictive [indexation] guidelines from total collapse'—see Cameron, *Unions in Crisis*, p. 273.
58 See E. A. Boehm and G. H. Moore, 'New Economic Indicators for Australia, 1949–1984', *Australian Economic Review*, 4th Quarter 1984, Tables 3–6.

59 Edited TGS, 1974–75, p. 44.
60 For details, see Plowman, 'Wage Indexation', Chs 5 f.
61 See also Boehm, 'Distortions in Wages', p. 44, Chart C.
62 ABS cat. *6312.0*; ACAC, National Wage Decisions (1975–78); and W. A. Howard, 'Australian Trade Unions in the Context of Union Theory', *Journal of Industrial Relations*, 19(3), (1977), pp. 255–73 at p. 271, using Department of Employment and Industrial Relations sources; and computations on these data.
63 This Statement is reproduced in E. Shann and D. Copland (eds), *Documents on Budgetary and Economic Policy*, Angus & Robertson, Sydney, 1931, at p. 17, quoted in J. O. Stone, '1929 and All That ...', *Australian Economic Review*, 3rd Quarter 1984, pp. 18–31 at p. 27.
64 See 'Vernon Report', Vol. I, p. 141 f.
65 See Downing and Isaac, '1961 Basic Wage', p. 489. E. A. Boehm, 'Money Wages, Consumer Prices, and Causality in Australia', *Economic Record*, 60(170), (1984), pp. 236–51 and p. 239, n. 12, provides a fuller citation of the literature on this point.
66 Downing and Isaac, '1961 Basic Wage', p. 487 f.
67 Source: Reserve Bank of Australia, *Statistical Bulletin*, January 1976.
68 Downing and Isaac, '1961 Basic Wage', p. 488.
69 ACAC, *Inquiry into the Principles of Wage Fixation*, AGPS, Canberra, 1978, Vol. II, at p. 17. The data are drawn from Exhibit M4, presented by the National Employers' Policy Committee, and the 'Source and Notes', pp. 15, 17, give ABS data sources and outline the methods of computation. The 1974–75 fall in the proportionate impact of indirect taxes less subsidies on changes in Australian consumer expenditure prices is consistent with the following data: excise duty and sales tax revenues of the Commonwealth for 1974–75, as a proportion of final private consumption expenditure, decreased from about 8.4 to 7.9 per cent. The following year, however, these revenue raisings increased to about 9.7 per cent of final private consumption expenditure (Australia, *Budget Paper No. 1*, 1975–76, p. 105; 1976–77, p. 115; ABS cat. *5204.0*).
70 Downing and Isaac, '1961 Basic Wage', p. 488.
71 ibid.
72 ibid., p. 488 f.
73 ibid., p. 482.
74 ibid., p. 483 f.
75 ibid., pp. 484 f, 490.
76 ibid., pp. 485, 493.
77 ibid.
78 167 CAR 18–41.
79 167 CAR 33.

80 Boehm, 'Distortions in Wages', p. 49.
81 Cameron, *Unions in Crisis*, p. 255.
82 See *Wage Indexation for Australia? A Discussion Paper*, AGPS, Canberra, 1974.
83 For example, see Plowman, *Wage Indexation*, pp. 152, 154 f, 186, where there is significant confusion on this point.
84 See 'New Economic Indicators', p. 43. Hereafter, the quarter is indicated by the numerical following the year.
85 F. Gelber, 'The Inter-Industry Effects of Cumulative Wage Indexation—A Critical Comment', *Australian Economic Papers*, 20(36), (1981), pp. 186–98 at p. 198.
86 Plowman, *Wage Indexation*, p. 152 f, 157, and Cameron, *Unions in Crisis*, pp. 277, 281, erroneously argue with reference to *ex post* data on industrial disputes prior to the introduction of wage indexation.
87 Such as reported by ABS cat. *6332.0*.
88 167 CAR 38.
89 See Plowman, *Wage Indexation*, pp. 84, 186.
90 TGS, 1974, Vol. II, p. 344.
91 See Plowman, *Wage Indexation*, p. 138.
92 For example, the assumption of Department of Labour (see note 82) that 'in the absence of wage indexation the adjustment of wages for increasing prices occurs after a lapse of time' (pp. 10, 22). Refer also to Boehm, 'Money Wages ... and Causality' (1984), p. 240, n. 14, and Cameron, *Unions in Crisis*, p. 264.
93 Boehm, 'Money Wages ... and Causality' (1984), discusses 'causality', and notes its usage 'in the sense of what Hicks (1979) calls "sequential causation"' (p. 237).
94 E. A. Boehm, 'Money Wages, Consumer Prices, and Causality in Australia', Research Paper No. 83, Department of Economics, University of Melbourne (1982), p. 13, and Boehm, 'Money Wages ... and Causality' (1984), p. 237, n. 8, where the results of other researchers are noted. Boehm notes that he attempts 'to identify the direction of causation between changes in wages and prices', but 'does not imply a complete explanation of the inflationary process' (p. 239).
95 167 CAR 32, 38.
96 167 CAR 38 f.
97 167 CAR 39.
98 J. Carmichael, J. Fahrer and J. Hawkins, 'Some Macroeconomic Implications of Wage Indexation: A Survey', Conference on Government Policies Towards Inflation, Macquarie University, North Ryde, (1983), p. 48, emphasis added.
99 See Boehm, 'Money Wages ... and Causality' (1984), p. 240.
100 Department of Labour and Immigration, *Wage Indexation for*

Australia? A Discussion Paper, AGPS, Canberra, 1974, pp. 22, 10.

101 Carmichael and others, 'Macroeconomic Implications of Indexation', p. 7.

102 ibid., p. 48, emphasis added.

103 Carmichael and others comment: '... empirical analysis of the effects of wage indexation has not been very extensive' (p. 47). Two Australian studies (by A. J. Phipps, 'The Impact of Wage Indexation on Wage Inflation in Australia: 1975:2–1980:2', *Australian Economic Papers*, 20(37), (1981), pp. 333–49; and C. N. Caton, E. A. Evans and H. N. Johnston, 'The Inflationary Process and the Impact of Wage Indexation on the Australian Economy', Fourth Conference of Economists, Canberra, (1974)) take a less critical view of the influence of indexation upon inflation.

104 TGS, 1974–75, p. 128.

105 167 CAR 31.

106 167 CAR 30.

107 167 CAR 30, 32, 35, 38 f.

108 167 CAR 32.

109 ibid.

110 The role of the increasing influence of 'white collar' unions is noted in Hughes, *Exit Full Employment*, p. 109, and D. Yerbury, 'Collective Negotiations, Wages Indexation and the Return to Arbitration', in G. W. Ford and others, *Australian Labour Relations: Readings*, Macmillan, Melbourne, 1980, p. 474 f.

111 Transcript, Vol. VIII, p. 1981.

112 Yerbury, 'Collective Negotiations', pp. 470, 481.

113 Boehm, 'Distortions in Wages', p. 49.

114 A comment in Stone, '1929 and All That ...' is relevant to this point: 'the maintenance of real wages for those who remain in employment simply means that the numbers of those fortunate people diminish relative to what they would otherwise have been, while the numbers of the unemployed grow' (p. 30).

115 This argument is further developed in Chapter 8.

Chapter 6: Wages as Costs and as Incomes, and Relative Labour Costs

1 Where gross pay, less income taxation before concessions, less other deductions, giving net pay, will usually be shown. (Allowance for concessions in the deduction of pay-as-you-earn taxation postdates the Whitlam period.)

2 Net taxation for a worker on male average weekly earnings was estimated using various issues of the *Statistical Report* of the Commissioner of Taxation. For the class interval in which annual income at male average weekly earnings occurred, the sum of net taxation pay-

able was extracted, and this was then divided by the number of tax-payers falling within this class interval, so deriving an estimate of average net taxation paid by individuals falling within this class interval. There are several deficiencies in this method:

(a) Class intervals are by 'taxable income', and this may not be the same as gross wage income (as 'gross income').
(b) Class intervals are not constant over the period.
(c) The position within each class interval of annual earnings at average male weekly earnings rate, of course, is not constant.
(d) For most years, separate relevant taxation data for males and for females are not available. Because most male taxpayers will be heads of families (and will thus have greater eligibility for taxation concessions than would most female taxpayers within this range), male taxation data is for the present purposes more relevant.

The above method will therefore tend to over-estimate net taxation for males at average weekly earnings. It would seem a major (and still hazardous) exercise to attempt to correct for these deficiencies. Gross taxation estimates are not subject to the same deficiencies and, as argued, are more relevant to the present analysis. For these reasons, attempts at greater sophistication were not undertaken.

3 Calculated from ABS cat. *6312.0*, and Table 6.1, column (a).
4 Calculated from Table 6.3, column (c).
5 Refer to Table 6.1, column (a).
6 For example, AGD, 3:1:586.
7 Transcript, 1974–75, Vol. VIII, p. 1983 f.
8 Calculated from Table 6.1, column (c).
9 Calculated from Table 6.3, column (a).
10 Calculated from Table 6.6, column (a).
11 Transcript, 1974–75, Vol. VIII, p. 1989, emphasis added.
12 'The possibility of the introduction of tax indexation in Australia' was touched upon by the ACTU Advocate in arguing for wage indexation during the 1974–75 National Wage Case (see ibid., p. 1976).
13 ibid., p. 1983 f.
14 ABS cat. *5204.0, 5206.0, 5620.0, 6304.0, 6312.0, 6319.0*, and AIDA, *Understanding Unemployment* and *AIDA Bulletin* (350), as explained in McGavin, 'Wages and Employment', Appendix 4.2.
15 Wage data are drawn from the ABS October Survey; taxation data refer to the fiscal year (ended 30 June). Where primary reference is to wage data, the calender year is cited; where reference is focused on taxation data, the fiscal year is cited. As the taxation rates for the previous fiscal year will have been applicable for eight months of the wage period ending October, it has been expedient to link October wage data with taxation data for the year ending the previous June.

16 As noted in Appendix 1.1, the term 'minimum wage' is reserved in this work for reference to that weekly rate determined by the various tribunals payable to employees falling within their jurisdiction, but who are not covered by a specific award category.
17 As of 23 May 1974, the female minimum wage was stated as a proportion of the male rate, rising to equality with the male rate as of 30 June 1975 (see the first section of Chapter 7).
18 See Chapter 5, note 45.
19 See 'The Skilled Metal Trades', in R. Blandy and S. Richardson (eds), *How Labour Markets Work: Case Studies in Adjustment*, Longman Cheshire, Melbourne, 1982, pp. 49–90.
20 ibid., p. 65.
21 Refer ABS cat. *6304.0*, June 1977, p. 15.
22 For example, AGD, 1:2:620, 1:3:1152, 2:2:394, AGWD 1975:141.
23 ACTU, *Decisions of the Australian Council of Trade Unions*, ACTU, Melbourne, 1971, 1973.
24 See BLMR, *Youth Wages, Employment and the Labour Force*, Research Report No. 3, AGPS, Canberra, 1983, p. 44.
25 ibid.
26 ibid.
27 ibid., p. 43.
28 C. R. Cameron, *Unions in Crisis*, Hill of Content, Melbourne, 1982, p. 118.
29 BLMR, *Youth Wages*, p. 46, includes a useful table showing twelve award wage variations subsequent to the Federal Metal Industry Award variation of 20 September 1972.
30 ibid., p. 55 f. See also Richard Blandy, 'Youth Unemployment', *Australian Bulletin of Labour*, 5(3), (1979), pp. 19–30, on deficiencies in the ABS series.
31 BLMR, *Youth Wages*, p. 52.
32 This would appear in part to derive from the established institutional practice of setting junior female rates as a higher proportion of female adult awards than was the case for junior males—a practice deriving from a period when female awards were below male awards (see ibid., p. 42).
33 'Teenage Unemployment: The Role of Wage Rates and Other Factors', 49th ANZAAS Conference, Auckland, NZ, 1979.
34 BLMR, *Youth Wages*.
35 ibid., p. 86.
36 ibid., pp. 89, 144 ff.
37 The term 'own price elasticity' refers to a measure of the responsiveness of quantity demanded of a factor (or of a product) to change in the price of that factor (or product).
38 BLMR, *Youth Wages*, p. 90.
39 Per capita employment data and ordinary-time earnings data are

used in the equation reported from Merrilees; full-time employment per capita data and average weekly earnings wage data are used in BLMR research—see W. Merrilees, 'Teenage Unemployment: The Role of Wage Rates and other Factors', 49th ANZAAS Conference, Auckland, NZ, January 1979, p. 28 f, and BLMR, *Youth Wages*, p. 143. All estimates are statistically significant at the 5 per cent level.
40 BLMR, *Youth Wages*, pp. 91, 146.
41 ibid., p. 91.
42 Merrilees, 'Teenage Unemployment', pp. 18, 24.
43 'The Role of Labour Costs in the Youth Labour Market: An Overview of the Evidence', Discussion Paper No. 65, Centre for Economic Policy Research, Australian National University, Canberra, 1983. For an alternative and critical viewpoint, see, P. N. Janankar and A. J. Neale, 'Relative Wages and the Youth Labour Market', Discussion Paper No. 29, Institute for Employment Research, University of Warwick, Warwick, 1985.
44 See, for example, R. G. Gregory and R. C. Duncan, 'The Labour Market in the 1970s', in W. E. Norton (ed.), *Conference in Applied Economic Research*, Reserve Bank of Australia, Sydney, 1980 (Chapter 5, Note 1), and Blandy, 'Youth Unemployment'.
45 See Chapter 7.
46 Dr K. Alford argues contrariwise ('Married Women's Employment and its Relation to Youth (Un)Employment', *Australian Economic Review*, 3rd Quarter 1979, pp. 37–46, and 'Cramming the Workforce and Neglecting their Children?', *Journal of Australian Political Economy*, No. 6, (1979), pp. 46–58). Alford's conclusion appears to proceed from her assertion of 'particularly severe' labour market segmentation (p. 47), leading to the 'non-substitutability of different categories of workers, including generally adult (married) women by junior females' (p. 55).
47 Cameron, *Unions in Crisis*, p. 118.

Chapter 7: An Economic Evaluation of the Implementation of Equal Pay for Women

1 127 CAR 1159.
2 147 CAR 177, and S. Eccles, 'The Role of Women in the Australian Workforce', in K. Hancock, Y. Sano, B. Chapman and P. Fayle (eds), *Japanese and Australian Labour Markets: A Comparative Study*, Australia–Japan Research Centre, Australian National University, Canberra, 1982, pp. 458–511, at pp. 486 ff.
3 147 CAR 178.
4 147 CAR 179 f, and Eccles, 'Role of Women', p. 487.
5 157 CAR 298 ff.
6 Australia, Women's Bureau of the Department of Employment and

Youth Affairs, *The Role of Women in the Economy*, Position Paper, OECD Conference on the Employment of Women, AGPS, Canberra, 1981, p. 30.

7 R. G. Gregory and R. C. Duncan, 'Segmented Labour Market Theories and the Australian Experience of Equal Pay for Women', *Journal of Post-Keynesian Economics*, Spring 1981, pp. 403–28, at p. 426.

8 Australia, *Role of Women*, p. 30.

9 See P. A. McGavin, 'Wages and Employment: An Economic Evaluation of the Wages Policy of the Whitlam Government', Doctoral Thesis, Department of Economics, University of Melbourne, 1984, Tables A4.3-10 and A4.3-11.

10 ibid., Appendix 7.1.

11 Again, however (as in Chapter 4, note 10), notice should be taken of possible different 'composition effects' as between federal and state award series.

12 127 CAR 1149, 1153.

13 127 CAR 1153, 147 CAR 178, 157 CAR 299.

14 147 CAR 177.

15 147 CAR 179.

16 157 CAR 299.

17 TGS, 1974, Vol. II, p. 348 f.

18 ibid., pp. 533–5.

19 ibid., p. 535 f.

20 TGS, 1974, Vol. III, p. 14.

21 See, for example, M. Power, 'Woman's Work is Never Done—by Men: A Socio-economic Model of Sex-typing in Occupations', *Journal of Industrial Relations*, 17(2), (1975), pp. 225–39; H. Moir and J. Selby Smith, 'Industrial Segregation in the Australian Labour Market', *Journal of Industrial Relations*, 21(3), (1979), pp. 281–91; Australia, *Role of Women*.

22 R. G. Gregory and R. C. Duncan, 'The Relevance of Segmented Labour Market Theories: The Australian Experience of the Achievement of Equal Pay for Women', Seventh Conference of Economists, Macquarie University, North Ryde, 1978 (see also 'Segmented Labour Market Theories' for an amended and edited version).

23 ibid. (1978), p. 30.

24 P. J. Sheehan, 'Real Wages and Unemployment: An Alternate View', in M. R. Fisher and others (eds), 'Real Wages and Unemployment', CAER Paper No. 4, Centre for Applied Economic Research, University of New South Wales, March 1978, p. 32. F. H. Gruen, 'Structural Unemployment as a Rival Explanation—A Survey of an Inconclusive Argument: International and Australian Aspects', Working Paper No. 63, Department of Economics, Research School of Social Sciences, Australian National University, Canberra, 1978,

at p. 21, remarks that 'A detailed economic and statistical study of equal pay has yet to be performed', and postulates the 'apparent anomaly' of 'change in the Australian female relative [wage which was] ... imposed administratively without any disemployment effects' as being explained by: (a) a 'trend towards greater female employment which is only weakly and partially affected by relative price changes', and (b) 'movement—on cost minimizing grounds—towards part-time employment', and (c) 'changing industry-mix' favouring females. Gruen's phrase 'apparent anomaly' suggests some perception of the issues. The present study, however, does not favour Gruen's first explanation, akin to Gregory and Duncan's, of the trend rate of growth in the female proportions of the work force as 'only weakly and partially' responsive to change in relative wages. Gruen's second and third suggestions are consistent with the evidence of research here considered.

25 The role of reduced average hours of employment is recognized by Gregory and Duncan (Appendix 5.1, note 1), p. 304 f, and 'Segmented Labour Market Theories', p. 414, but is subsequently and (in the present author's view) unsatisfactorily set aside (ibid., p. 421 f). Sheehan also makes some recognition of the point, 'An Alternate View', p. 32, and Sheehan and others, 'Recent Empirical Work', p. 42. Gruen, 'Structural Unemployment', p. 21, also makes relevant mention of a movement on cost minimizing grounds towards part-time employment.

26 See (Appendix 5.1, note 2), p. 178.

27 These are reported in McGavin, 'Wages and Employment', Table A7.2-2.

28 There are, however, several points that should be noted concerning Gregory and Duncan's ordinary least squares estimations:

(a) A scan down the R^2 column of the tables in the 1978 and 1981 papers of Gregory and Duncan (respectively, p. 37 and p. 418) isolates the most potentially significant R^2 as attaching to 'manufacturing' employment, where the dependent variable is the additional growth rate of female employment. That is, where market influence would be expected to be stronger, the highest fit is observed in regression between the additional growth rate of female employment and the adult male unemployment rate and female relative award earnings.

(b) The lowest fit in regressions between the male unemployment rate, female relative wages, and growth in female employment occurs under the dependent variable headings of 'public authorities and community services'. This is not surprising, because these are comparatively non-market areas, and in these areas one should least expect a response to variation in labour market conditions and to changing factor price relativities.

(c) It is not surprising, therefore, to observe that for Gregory and Duncan's government/public authority equations for the growth, additional growth, and sex composition growth in female employment, the independent variable with the highest *t* value is 'time'. The requisite information to assess levels of significance is not given, but Gregory and Duncan note ('Achievement of Equal Pay', p. 25) that none of the co-efficients for 'public authorities and community services' is significant at 5 per cent.

(d) This is clearly not so for 'manufacturing', where the equations for the additional growth in female employment, and for additional growth in female employment due to industry structure change, show co-efficients attaching to relative wage as negative and significant.

(e) It is most interesting to notice that these respective co-efficients are shown as −0.136 and −0.125 in the 1978 paper, and as −0.65 and −0.39 in the 1981 paper. No clues are given for these differences in the estimated co-efficients attaching to the female relative wage variable. The 1978 paper includes an 'RWL' variable, which may mean 'relative wage lagged', and the 1981 paper includes an 'RW-1' variable, indicating at p. 420 that the lag is set at 18 months. Given their re-estimations, it is hardly surprising that the authors should change their description of substitution responses from 'trivial' (1978, p. 30) to 'very small' (1981, p. 426).

29 For this algorithm, see Chapter 4, note 39, pp. 49–51.
30 Gregory and Duncan, 'Achievement of Equal Pay', p. 18.
31 Gregory and Duncan, 'Segmented Labour Market Theories', pp. 403, 405.
32 ibid., p. 426.
33 ibid., p. 422, and Sheehan, 'An Alternate View', p. 32. A study by S. Eccles, 'Female Employment: Real and Apparent Gains', *Australian Bulletin of Labour*, 6(3), (1980), pp. 172–85, using per capita data for all employed persons and for full-time employed persons, goes some distance towards meeting the present author's criticisms. Eccles documents and describes the shift between the 1960s and the 1970s in relative importance of the 'rate component' and the 'structural component' for change in female employment (pp. 178 ff). Indeed, she reports for 1974–79 a shift to a negative estimate of change in female per capita employment shares by industry sector ('rate component') (p. 178). For change in female full-time employment, Eccles derives negative rate component estimates for both 1971–79 and 1974–79 (p. 179).
34 The period discussed in this section, 1973–77, corresponds to Gregory and Duncan's periodization.

35 The respective figures (in millions) were: 209.3 to 205.3 and 2.9 to 4.2 hours.
36 All data presented in the above sub-section are computed from information kindly supplied by the ABS.
37 See 'An Alternate View'.
38 See 'Labour Market 1970s', in Norton, *Conference*.
39 See 'Achievement of Equal Pay' and 'Segmented Labour Market'.
40 This possibility is in fact mentioned by Gregory and Duncan, 'Segmented Labour Market Theories', p. 415. P. Sheehan and others, 'An Assessment of Recent Empirical Work Relevant to Macroeconomic Policy in Australia', *Australian Economic Review*, 1st Quarter 1979, p. 39, note the growth of the government sector and the decline of the private sector, and suggest further investigation. But in interpreting their Chart E (p. 41), they align themselves with Gregory and Duncan in emphasizing cyclical influences (further discussed in the next section).
41 Clearly, the implication here is contrary to the conclusions of several Australian researchers concerning the segmentation of the female labour market. However, Gregory and Duncan's research for the period up to 1978 on the changing patterns of male and female proportions in occupational categories appears to support the view that the pattern of occupational specialization by males and females is not constant. Their data, 'Achievement of Equal Pay', p. 34, show for 1966–71 that 67 per cent of the additional growth rate of the female work force was due to change in the female representation in occupations; while for 1971–78 the same proportion was 40 per cent. That is, the role of change in female proportions in occupational categories has not been constant, and in the latter period the shift has been towards reduction in the relative role of increasing female proportions in occupational groupings. On this question see P. A. McGavin, 'The Measurement of the Occupational and Industrial Segregation of Women: A Re-appraisal', *Journal of Industrial Relations*, 25(3), (1983), pp. 339–46.
42 These headings are drawn by the ABS from the 1978 Standard Industry Classification and they are described as follows:

Community Services: health services; educational and cultural services; welfare services; research, professional and political associations; and police, and garbage disposals.

Other: electricity, gas, water authorities; and public and defence authorities (that is, federal, state, and local government, public and semi-government authorities).

43 The dominant role of government employment, and particularly full-time government employment, in the growth of female employment is widely remarked in the literature (see McGavin, 'Wages and Employment', p. 235, n. 12).

44 Gregory and Duncan, 'Segmented Labour Market Theories', p. 419, mention that the sizeable trend towards female employment is, to a lesser extent and amongst other things, being generated by 'an industry-mix effect favourable to female employment in the private sector'.
45 See R. G. Gregory and R. C. Duncan, 'Equal Pay for Women: A Reply', *Australian Economic Papers*, 22(40), (1983), pp. 60–4.
46 See 'Authors' Reply', in W. E. Norton (ed.), *Conference in Applied Economic Research*, Reserve Bank of Australia, Sydney, 1980, p. 375.
47 Sheehan, 'An Alternate View', p. 32.
48 Gregory and Duncan, 'Achievement of Equal Pay', p. 30, and 'Segmented Labour Market Theories', p. 426.
49 R. H. Snape, 'Australian Unemployment—Is it Created by Costs or by Demand?', in Committee for Economic Development of Australia, *Growth*, No. 31, (1981), pp. 20–35, at p. 26.
50 Refer to P. A. McGavin, 'Equal Pay for Women: A Postscript', *Australian Economic Papers*, 22(40), (1983), pp. 65–7, where the confusion of Gregory and Duncan 'A Reply' (note 45) is explained.
51 Some evidence of this is presented in Table A5.1-4 of Appendix 5.1 of this book, where an increase in the proportion of investment in capital equipment may be noticed—compare column (b) with columns (a) + (b). See also note 36 of Appendix 5.1.
52 The phrase 'shade' derives from the 'Report from the Secretary of State for the Home Department on the Wages Boards and Industrial Conciliation and Arbitration Acts of Australia and New Zealand', ed. 4167, *Accounts and Papers*, lxxi, 327—quoted in D. Pope, 'Wage Regulation and Unemployment in Australia: 1900–30', *Australian Economic History Review*, 22(2), (1982), p. 117, n. 28. It is interesting to notice that A. B. Piddington, in his Royal Commissioner Report to the New South Wales Government of 31 October 1913, makes similar observations: 'The principle of equal pay for equal work which is so strongly championed by advocates of women's progress outside the ranks of industry is in general discredit amongst the great and growing host of women workers in the ordinary industrial concerns of this country.' 'In Victoria, the Commercial Clerks' Board, on which women were not represented, deliberately fixed equal pay for women working as clerks in order to improve the chances of men clerks, and an appeal was brought by women clerks to the Industrial Appeals Court on the ground that the Determination of the Board would oust them from employment. They, therefore, asked for a lower wage to be fixed for women clerks, and the Court upheld the Appeal and granted their request' (see 'Final Report of the Royal Commission of Inquiry on Industrial Arbitration', New South Wales Government Printer, December 1913, reproduced in NSW *Parliamentary Papers*, Vol. II, First and Second Sessions of

1913, pp. xxxvii and xxxix).

53 Note that the author makes no argument against women receiving equal (or greater) pay than men, but only about the arbitrary regulation of the relative wage. It may be noticed that this argument was also canvassed by Piddington (above), who quotes Judge Heydon (*Boot Trade Case*, 1911, AR 589), 'Before the [1908] Acts, women had a common law right to earn their living in any honest way they could ... Yet here it is admitted that the amendment [of the Act] asked for is intended to prevent and would prevent the competition of women with men in that branch of factory work' (p. xxxvii).

54 See P. A. McGavin, 'A Christian Perspective on the Economics of Work and Welfare', in G. H. Brennan and J. K. Williams (eds), *Chaining Australia: Church Bureaucracies and Political Economy*, Centre for Independent Studies, St Leonards, NSW, 1984, pp. 41–79.

Chapter 8: Wages and the Social Welfare System

1 ALP, *Policy Speech 1972*, Canberra, 1972, p. 6.

2 For example, AGD 1:1:375, 1:3:1217, 2:1:196, 2:2:879f.

3 For example, Hayden, Speech, 28 July 1973.

4 For example, Hayden, Speech, 2 August 1974.

5 BLMR, *Youth Wages, Employment and the Labour Force*, Research Report No. 3, AGPS, Canberra, 1983, p. 45, and ABS cat. *6312.0* and *6304.0*.

6 147 CAR 14 (NSW), and BLMR, *Youth Wages*, p. 44, using ACTU sources.

7 R. G. Gregory and R. C. Duncan, 'High Teenage Unemployment: The Role of Atypical Labour Supply Behaviour', *Economic Record*, 56(155), (1980), pp. 316–30.

8 ibid., p. 326.

9 ibid., p. 328.

10 For a summary, see BLMR, *Youth Wages*, pp. 28 ff.

11 ibid., p. 30.

12 B. Hughes, 'Labour Force Participation: What Are the Issues?', in BLMR, *Labour Force Participation in Australia*, Monograph Series No. 1, AGPS, Canberra, 1984, pp. 1–11, at pp. 2, 6.

13 ibid., p. 6.

14 The more complex model of Gregory and Duncan, 'High Teenage Unemployment', is an attempt to capture what they see as the segmentation of full-time and part-time teenage labour markets deriving from the income tests applying to unemployment benefits. They attempted to capture this effect by introducing into their last two equations the multiple of real weighted unemployment benefits and the part-time labour force participation rates of teenagers. The resultant co-efficients are then combined with the co-efficients attaching to

unemployment benefits. This 'aggregate co-efficient attaching to the level of unemployment benefits ... [for] equations 5(a) and 5(b) ... is positive for males after 1969 and for females after 1972' (p. 328 f). The 'aggregate co-efficient' attaching to unemployment benefits at July 1974 is calculated at 0.10 for males and 0.07 for females (equations 5(a) and 5(b), respectively). This derives *ceteris paribus* increases in labour force participations following an increase of $5 in real unemployment benefits of 0.48 per cent for males and 0.34 per cent for females, aged 15–19 years. Notice that after March 1973 the question of weighting of age-specific unemployment benefits does not arise, as from that date a common rate applied.

15 ibid., p. 327 f.

16 Calculation: 5 × 0.18 = 0.90; 5 × 0.15 = 0.75. ABS cat. *6204.0*, 1978, p. 28.

17 P. A. McGavin, 'School Participation of Australians Aged Sixteen: An Analysis of Youth Unemployment', *Economic Record*, 57(159), (1981), pp. 379–81.

18 BLMR, *Youth Wages*, p. 88.

19 J. P. Smith, 'Education Participation and Financial Incentives', Working Paper of the Department of Education and Youth Affairs—Office of Youth Affairs (now located in the Department of Prime Minister and Cabinet), Canberra, 1984, pp. 45–8.

20 Gregory and Duncan, 'High Teenage Unemployment', p. 326.

21 Commonwealth Department of Education, *Statistical Monograph*, No. 3, July 1980, and data kindly supplied by the Department. DSS, *Annual Report*, 1978–79, p. 112. ABS cat. *6302.0*, *6304.0*, *6401.0*, various issues, and data kindly supplied by the Australian Bureau of Statistics.

22 See Gregory and Duncan, 'High Teenage Unemployment', Figure 4, p. 323.

23 One should, however, note that we may expect there to be a relationship between the rate of change in $\mathbf{W}_m$ and job opportunities.

24 Another relevant contribution is by Dr W. Merrilees, 'The Effects of Labour Market Conditions on School Enrolment Rates', *Australian Economic Review*, 3rd Quarter 1981, pp. 56–60. The papers by Merrilees and by McGavin were prepared independently with (so far as this author is aware) neither author having knowledge of the other's work. Merrilees attempts to find results different from McGavin: 'Unemployment benefits have very little effect on school enrolment rates' (p. 58). The results of Merrilees are not commensurable with those of McGavin—in particular, the use of different variables, the introduction of data in levels, and the introduction of lags. The Durbin-Watson statistic reported in Merrilees' estimates of female school enrolment equations (p. 60) clearly suggests autocorrelation

(as also for the males 15 years school enrolment equations) (p. 59). The males 16 years and males 17 years equations (p. 59) appear to be trend-dominated. Interestingly, however, Merrilees's results for males aged 16 years qualitatively agree with the argument of McGavin, and he writes, 'The sharp rises in [unemployment] benefits over the 1972 to 1974 period induced about 5000 [males aged 16 years] to leave school early' (p. 59). As noted earlier in this sub-section, modelling of the schooling decisions of 16-year-olds may be expected to be simpler, as teenagers of this age have not entered into the investment entailed in the additional schooling experience of 17- and 18-year-olds (who may be near to attaining the HSC certificate).

Equation (8.1) was also estimated with the unemployment benefits variable removed, and this led to significant reduction in the explanatory power of the formulation. Of course, the dummy variable also then becomes non-significant. In an earlier paper ('An Economic Framework for Explaining Teenage Unemployment', *Australian Bulletin of Labour*, 7(1), (1980), pp. 18–30), Merrilees argues that Gregory and Duncan's correlation of unemployment benefits and teenage labour force participation may be spurious (pp. 24 f, 30). Equation (8.1) does suggest that the **B** variable at 1973 'creates something akin to a dummy variable' (Merrilees, p. 30). However, the performance of this equation hardly permits the ascription 'spurious' to the hypothesis of correlation.

25 BLMR, *Youth Wages*, p. 96.

26 These estimates are derived by taking the increase in unemployment benefits in 'real' terms of about \$5, times the respective co-efficients of these equations. The calculations are as follows: for males, \$5(0.66) = 3.30, and for females \$5(1.15) = 5.75.

27 Source: Australia, Department of Education, *Statistical Monograph* No. 3, July 1980: age participation rates (per cent), Australia, all schools: 1973, 16 years of age, males 56.9, females 51.4.

28 The calculations are as follows: for males, 68 186 (0.031) = 2114, and for females, 59 291(0.057) = 3380. Population estimates derived from ABS cat. *4202.0*, 1973, pp. 5, 23.

29 ABS cat. *6204.0*, 1978, p. 42.

30 These conclusions point to the enormity of the issues requiring examination when considering the relationship of wages and welfare. An adequate consideration requires more than an examination of the whole gamit of economic policy formulation and execution. It requires an examination of the range of economic policies within a context of overall social policy (and, in the author's view, within the context of one's total cosmology).

The statement, '... from these analytical perspectives, Government policy changes in transfer payments as they affected Australian youth were misconceived', clearly draws on a partial analysis, only.

It may therefore be argued that the analytical perspectives employed deserve further examination because the approach adopted is a partial economic analysis, only. A more fundamental criticism would be to say that the analytical perspective is inadequate because it is economic only, where a wider perspective of social (including political) analysis is required. The larger question of social policy has engaged the author's attention, and is in some measure implicit in the conclusions drawn from a partial and restricted economic analysis.

The author's view is that social policy ought not to deal with people on an individual basis which is independent of the family and community contexts. This view is implicit in the author's criticism levelled at the Whitlam Government's welfare policy. Government welfare policy sought from a national level to grant to people an economic independence which was detached from family and local community relations (and, one may say, detached also from macro-economic circumstances). It may be argued that earlier governments sought to exercise a central influence along these lines. But the active pursuit of this approach to welfare policy gained a sharp stimulus with the advent of the Whitlam Government. The large increases in the provision of unemployment benefits for youths manifest this shift in Australian government policy. And the widely-remarked growth in youth detachment from family and community networks of mutual obligation and support (in the author's view) demonstrate the effects of a social policy administration that grants to individuals an economic independence which is not tied to local networks of social and material obligation and support.

Comments of this kind are, indeed, critical of the whole notion of the 'welfare state' and of the social policy implicit in the administration of the welfare state. The need for governments to exercise an active concern for the social support of individuals is not questioned. What is questioned is a central administration of social welfare which deals with people atomistically. It is the author's view that central welfare administration of this kind generates a dysfunctional growth of social detachment in individuals who are the subject of such welfare administration.

The criticism directed at the Whitlam Government's policy concerning youth unemployment benefits therefore implies a larger criticism of the whole notion of the provision of 'social security' by the instrument of the 'welfare state'. Within the confines of partial economic analysis, the social security policy of the Whitlam Government may be judged as being 'economically misconceived'. Such a judgement does not proceed from a lack of interest in, and of concern for, social and material provision for individuals within society. Nor is this judgement bereft of links with an overall social policy framework. The issues involved are, however, very wide—much wider than the subject matter of this book. For these reasons, the economic aspects of the policies as they relate to wider issues of social policy in general are not given direct and extensive treatment.

31 ABS cat. *6204.0*, 1978, p. 71.

32 C. R. Cameron, *Unions in Crisis*, Hill of Content, Melbourne, 1982, p. 118.

33 The data of BLMR, *Retired, Unemployed or at Risk: Changes in the Australian Labour Market for Older Workers*, Research Report No. 4, AGPS, Canberra, 1983, Table 6.8, p. 44, show a tendency for women, 55–59 years (female eligibility for the aged pension commences at 60 years of age), to increase full-time employment during 1972 to 1975, but for unmarried women of this age group to decrease full-time employment (the decision of unmarried women may be nearer the decision as made by men, married and unmarried). Over this period these data also show a (strong) tendency for married women, 55–59 years, to increase part-time labour force employment, whereas for unmarried women of this age group the tendency appears to be in the reverse direction (again linking the indications of their behaviour with that of men). (Notice that this change in married women's labour market behaviour coincides with a change in the labour market status of men—refer, Y. Dunlop and L. S. Williams, 'Declining Labour Force Participation Rates at Older Ages', Conference Paper No. 24, BLMR, Canberra, 1983, p. 16.) These indications are consistent with the findings of C. Brooks, D. Sams and L. S. Williams ('An Econometric Model of Fertility, Marriage, Divorce and Labour Force Participation for Australian Women, 1921–22 to 1975–76', Working Paper BP-29, IMPACT Project, University of Melbourne, 1982), who report for older unmarried, but not for married, females a strong and significant negative relationship between aged and invalid pensions and labour force participation (Brooks and others, p. 60, and Dunlop and Williams, pp. 14, 21).

34 D. W. Kalisch and L. S. Williams, 'The Labour Force Experience of Older Workers', Working Paper No. 16, BLMR, Canberra, 1982.

35 This is average weekly earnings 'per employed male unit', as explained in Appendix 1.1.

36 See Table 8.5. For sources, see the following note and DSS, *Annual Report*, 1978–79, pp. 108, 112.

37 Changes in the eligibility and administration of invalid pensions are detailed in a DSS research paper—'Developments in Social Security: A Compendium of Legislative Changes since 1908', Research Paper No. 20, DSS, Canberra, 1983, pp. 40–6. Substantial changes in the administration of unemployment benefits did not occur during the Whitlam period (pp. 102–5).

38 Sources: Kalisch and Williams, 'Labour Force Experience', p. 13,

using data from AES, DSS, and the Office of the Commissioner for Taxation.

39 One change of the Whitlam Government which may have operated in the direction of encouraging continued labour force participation was the decision effective as of 16 March 1973 to increase unemployment benefits for single and married couples to $21.50 and $37.50, respectively—thus bringing them into line with the corresponding aged and invalid pension rates. During the five years prior to the advent of the Whitlam Government, unemployment benefits as a proportion of aged and invalid pensions had been as low as 58 per cent for single people, and 73 per cent for a married couple (DSS, *Annual Report*, 1978–79, pp. 108, 112). The McMahon Government had sharply increased these proportions to 85 and 72 per cent, respectively, on 5 October 1972. The Whitlam Government decision establishing, on 16 March 1973, a parity between unemployment benefits and pension rates eliminated a difference which may have acted as an incentive for older workers to seek aged or invalid retirement rather than continuing in the labour force.

40 DSS, 'Developments in Social Security', p. 143. In October 1973 the Whitlam Government abolished the means test for persons aged 75 years and over, and extended this exemption to persons aged 70–74 years from May 1975 (AGD 1:3:1217, AGWD 1975:220).

41 BLMR, *Retired or at Risk*, p. 42. Data showing the continuance of this decline through to 1980 are reproduced in McGavin, 'Wages and Employment', Table 8.6.

42 The category 'unemployment benefit recipients' is inapplicable for this age group.

43 Data to 1980 are shown in BLMR, *Retired or at Risk*, p. 42 f, and are reproduced in P. A. McGavin, 'Wages and Employment: An Economic Evaluation of the Wages Policy of the Whitlam Government', Doctoral Thesis, Department of Economics, University of Melbourne, 1984, Tables 8.6 and 8.7.

44 This growth was sustained through to 1980, when about 35 per cent of Australian men, 60–64 years, were in receipt of service and invalid pensions (see previous note).

45 Dunlop and Williams, 'Declining Participation', p. 11, note a significant increase in the proportion of the population aged 60–64 eligible for a service pension, as World War II service veterans moved through this age bracket.

46 Data to 1980 are found in BLMR, *Retired or at Risk*, p. 43, and are reproduced in McGavin, 'Wages and Employment', Table 8.8.

47 P. P. Stricker and P. Sheehan, *Hidden Unemployment: The Australian Experience*, Institute of Applied Economic and Social Research, University of Melbourne, Parkville, 1981, at pp. 83 f, 88.

48 ibid., p. 84.
49 ibid., p. 90.
50 ibid., p. 124.
51 ibid., p. 128.
52 ibid., see Figure 6.5, p. 128.
53 ibid., pp. 117, 128.
54 Notice that the terms 'voluntary' and 'involuntary' were first given Australian usage in Stricker and Sheehan (ibid., pp. 110, 117), and only subsequently used by Dunlop and Williams, 'Declining Participation'.
55 *Hidden Unemployment*, p. 128.
56 See note 33.
57 The *t* statistic is significant at 10 per cent; 5 per cent is the conventional level of statistical significance.
58 BLMR, *Retired or at Risk*, p. 88.
59 Dunlop and Williams, 'Declining Participation,' p. 3 f, note the results of Australian research to be consistent with overseas work of M. J. Boskin ('Social Security and Retirement Pensions', *Economic Enquiry*, 15(1), (1977), pp. 1–25) and A. Zabalza, C. Pissarides and M. Barton ('Social Security and the Choice Between Full-time Work, Part-time Work and Retirement', *Journal of Public Economics*, 14, (1980), pp. 245–76). An interesting paper by M. Carter and R. G. Gregory ('Government Pensions, Benefits and the Distribution of Employment for Males during a Recession', Tenth Conference of Economists, Australian National University, Canberra, 1981) offers a preliminary assessment of the use of income support by males withdrawing from the labour force. Using 1976 Census data, Carter and Gregory estimate (for males aged 60–64 years) that 'a one percentage point increase in the unemployment rate of males 25–44 years reduces the participation rate by ... 0.9 ... percentage points' (p. 18 and Table 3). The R^2 for this equation is, however, only 0.31, and a Durbin-Watson statistic is not reported. Census data as to the number of males receiving government pensions and benefits by age group are not available, and the results which Carter and Gregory present in their Table 7 are for males as a group (pp. 20, 33). The present author agrees with Carter and Gregory's judgement that their 'regression equations ... need more work' (p. 23). Their paper (like the book by Stricker and Sheehan which they acknowledge as having stimulated their work) represents a useful contribution to the development of Australian research on the labour force participation decision of older Australians, but is superseded by the work of W. Merrilees ('Pension Benefits and the Decline in Elderly Male Labour Force Participation', Working Papers in Economics No. 63, Department of Economics, University of Sydney, 1982) and Dunlop and Williams, 'Declining Participation'.

60 The behaviour of unmarried older women appears to conform to the pattern of older males, and the econometric evidence of Dunlop and Williams, 'Declining Participation', pp. 15, 21, confirms this observation.

61 For example: The findings of at least six US studies are cited in R. L. Clark and J. J. Spengler, *The Economics of Individual and Population Aging*, Cambridge University Press, Cambridge, 1980, pp. 91–9. See also D. R. Maki and Z. A. Spindler, 'The Effects of Unemployment Compensation on the Rate of Unemployment in Great Britain', *Oxford Economic Papers*, 27, (1975), pp. 440–54, and Z. A. Spindler and D. R. Maki, 'More on the Effects of Unemployment Compensation on the Rate of Unemployment in Great Britain', *Oxford Economic Papers*, 31, (1979), pp. 147–64; H. G. Grubel and others, 'Real and Insurance-induced Unemployment in Canada', *Canadian Journal of Economics*, 8, (1975), pp. 174–91; K. G. Grubel and D. R. Maki, 'The Effects of Unemployment Benefits on US Unemployment Rates', *Weltwirtschaftliches Archiv*, 112, (1976), pp. 274–97; H. G. Grubel and M. A. Walker, 'Unemployment Insurance: Global Evidence of its Effects on Unemployment', Fraser Institute, Vancouver, Canada, 1978; D. O. Parsons, 'The Decline in Male Labour Force Participation', *Journal of Political Economy*, 88, (1980), pp. 117–34; and Boskin, 'Social Security', and Zabalza and others, 'Social Security and Choice'.

62 See Appendix 1.1 on this distinction.

63 ALP, *Policy Speech 1972*, p. 10.

Chapter 9: Wages and Employment: An Economic Evaluation of the Whitlam Government Wages Policy

1 Edited TGS, 1974–75, p. 128.

2 ALP, *Policy Speech 1972*, Canberra, 1972, p. 10.

3 Although with greater qualification than is introduced by the present author, this verdict has also been made by one of the Prime Minister's chief advisers, Professor F. H. Gruen. After surveying influences which mitigate the blame attributed to the wages policies of the Whitlam Government, Gruen nevertheless concedes: '[This] is not to deny that Labor's wage policies were unwise and contributed their share to the inflationary pressures generated' ('What Went Wrong? Some Personal Reflections on Economic Policies under Labor', *Australian Quarterly*, December 1976, pp. 15–32, at p. 22).

4 For example, TGS, 1974–75, p. 44.

5 For example, Cameron, Speech, 18 November 1974.

6 This paragraph finds so many echoes in Mr J. O. Stone's (August) 1984 Shann Memorial Lecture (see, for example, '1929 and All That ...', *Australian Economic Review*, 3rd Quarter 1984, pp. 18–31, at pp.

28, 30) that I take the opportunity of noting that this chapter first took written form in February 1984. Reading Stone's lecture has influenced only footnote annotations to the penultimate draft of this work. Stone's conclusions (like my own) are not 'new'—as I later remark, 'they simply apply well-known tools of economic analysis'. Whilst scanning my notes on the literature during late editorial work on this book, this point was further underscored when I noticed Professor W. M. Corden's 1977 remarks (last read, I think, in 1980) which my comments reproduce almost verbatim (see 'Macro-economic Policy Options for Australia', *Economic Papers*, 55, (1977), pp. 25–34, at pp. 28 f, 32 f).

7 During the five years over which this study was in progress, close attention to newspapers on this question has revealed no evidence of unemployed persons or of coalitions of unemployed people making a causal link between wages and employment. I could dig up two or three 'Letters to the Editor' written by small business entrepreneurs and occasional reports of comments made by business representatives. But that is about all. These conclusions also apply to my survey of newspaper coverage of wages policy issues during the Whitlam period.

8 This particular image occurred to me in 1981 whilst listening to a particularly melodramatic concert piece played on the grand 'romantic' organ at St Patrick's Cathedral, Melbourne. The image finds a remarkable correspondence in the recall by Stone in his 1984 Memorial Lecture of a remark made by Professor E. Shann in 1928: 'Democracy is always hopeful of disposing of economic facts by manipulation' (quoted in Stone, '1929 and All That ...', p. 20). (Clearly the term 'democracy' is not being used in a text-book sense.)

9 For example, R. G. Gregory and R. C. Duncan, 'Segmented Labour Market Theories and the Australian Experience of Equal Pay for Women', *Journal of Post-Keynesian Economics*, Spring 1981, pp. 403–28, at p. 422.

10 Refer to the argument in Chapter 2.

11 For example: (a) During the last year of the Whitlam Government (1975), the share of wages in GDNFP(sa) was about 61 per cent (an increase of about 7.5 per cent on the modal share going to wages between 1959–60 and 1972–73), while the 12.5 per cent share for 1975 of profits in GDNFP(sa) was a fall of about 22 per cent on the modal share going to profits between 1959–60 and 1972–73 (computed from Table 5.2). (b) During the last year of the Whitlam Government (1975), real unit labour costs had increased by almost 7 per cent on their 1972 level (computed from Treasury RES, September 1978, p. 25).

Appendix 1.1: An Outline of Australian Institutions of Wage Determination

1 Para. (xxxv) of S. 51 of the Constitution of the Commonwealth of Australia gives the federal Parliament power to make laws with respect to 'Conciliation and arbitration for the prevention and settlement of industrial disputes extending beyond the limits of any one State'. A party engaged in industrial disputation satisfying this criterion may bring the dispute to the Australian Conciliation and Arbitration Commission. There has been a progressive extension of the meaning of the terms used in s.51(xxxv), and this has extended the industrial area over which federal awards operate (see R. M. Eggleston in R. Else-Mitchell (ed.), *Essays on the Australian Constitution*, Law Book Company, Sydney, 1961). Descriptions of the various state tribunals covering employment conditions may be found in *Labour Report* No. 58, 1973, pp. 125 ff (ABS cat. *6.7*).

For males, the proportion of employees under federal awards remained approximately stable between 1954 and 1974 (at about 44 per cent). There has been, however, a growth in the proportion of females under state awards (to 62 per cent at 1974). With the increase in the proportion of females to total employees, there has therefore been some reduction in the proportion of all employees affected by federal awards (to about 39 per cent at 1974). For females, the proportion of employees covered by 'unregistered collective agreements' or 'not affected by awards' remained unchanged over two decades (about 8 per cent at 1974). For males, however, there has been growth in this category (to about 16 per cent at 1974), most of this growth apparently being in male employees 'not affected by awards, etc.' (refer, ABS cat. *6315.0*, May 1974, p. 3).

Appendix 5.1: Real Wage Overhang and Employment: A Critique of Dissent

1 'The Labour Market in the 1970s', in W. E. Norton (ed.), *Conference in Applied Economic Research*, Reserve Bank of Australia, Sydney, 1980, pp. 256–319.

2 ibid., p. 295. Gregory and Duncan appear to treat output as an exogenously-determined variable (for example, pp. 279, 286 f, 289). Other Australian authors who seem to adopt this position include: F. H. Gruen, 'What Went Wrong? Some Personal Reflections on the Economic Policies under Labor', *Australian Quarterly*, December 1976, pp. 15–32; P. A. Riach and G. M. Richards, 'The Lessons of the Cameron Experiment', *Australian Economic Papers*, 18(32), (1979), pp. 21–35; and B. Hughes, *Exit Full Employment*, Angus & Robertson, Sydney, 1980. Gruen's 1976 paper is in part answered by

his 1980 'Comment' in Norton, *Conference*; Riach and Richards by R. H. Snape, 'Wages Policy and the Economy in the Seventies and Beyond', in K. Hancock (ed.), *Incomes Policy in Australia*, Harcourt Brace Jovanovich, Sydney, 1981, pp. 171–93; and Hughes by E. A. Boehm's review of Hughes's book in *Economic Record*, 57(159), (1981), p. 386 f.

3 See note 1, pp. 285–7.

4 Gregory and Duncan (p. 286), speaking to their Table 1 ('Labour Market 1970s', p. 283), describe Treasury's 1978 estimates (see RES (Chapter 5, note 4)) as being 'based on old data'. The significance of the revisions mentioned by C. I. Higgins, 'Comment', in Norton, *Conference*, p. 352, n. 11, is unclear, for the government submitted the 1978 estimates before the Arbitration Commission in 1980 (see *National Wage Case, May 1980*, AGPS, Canberra, Vol. II, p. 121). Revisions introduced in Treasury (1983)—see Table 5.1—do not change the picture for the Whitlam period.

5 Refer to Table A5.1–2, where this incidence is indicated by asterisks for productivity growth estimates which exceed output growth estimates—years 1974–75 to 1976–77 only.

6 For definitions and data, see Treasury, RES, September 1978 and October 1983.

7 'Authors' Reply', in Norton, *Conference*, pp. 370–9, at p. 374.

8 Refer to 'Comments' by R. Blandy, p. 329, and by F. H. Gruen, pp. 333, 338, in Norton, *Conference*, as well as by Higgins, pp. 348, 351 f, and by Snape, p. 362 f.

9 RES, September 1978 and October 1983.

10 As recommended in the 1976 *Report of the Working Party on the Measurement of Labour Productivity*, AGPS, Canberra, pp. 14–16; S. M. Bonnell, 'The "Real Wage Overhang" and the Wage Share of Output', *Australian Bulletin of Labour*, 5(4), (1979), p. 30; Gregory and Duncan, 'Labour Market 1970s', p. 274, n. 11; and Higgins, 'Comment', p. 352, n. 11.

11 Gruen, 'Comment', Table I, p. 334.

12 ibid., p. 333.

13 ibid., p. 335.

14 Gregory and Duncan, 'Authors' Reply', in Norton, *Conference*, p. 374.

15 Gregory and Duncan, 'Labour Market 1970s', p. 283.

16 Gregory and Duncan, 'Authors' Reply', p. 374.

17 A problem of which Gregory and Duncan are not unaware—ibid., p. 374.

18 The Durbin-Watson statistic for Gruen's Equation (3) is 1.29.

19 Gregory and Duncan, 'Authors' Reply', p. 373 f.

20 Gregory and Duncan, 'Labour Market 1970s', p. 283.

21 Absence of evidence of a recession decline in productivity growth

is also indicated using the data of Treasury, RES, September 1978, p. 24, where annual average hourly labour productivity growth estimates for 1967–68 to 1973–74 are shown as 3.9 per cent, and for 1973–74 to 1976–77 as 4.0 per cent.

22 See Snape, 'Comment' in Norton, *Conference*, p. 361 f. According to 'Okun's law', productivity and output move in the same direction.

23 Gregory and Duncan, 'Labour Market 1970s' in Norton, *Conference*, pp. 276 ff.

24 See, for example, R. G. Hawkins, 'Business Fixed Investment' in *Conference*, pp. 193–231, and 'Summary Discussion' at p. 250.

25 ibid., pp. 206, 215, 222 f.

26 Gregory and Duncan, 'Labour Market 1970s', in Norton, *Conference*, p. 278, n. 13.

27 For example, AGD 3:1:197, 2:4:1197.

28 Gregory and Duncan, 'Labour Market 1970s', in Norton, *Conference*, p. 278, n. 13. It is unclear how Gregory and Duncan get their 7–8 per cent (p. 288). The above data suggest a figure of about 4.5 per cent.

29 Higgins, 'Comment', in Norton, *Conference*, p. 344.

30 Gregory and Duncan, 'Labour Market 1970s', in Norton, *Conference*, p. 277 f.

31 Higgins, 'Comment', p. 344, n. 3.

32 Treasury, *Job Markets: Economic and Statistical Aspects of the Australian Market for Labour*, Treasury Economic Paper No. 4, AGPS, Canberra, 1979, p. 33, n. 3.

33 Gregory and Duncan, 'Labour Markets 1970s', in Norton, *Conference*, p. 278.

34 ibid., Figure 10, p. 277.

35 Suggestions consistent with the above evidence of 'capital deepening' are found in the Department of Industry and Commerce publication, *Journal of Industry and Commerce*, March 1978, where the results of a survey of manufacturing firms (details of which are not reported) are summarized in the following terms: 'The bulk of capital investment since 1974 has been directed at labour replacement with little investment in increments to capacity ... Capital investment has been directed at labour replacement' (p. 11).

36 'AGD 2:4:1197. Gregory and Duncan recognize this in 'Labour Markets 1970s', pp. 276 f, 280, 'over a period when investment can occur', and 'if there is sufficient time for investment to occur'. But they still infer that 'discussion has been directed towards the wrong relative price' (p. 278).

Appendix 8.1: The Contribution of Changes in Welfare to Stagflation: An Illustrative First-Estimate

1 See Y. Dunlop & L. S. Williams, 'Declining Participation Rates at Older Ages', Conference Paper No. 24, BLMR, Canberra, 1983.

2 ibid., p. 10, n. (a).

3 Estimation was by the generalized least squares method, using data for the period 1966:3 to 1981:4. The author gratefully acknowledges clarification by Dr L. S. Williams that the reported co-efficients of Dunlop and Williams are calculated at sample means.

4 The method of computation (briefly explained in the text) is as follows:

(a) Take the co-efficient on **G** for the relevant age group as reported by Dunlop and Williams, 'Declining Participation', p. 10, times $(1-\lambda)$ for the relevant year (λ is found in ABS, cat. *6204.0*, August, 1978, p. 40), deriving $\eta_{\lambda,g}$ for the relevant year.

(b) Calculate third-quarter percentage changes in **G** from Table 8.2.

(c) Multiply (a) by (b) to derive an estimate for the relevant year of the change in male labour force participation as a result of increases during that year in **G**.

5 Because the estimates are used for orders-of-magnitude purposes only, the following estimation procedure was used to obtain labour force figures for males aged 60–64 years for each of the three years, 1973–75: Employment of males in the 60–64 year cohort is reported in ABS cat. *6204.0*, 1978, p. 45. Unemployment of males is reported only for the '55 years and over' cohort. Due to the insufficiency of the sample, this is reported at 1974 for persons only (males plus females). A 1974 estimate of unemployed males, 55 years and over, is derived by taking 70 per cent of persons unemployed in that group. For the years 1973–75, estimates of males, 60–64 years, unemployed are derived by taking 25 per cent of unemployed males, 55 years and over. This method derives for males, 60–64 years, labour force estimates as follows: 1973, 200 800; 1974, 197 100; 1975, 187 400.

Labour force participation rates (per cent) for that cohort were: 1973, 76.1; 1974, 72.4; 1975, 68.6 (ABS cat. *6204.0*, 1978, p. 40). Population estimates for males, 60–64 years, are taken from ABS cat. *3201.0*: 1973, 264 392; 1974, 272 869; 1975, 279 030.

These population estimates were then multiplied by the co-efficients of Table A8.1–2 to obtain estimates of the reduction in the male labour force: 1973, 1057; 1974, 3002; 1975, 2232.

These estimates were rounded to the nearest 100 for use in this Appendix.

6 Sources and Notes to Table A8.1–4:

(a) Males aged 60–64 years withdrawing from the labour force as a result of the attraction of increases in **G**, as per Table 8.1–3.

(b) Annual real value of G calculated using the four-quarter mean weekly G (married rate), derived from Table 8.2.
(c) Annual real value of third-quarter minimum (male) wage, derived from Table 6.10.
(d) Derived by multiplying (a) times (b).
(e) Derived by multiplying (a) times (c).

Bibliography

Australian Bureau of Statistics (ABS) References

cat. 1311.0 *Time Series Data on Magnetic Tape and Microfiche*, quarterly, various issues

cat. 3201.0 *Estimated Age Distribution of the Population: States and Territories of Australia*, annual, various issues

cat. 4202.0 *Schools, Australia*, annual, various issues

cat. 5204.0 *Australian National Accounts: National Income and Expenditure*, annual, various issues

cat. 5206.0 *Quarterly Estimates of National Income and Expenditure, Australia*, quarterly, various issues

cat. 5207.0 *Historical Series of Quarterly Estimates of National Income and Expenditure, Australia*, annual, various issues

cat. 5620.0 *General Insurance, Australia*, annual, various issues

cat. 5626.0 *New Capital Expenditure by Private Enterprise in Selected Industries, Australia*, quarterly, various issues

cat. 6203.0 *The Labour Force, Australia*, monthly, various issues

cat. 6204.0 *The Labour Force*, annual, various issues

cat. 6214.0 *Civilian Employees, Australia*, irreg., various issues

cat. 6302.0 *Average Weekly Earnings, Australia*, quarterly, various issues

cat. 6304.0 *Earnings and Hours of Employees, Australia*, annual, various issues

cat. 6312.0 *Wage Rates, Australia*, monthly, various issues

cat. 6314.0 *Wage Rates Indexes, Australia*, irreg.

cat. 6315.0 *Incidence of Industrial Awards, Determinations and Collective Agreements, Australia*, irreg.

cat. 6319.0 *Survey of Superannuation, Australia*, irreg.

cat. 6322.0 *Industrial Disputes, Australia*, quarterly, various issues

cat. 6401.0 *Consumer Price Index*. quarterly, various issues

cat. 6.7 *Labour Report*, No. 58, 1973

Other References

Alford, K., 'Married Women's Employment and its Relation to Youth (Un)Employment', *Australian Economic Review*, 3rd Quarter 1979, pp. 37–46.

———, 'Cramming the Workforce and Neglecting their Children?', *Journal of Australian Political Economy*, No. 6, November 1979, pp. 46–58.

Australia, *Australian Government Digest*, AGPS, Canberra [replaced, 1975 with *Australian Government Weekly Digest*], various issues.

———, *Budget Speech and Statements*, AGPS, Canberra, various years.

———, Department of Employment and Youth Affairs, *Monthly Review of the Employment Situation*, monthly, various issues.

———, *Report of the Committee of Economic Enquiry* ('Vernon Report'), Government Printer, Canberra, 1965, Volumes I and II.

———, *Report of the Working Party on the Measurement of Labour Productivity* (tabled November 1975), AGPS, Canberra, 1976.

———, *National Wage Case, May 1980, Submissions by the Commonwealth Government*, Volumes 1 and 2, AGPS, Canberra, 1980.

———, Women's Bureau of the Department of Employment and Youth Affairs, *The Role of Women in the Economy*, Position Paper, OECD Conference on the Employment of Women, AGPS, Canberra, 1981.

———, National Economic Summit Conference, *Information Paper on the Economy*, AGPS, Canberra, April 1983.

Australian Conciliation and Arbitration Commission, *Commonwealth Arbitration Reports*, AGPS, Canberra, various issues.

———, *Transcripts of National Wage Cases* (cited as *Transcript*, year, volume, page—and, for government submissions, *Transcript of Government Submissions*.

———, *Inquiry into the Principles of Wage Fixation*, AGPS, Canberra, 1978.

Australian Council of Trade Unions, *Decisions of the Australian Council of Trade Unions*, ACTU, Melbourne, various issues.

Australian Industries Development Association, *Understanding Unemployment*, Melbourne, 1978.

———, 'The True Cost of Labour', *AIDA Bulletin*, No. 350, April 1983, pp. 9–12.

Australian Labor Party, *Policy Speech 1972*, Canberra, 1972.

Blandy, R. J., 'Youth Unemployment', *Australian Bulletin of Labour*, 5(3), (1979), pp. 19–30.

———, 'Comment', in W. E. Norton (ed.), *Conference in Applied Economic Research*, Reserve Bank of Australia, Sydney, 1980, pp. 326–32.

Blandy, R. and Richardson, S. (eds), *How Labour Markets Work: Case*

Studies in Adjustment, Longman Cheshire, Melbourne, 1982.

Boehm, E. A., 'Distortions in Relative Wages: The Inflationary Consequences and Policy Implications', *Australian Economic Review*, 4th Quarter 1974, pp. 39–50.

———, 'Money Wages, Consumer Prices, and Causality in Australia', *Research Paper* No. 83, Department of Economics, University of Melbourne, March 1982.

———, 'Understanding Business Cycles: A Critical Review of Theory and Fact', Research Paper No. 84, Department of Economics, University of Melbourne, June 1982.

———, 'The Price–Cost Cycle and the Business Cycle', *Research Paper* No. 93, Department of Economics, University of Melbourne, May 1983.

———, 'Money Wages, Consumer Prices, and Causality in Australia', *Economic Record*, 60(17), (September 1984), pp. 236–51.

Boehm, E. A. and Moore, G. H., 'New Economic Indicators for Australia, 1949–1984', *Australian Economic Review*, 4th Quarter 1984, pp. 34–56.

Bonnell, S. M., 'The "Real Wage Overhang" and the Wage Share of Output', *Australian Bulletin of Labour*, Volume 5, No. 4, September 1979, pp. 27–47.

Boskin, M. J., 'Social Security and Retirement Pensions', *Economic Inquiry*, Vol. 15, No. 1, (1977), pp. 1–25.

Brooks, C., Sams, D. and Williams, L. S., 'An Econometric Model of Fertility, Marriage, Divorce and Labour Force Participation for Australian Women, 1921/22 to 1975/76', Working Paper BP-29, IMPACT Project, University of Melbourne, Parkville, May 1982.

Bureau of Labour Market Research, *Youth Wages, Employment and the Labour Force*, Research Report No. 3, AGPS, Canberra, March 1983.

———, *Retired, Unemployed or at Risk: Changes in the Australian Labour Market for Older Workers*, Research Report No. 4, AGPS, Canberra, July 1983.

———, *Labour Force Participation in Australia*, Monograph Series No. 1 (A. J. Kaspura (ed.)), AGPS, Canberra, 1984.

Cameron, C. R., *Unions in Crisis*, Hill of Content, Melbourne, 1982.

Carmichael, J., Fahrer, J. and Hawkins, J., 'Some Macroeconomic Implications of Wage Indexation: A Survey', Conference on Government Policies Towards Inflation, Macquarie University, North Ryde, September 1983.

Carter, M. and Gregory, R. G., 'Government Pensions, Benefits and the Distribution of Employment for Males during a Recession', Tenth Conference of Economists, Australian National University, Canberra, August 1981.

Caton, C. N., Evans, E. A. and Johnston, H. N., 'The Inflationary Process and the Impact of Wage Indexation on the Australian Economy',

Fourth Conference of Economists, Canberra, August 1974.

Clark, R. L. and Spengler, J. J., *The Economics of Individual and Population Aging*, Cambridge University Press, Cambridge, 1980.

Commissioner for Taxation, *Annual Report* and *Taxation Statistics*, AGPS, Canberra, various issues.

Corden, W. M., 'Macro-economic Policy Options for Australia', *Economic Papers*, No. 55, October 1977, pp. 25–34.

———, 'Wages and Unemployment in Australia', *Economic Record*, Vol. 55, No. 148, March 1979, pp. 1–19.

———, 'Wages, Inflation and Unemployment' *Australian Economic Review*, 1st Quarter 1979, pp. 69–70.

———, 'The Wages Push and Macro-economic Policy: The Dilemmas Ahead', *Economic Record*, Vol. 58, No. 161, June 1982, pp. 111–17.

Department of Education, *Statistical Monograph*, Canberra, various issues.

Department of Labour and Immigration, *Wage Indexation for Australia? A Discussion Paper*, AGPS, Canberra, 1974.

Department of Social Security, *Annual Report*, AGPS, Canberra, various issues.

———, 'Developments in Social Security: A Compendium of Legislative Changes Since 1908', Research Paper No. 20, June 1983.

Doeringer, P. B. and Piere, H. J., *Internal Labour Markets and Manpower Analysis*, Heath, Lexington, Mass., 1971.

Downing, R. I. and Isaac, J. E., 'The 1961 Basic Wage Judgement and Wage Policy', *Economic Record*, Vol. 37, No. 80, December 1961, pp. 480–94.

Dunlop, Y. and Williams, L. S., 'Declining Labour Force Participation Rates at Older Ages', Conference Paper No. 24, Bureau of Labour Market Research, Canberra, July 1983.

Eccles, S., 'Female Employment: Real and Apparent Gains', *Australian Bulletin of Labour*, 6(3), (1980), pp. 172–85.

———, 'The Role of Women in the Australian Workforce', in K. Hancock and Y. Sano (eds), *Japanese and Australian Labour Markets: A Comparative Study*, Australia–Japan Research Centre, Australian National University, Canberra, 1982, pp. 458–511, 521–6.

Eggleston, R. M., 'Industrial Relations', in R. Else-Mitchell (ed.), *Essays on the Australian Constitution*, 2nd edn, Law Book Company, Sydney, 1961, pp. 221–46.

Fisher, M. R., Gruen, F. H., Sheehan, P. J. and Stammer, D. W. (eds), 'Real Wages and Unemployment', CAER Paper No. 4, Centre for Applied Economic Research, University of New South Wales, March 1978.

Ford, G. W., Hearn, J. M. and Lansbury, R. D., *Australian Labour Relations: Readings*, 3rd edn, Macmillan, Melbourne, 1980.

Gelber, F., 'The Inter-industry Effects of Cumulative Wage Indexation—A Critical Comment', *Australian Economic Papers*, 20(36), (June 1981), pp. 186–8.

Gregory, R. G. and Duncan, R. C., 'The Relevance of Segmented Labour Market Theories: The Australian Experience of the Achievement of Equal Pay for Women', Seventh Conference of Economists, Macquarie University, Sydney, 1978.

———, 'The Labour Market in the 1970s', in W. E. Norton (ed.), *Conference in Applied Economic Research*, Reserve Bank of Australia, Sydney, 1980, pp. 256–319.

———, 'Authors' Reply', in W. E. Norton (ed.), *Conference in Applied Economic Research*, Reserve Bank of Australia, Sydney, 1980, pp. 370–9.

———, 'High Teenage Unemployment: The Role of Atypical Labour Supply Behaviour', *Economic Record*, 56(155), (December 1980), pp. 316–30.

———, 'Segmented Labour Market Theories and the Australian Experience of Equal Pay for Women', *Journal of Post-Keynesian Economics*, (Spring 1981), pp. 403–28.

———, 'Equal Pay for Women: A Reply', *Australian Economic Papers*, 22(40), June 1983, pp. 60–4.

Grubel, H. G. and Maki, D. R., 'The Effects of Unemployment Benefits on US Unemployment Rates', *Weltwirtschaftliches Archiv*, 112, (1976), pp. 274–97.

Grubel, H. G., Maki, D. and Sax, S., 'Real and Insurance-induced Unemployment in Canada', *Canadian Journal of Economics*, 8, (1975), pp. 174–91.

Grubel, H. G. and Walker M. A., 'Unemployment Insurance: Global Evidence of its Effects on Unemployment', Fraser Institute, Vancouver, Canada, 1978.

Gruen, F. H., 'What Went Wrong? Some Personal Reflections on Economic Policies under Labor', *Australian Quarterly*, December 1976, pp. 15–32.

——— (ed.), for the Academy of the Social Sciences in Australia, *Surveys of Australian Economics*, Volume I, Allen & Unwin, Sydney, 1978.

———, 'Structural Unemployment as a Rival Explanation—A Survey of an Inconclusive Argument: International and Australian Aspects', Working Paper No. 63, Department of Economics, Research School of Social Sciences, Australian National University, Canberra, July 1978.

——— (ed.), *Surveys of Australian Economics*, Volume II, Allen & Unwin, Sydney, 1979.

———, 'Comment', in W. E. Norton (ed.), *Conference in Applied Economic Research*, Reserve Bank of Australia, Sydney, 1980, pp. 332–9.

Hancock, K. (ed.), *Incomes Policy in Australia*, Harcourt Brace Jovanovich, Sydney, 1981.

Hancock, K. and Sano, Y. (eds), *Japanese and Australian Labour Markets: A Comparative Study*, Australia–Japan Research Centre, Australian National University, ANU Press, Canberra, 1982.

Hawkins, R. G., 'Business Fixed Investment', in Norton, pp. 193–231.

Higgins, C. I., 'Comment', in W. E. Norton (ed.), *Conference in Applied Economic Research*, Reserve Bank of Australia, Sydney, 1980, pp. 340–57.

Howard, W. A., 'Australian Trade Unions in the Context of Union Theory', *Journal of Industrial Relations*, 19(3), (1977), pp. 255–73.

Hughes, B., *Exit Full Employment*, Angus & Robertson, Sydney, 1980.

———, 'Real Wages and Unemployment', in Committee for Economic Development of Australia, *Growth*, No. 31, April 1981, pp. 36–47.

———, 'Labour Force Participation: What Are the Issues?', in Bureau of Labour Market Research, *Labour Force Participation in Australia*, Monograph Series No. 1, AGPS, Canberra, 1984, pp. 1–11.

Institute of Applied Economic and Social Research, unauthored comment in *Australian Economic Review*, Melbourne, quarterly, various issues.

Isaac, J. E., *Wages and Productivity*, Cheshire, Melbourne, 1967.

———, 'Compulsory Arbitration and Collective Bargaining Reconsidered', *Journal of Industrial Relations*, Vol. 16, No. 1, March 1974, pp. 1–12.

———, 'Economics and Industrial Relations', Edward Shann Memorial Lecture in Economics, University of Western Australia, August 1982.

Janankar, P. N. and Neale, A. J., 'Relative Wages and the Youth Labour Market', Discussion Paper No. 29, Institute for Employment Research, University of Warwick, Warwick, 1985.

Johnston, H. N., Campbell, R. B. and Simes, R. M., 'The Impact of Wages and Prices on Unemployment', *Economic Papers*, No. 60, (December 1978), pp. 18–37.

Jonson, P. D. and Taylor, J. C., 'Inflation and Economic Stability in a Small Open Economy: A Systems Approach', in K. Brunner and A. H. Meltzer (eds), *The Problem of Inflation*, Carnegie Rochester Conference Series on Public Policy (supplementary series to *Journal of Monetary Economics*), No. 8, (1978), pp. 289–323.

Kalish, D. W. and Williams, L. S., 'The Labour Force Experience of Older Workers', Working Paper No. 16, Bureau of Labour Market Research, Canberra, December 1982.

Keynes, J. M., *The General Theory of Employment, Interest, and Money*, Macmillan, London (1936; 1964 edn).

McGavin, P. A., 'School Participation of Australians Aged Sixteen: An Analysis of Youth Unemployment', *Economic Record*, (December 1981), pp. 379–81.

———, 'Equal Pay for Women: A Re-assessment of the Australian Experience', *Australian Economic Papers*, (June 1983), pp. 48–59.

———, 'Equal Pay for Women: A Postscript', *Australian Economic Papers*, (June 1983), pp. 65–7.

———, 'The Measurement of the Occupational and Industrial Segregation of Women: A Re-appraisal', *Journal of Industrial Relations*, (June 1983), pp. 339–46.

———, 'A Christian Perspective on the Economics of Work and Welfare', in G. H. Brennan and J. K. Williams (eds), *Chaining Australia: Church Bureaucracies and Political Economy*, Centre for Independent Studies, St Leonards, NSW, August 1984, pp. 41–79.

———, 'Wages and Employment: An Economic Evaluation of the Wages Policy of the Whitlam Government', Doctoral Thesis, Department of Economics, University of Melbourne, November 1984.

Maki, D. R. and Spindler, Z. A., 'The Effects of Unemployment Compensation on the Rate of Unemployment in Great Britain', *Oxford Economic Papers*, 27, (1975), pp. 440–54.

Merrilees, W., 'Teenage Unemployment: The Role of Wage Rates and Other Factors', 49th ANZAAS Conference, Auckland, NZ, January 1979.

———, 'An Economic Framework for Explaining Teenage Unemployment', *Australian Bulletin of Labour*, 7(1), (December 1980), pp. 18–30.

———, 'The Effects of Labour Market Conditions on School Enrolment Rates', *Australian Economic Review*, 3rd Quarter 1981, pp. 56–60.

———, 'Pension Benefits and the Decline in Elderly Male Labour Force Participation', Working Papers in Economics No. 63, Department of Economics, University of Sydney, September 1982.

Miller, P. W., 'The Role of Labour Costs in the Youth Labour Market: An Overview of the Evidence', Discussion Paper No. 65, Centre for Economic Policy Research, Australian National University, Canberra, March 1983.

Moir, H. and Selby Smith J., 'Industrial Segregation in the Australian Labour Market', *Journal of Industrial Relations*, 21, (September 1979), pp. 281–91.

Nieuwenhuysen, J. P. and Sloan, J., 'Wages Policy', in F. H. Gruen (ed.), *Surveys of Australian Economics*, Volume I, Allen & Unwin, Sydney, 1978, pp. 91–131.

Norton, W. E. (ed.), *Conference in Applied Economic Research*, Reserve Bank of Australia, Sydney, 1980.

———, *The Deterioration in Economic Performance*, Occasional Paper No. 9, Reserve Bank of Australia, Sydney, September 1982.

Norton, W. E., Garmston, P. M. and Brodie, M. W., *Australian Economic Statistics, 1949–50 to 1982–83: Tables*, Occasional Paper

No. 8A, Reserve Bank of Australia, May 1983.

Parsons, D. O., 'The Decline in Male Labour Force Participation', *Journal of Political Economy*, 88, (1980), pp. 117–34.

Phipps, A. J., 'The Impact of Wage Indexation on Wage Inflation in Australia: 1975(2)–1980(2)', *Australian Economic Papers*, 20(37), (December 1981), pp. 333–49.

Piddington, A. B., 'Final Report of the Royal Commission of Inquiry on Industrial Arbitration', New South Wales Government Printer, December 1913 (reproduced in NSW *Parliamentary Papers*, Volume II, First and Second Sessions of 1913).

Pitchford, J. D., 'Wage Policy and Distribution Theory', *Economica*, xxxiv, (May 1967), pp. 167–80.

Plowman, D. H., *Wage Indexation: A Study of Australian Wage Issues, 1975–80*, Allen & Unwin, Sydney, 1981.

Pope, D., 'Wage Regulation and Unemployment in Australia: 1900–30', *Australian Economic History Review*, 22(2), (September 1982), pp. 103–26.

Power, M., 'Woman's Work Is Never Done—by Men: A Socio-economic Model of Sex-typing in Occupations', *Journal of Industrial Relations*, Vol. 17, No. 2, June 1975, pp. 225–39.

Prices Justification Tribunal, *Annual Report*, AGPS, Canberra, various issues.

Reserve Bank of Australia, *Statistical Bulletin*, various issues.

Riach, P. A. and Richards, G. M., 'The Lessons of the Cameron Experiment', *Australian Economic Papers*, 18(32), (1979), pp. 21–35.

Richardson, S., 'The Skilled Metal Trades', in R. Blandy and S. Richardson (eds), *How Labour Markets Work: Case Studies in Adjustment*, Longman Cheshire, Melbourne, 1982, pp. 49–90.

Salter, W. E. G., *Productivity and Technical Change*, Cambridge University Press, London, 1966.

Scherer, P., 'Insubstantial Compliance: Changes in Composition and Distribution of Earnings Under Wage Indexation, 1975–1980', Tenth Conference of Economists, Australian National University, August 1981.

Sheehan, P. J., 'Real Wages and Unemployment: An Alternate View', in M. R. Fisher and others (eds), 'Real Wages and Unemployment', CAER Paper No. 4, Centre for Applied Economic Research, University of New South Wales, March 1978, pp. 19–49.

Sheehan, P., Derody, B. and Rosendale, P., 'An Assessment of Recent Empirical Work Relevant to Macroeconomic Policy in Australia', *Australian Economic Review*, 1st Quarter 1979, pp. 33–61.

Sloan, J., 'Decentralised versus Centralised Wage Fixation', *Economic Papers*, 2(2), August 1983, pp. 8–13.

Snape, R. H., 'Productivity, Costs and Employment', *Australian Economic Review*, 2nd Quarter 1979, pp. 65–71.

———, 'Comment', in W. E. Norton (ed.), *Conference in Applied Economic Research*, Reserve Bank of Australia, Sydney, 1980, pp. 359–67.

———, 'Australian Unemployment—Is it Created By Costs or by Demand?', in Committee for Economic Development of Australia, *Growth*, No. 31, April 1981, pp. 20–35.

———, 'Wages Policy and the Economy in the Seventies and Beyond', in K. Hancock (ed.), *Incomes Policy in Australia*, Harcourt Brace Jovanovich, Sydney, 1981, pp. 171–93.

Spindler, Z. A. and Maki, D. R., 'More on the Effects of Unemployment Compensation on the Rate of Unemployment in Great Britain', *Oxford Economic Papers*, 31, (1979), pp. 147–64.

Stone, J. O., '1929 and All That ...', *Australian Economic Review*, 3rd Quarter 1984, pp. 18–31.

Stricker, P. P. and Sheehan, P., *Hidden Unemployment: The Australian Experience*, Institute of Applied Economic and Social Research, University of Melbourne, Parkville, 1981.

Treasury [The Australian], *Round-up of Economic Statistics*, AGPS, Canberra, monthly, various issues.

———, *Treasury Information Bulletin*, quarterly, various issues.

———, 'The Measurement of Real Unit Labour Cost', Supplement to *Round-up of Economic Statistics*, AGPS, Canberra, September 1978, pp. 15–26.

———, *Job Markets: Economic and Statistical Aspects of the Australian Market for Labour*, Treasury Economic Paper No. 4, AGPS, Canberra, 1979.

———, 'Factor Shares and Real Unit Labour Costs', Supplement to *Round-up of Economic Statistics*, AGPS, Canberra, October 1983, pp. 27–46.

Trivedi, P. K. and Baker, G. M., 'Equilibrium Unemployment in Australia: Concepts and Measurement', Discussion Paper No. 59, Centre for Economic Policy Research, Australian National University, Canberra, December 1982 (a revised and edited version published in *Economic Record*, 61(174), (1985)).

Vernon Report (1965), see entry under Australia, *Report of Committee of Economic Enquiry*.

Wilson, G. W., 'The Economics of the Just Price', *History of Political Economy*, 7(1), (1975), pp. 56–74.

Yerbury, D., 'Collective Negotiations, Wage Indexation and the Return to Arbitration: Some Institutional and Legal Developments During the Whitlam Era', in G. W. Ford and others, *Australian Labour Relations: Readings*, 3rd edn, Macmillan, Melbourne, 1980, pp. 462–503.

Zabalza, A., Pissarides, C. and Barton, M., 'Social Security and the Choice Between Full-time Work, Part-time Work and Retirement', *Journal of Public Economics*, 14, (1980), pp. 245–76.

List of Tables and Figures

Tables

Chapter 6

Figures

Index